Adenauer

PROFILES IN POWER

General Editor: Keith Robbins

Adenauer

Ronald Irving

An imprint of **Pearson Education**

London • New York • Toronto • Sydney • Tokyo • Singapore • Hong Kong • Cape Town
New Delhi • Madrid • Paris • Amsterdam • Munich • Milan • Stockholm

PEARSON EDUCATION LIMITED

Head Office:
Edinburgh Gate
Harlow CM20 2JE
Tel: +44(0)1279 623623
Fax: +44(0)1279 431059

London Office:
128 Long Acre
London WC2E 9AN
Tel: +44(0)20 7447 2000
Fax: +44(0)20 7240 5771
Website: www.history-minds.com

―――――――――――――――

First pubilshed in Great Britain in 2002

ISBN 0 582 06824 X

British Library Cataloguing in Publication Data
A CIP catalogue record for this book can be obtained from the British Library

Library of Congress Cataloguing in Publication Data
A CIP catalogue record for this book can be obtained from the
Library of Congress

10 9 8 7 6 5 4 3 2 1

Typeset by Fakenham Photosetting Limited in 10/12 pt Janson Text
Produced by Pearson Education Asia Pte Ltd,
Printed in Malaysia, LSP

The Publishers' policy is to use paper manufactured from sustainable forests.

To My Grandchildren

CONTENTS

CONTENTS

List of Abbreviations

BDI	Bundesverband der Deutschen Industrie
BHE	Block der Heimatvertriebenen und Entrechteten
BP	Bayernpartei
BVP	Bayerische Volkspartei
CAP	Common Agricultural Policy
CDU	Christlich Demokratische Union
CSU	Christlich-Soziale Union
DDP	Deutsche Demokratische Partei
DGB	Deutscher Gewerkschaftsbund
DNVP	Deutschnationale Volkspartei
DP	Deutsche Partei
DVP	Deutsche Volkspartei
ECSC	European Coal and Steel Community
EDC	European Defence Community
EEC	European Economic Community
FAZ	*Frankfurter Allgemeine Zeitung*
FDP	Freie Demokratische Partei
GB	Gesamtdeutscher Block
GB/BHE	Gesamtdeutscher Block/Block der Heimatvertriebenen und Entrechteten
GDP	Gesamtdeutsche Partei
NATO	North Atlantic Treaty Organizaion
NSDAP	Nationalsozialistische Deutsche Arbeiterpartei
OEEC	Organization for European Economic Cooperation
Spiegel	*Der Spiegel*
SPD	Sozialdemokratische Partei Deutschlands
SRP	Sozialistische Reichspartei
WAV	Wirtschaftliche Aufbauvereinigung
VDB	*Verhandlungen des Deutschen Bundestages*
Welt	*Die Welt*
Zeit	*Die Zeit*

Preface

This book reached the publishers later than intended. I am therefore extremely grateful to Professor Keith Robbins, Editor of the 'Profiles in Power' series, and Heather McCallum, Editor-in-Chief at Pearson, for waiting so patiently for the manuscript. In carrying out my research, I have received invaluable help from the Librarians of the Konrad-Adenauer-Stiftung, Bonn, St Antony's College, Oxford, the German Historical Institute, London, and the Europa Institute, University of Edinburgh; and also from the Adenauer Foundation in London. In addition, I am very grateful to the following, who read the draft manuscript and made a number of valuable suggestions: Professor William Paterson, Director of the Institute of German Studies, University of Birmingham, Mr Richard McAllister, Senior Lecturer in Politics, University of Edinburgh, and Mrs Alison Mayne, former Exhibitioner in German and History at St Hilda's College, Oxford. Alison, who happens to be my eldest daughter, also proofread the whole book with her usual thoroughness. Finally, I am indebted to another daughter, Mrs Jane Thain, a computer expert par excellence, who made a superb job of word-processing the manuscript, including notes, references, bibliography and German dialectical marks. Without the invaluable help given by all of these, my book would never have reached the point of publication. Any errors of fact and judgement are of course mine.

Ronald Irving

University of Edinburgh

Chronology

1871	Foundation of Second German Empire
1876	Born, 5 January, Cologne (3rd of 5 children)
1894	Passed *Abitur* at Aposteln Gymnasium
1894–97	Law student at Universities of Freiburg, Munich and Bonn.
1897–1906	Legal official in Cologne
1904	Married Emma Weyer: children – Konrad (1906), Max (1910), Rhia (1910).
1906	Elected a Deputy Mayor of Cologne
1909	Elected First Deputy Mayor of Cologne
1914–18	The Great War
1916	Death of first wife
1917	Elected Mayor of Cologne for 12 years
1918	November: Kaiser Wilhelm II abdicated; Germany a Republic; Armistice
1919–1933	The Weimar Republic
1919	June: Treaty of Versailles
	September: Adenauer married Auguste (Gussie) Zinsser: children – Paul (1923), Lotte (1925), Libeth (1928), Georg (1931)
1921	Elected President of Prussian State Council (re-elected annually till 1933)
1921 & 1926	Possible Chancellor-candidate
1929	Elected Mayor of Cologne for a further 12 years. Wall Street Crash
1933–45	Third Reich (January 1933: Hitler Chancellor. April 1945: Hitler's suicide)
1933	Dismissed as Mayor of Cologne by Nazis
1939–45	Second World War
1944	Imprisoned for 3 months after July Plot (failed attempt to assassinate Hitler)
1945	May: Germany's unconditional surrender. Reappointed Mayor of Cologne (May); dismissed (October)

1946	Chairman of CDU, British Zone
1948	Death of second wife. Currency reform (new *Deutschmark*)
1948–49	Chairman of Parliamentary Council (drew up Federal Republic's Constitution, the Basic Law). Berlin Blockade. NATO founded
1949	First Bundestag Election. CDU/CSU leading party; Adenauer elected Chancellor.
1950	May: Schuman Plan for European Coal and Steel Community. Implemented by Treaty of Paris, 1951
	June: outbreak of Korean War (lasted till 1953)
	October: Pleven Plan for European Defence Community
	October: First National Congress of CDU. Elected Chairman (retained office till 1966)
1951	March: Federal Republic allowed Foreign Ministry (Foreign Minister as well as Chancellor till 1955)
	May: Federal Republic joined Council of Europe
1952	May: Treaty of Paris (EDC) and General Treaty (important step towards West German sovereignty)
1953	Second Bundestag Election. Major success for Christian Democrats
1955	Federal Republic sovereign state. Joined NATO
1957	Saarland returned to Germany
	Treaties of Rome (Euratom and European Economic Community)
	third Bundestag Election. Christian Democrats won absolute majority
1959	Presidential Election
196	Berlin Wall built (August)
	fourth Bundestag Election. Setback for Christian Democrats, though still leading party
1962	*Spiegel* Affair
1963	January: De Gaulle rejected UK's application to join EEC. Franco-German Treaty
	fall (May: dismissed by parliamentary party. October: Erhard succeeded as Chancellor)
1965	Fifth Bundestag Election (Christian Democrats won under Erhard)
1967	Death, 19 April

Introduction

Biography is the one thing needful for the study of history.

Thomas Carlyle

Any man who has, like Adenauer, had an era named after him[1] is worthy of a 'Profiles in Power' biography. For this series aims not only to present life histories of interesting men and women, but also to set them in the context of their times. It also aims to do something which is more difficult – to assess how exactly they influenced the major developments of their times.

Konrad Adenauer's life (1876–1967) spanned four very different periods in German history. He was born and brought up in the Prussian-dominated Second German Empire (1871–1918). He played an important role as Mayor of Cologne and a minor one as a national politician in Germany's first attempt at democracy, the Weimar Republic (1919–33). He survived the twelve years of Hitler's Third Reich (1933–45). Then in 1949, aged seventy-three, he became the first Chancellor of the Federal Republic of Germany, retaining that office for fourteen years.

The domestic and foreign policies implemented in the 'Adenauer era' (1949–63) were of immense importance in Germany's second attempt at liberal democracy and first attempt at full integration with the West – through her commitment to the American-led Atlantic Alliance and to West European, and especially Franco-German, reconciliation. Adenauer has been praised by many as a democrat and reconciler, but criticized by others for his autocratic behaviour and the rigidity of his policies. Certainly, in the final years of his Chancellorship, at home he seemed to give up listening to the advice of his colleagues, and abroad to become unnecessarily subservient to General de Gaulle and unduly simplistic in his hardline anti-Communism as the era of détente opened.

The 'Adenauer era' certainly saw a remarkable degree of social and economic reconstruction in West Germany, and of international reconciliation (except with the Communists) after the devastation and distrust caused by the Second World War. But how far was Adenauer merely a product of his times? And how far did he influence the years with which his name is associated? These are the difficult questions which this book will attempt to answer.

The times of course tend to produce the man. The Germans were ready for an 'Adenauer'. They had lost all faith in the great *Weltanschauungen*. Too many millions had died for 'my country right or wrong', for 'my fatherland', for an 'infallible leader' – for 'ein Reich, ein Volk, ein Führer'. Others recognized the sterility of inter-confessional rivalry and inter-class rigidity. Adenauer was thus able to take advantage of the historical circumstances of the post-war period. He, like the vast majority of his fellow citizens, wanted to put the past behind him; to reduce religious and social differences; to learn from the failures of the Weimar Republic; to commit Germany *genuinely* (albeit initially of course only West Germany) to liberal democracy, that is to say to democracy in terms of *political culture* and *attitudes*, and not just in the words of the Constitution; and to work in partnership with the other European liberal democracies rather than trying always to dominate or rival them. The times, then, were ripe for the man. The tide was flowing in the direction Adenauer wanted. The man at the tiller may at times have been rather autocratic. But the vast majority of the passengers were quite happy about the ship's destination and were prepared to forgive the skipper for his tendency to behave at times as a martinet.

Note and references

1   See many books with 'Adenauer era' in their titles in the Bibliography, e.g. W. Bührer (1993), A. Doering-Manteuffel (1988), R. Hiscocks (1966), K. Knipping and K. Müller (1995), J. Kupper (1985), K. Ruhl (1985), H.P. Schwarz (1981 and 1983) and K. Sontheimer (1991).

Chapter One

Konrad Adenauer:
Youth, Education, Marriage and Early Career

The child is the father of the man.

Wordsworth

Background and upbringing

Konrad Adenauer was born in Cologne on 5 January 1876, the third son
of Johann Konrad Adenauer and Maria Christiana Helena Scharfenberg.
His parents had married in Cologne in August 1871. They had two sons
before Konrad, August born in 1872 and Hans born in 1874, and two
daughters after him, Lilli born in 1879 and a girl who died in infancy in
1882. Like his near contemporary and future political friend Charles de
Gaulle, Adenauer was greatly influenced by his parents. His father was a
junior civil servant in the Court of Appeal in Cologne. He had previously
(1851–68) been a regular soldier in the Prussian Army (the Rhineland
then being part of Prussia, as it had been since the Treaty of Vienna, 1815).
Johann Konrad seems to have been authoritarian, orderly, efficient, punc-
tual and humourless – perhaps what one might expect of a Prussian soldier turned minor civil servant. He was also devoutly Catholic, patriotic
and very ambitious for his sons.[1]

Considering his humble origins Johann Konrad Adenauer had done
well, although he was always relatively poor and never emerged from the
lower middle class. Certainly, prior to Johann Konrad, there had been no
signs of upward mobility in the Adenauer family. The name Adenauer (or
Adeneuer) can be traced back to the sixteenth century in the Eifel region
of the Rhineland. Konrad Adenauer's ancestors probably came from the

village of Flerzheim. By 1835 Adenauer's grandfather, Franz, born in 1810, was running a small bakery in Messdorf near Bonn. Franz Adenauer married in 1831, his wife aged twenty-seven being six years older than he. They had three children, of whom one was Konrad Adenauer's father, Johann Konrad, but Johann Konrad's mother died in 1837 soon after the birth and death of her fourth child. Worse was to come, for his father, who had remarried two months after the death of his first wife (not unusual in those days when life expectancy was so short), died after a fall from a fruit tree in 1840 before he had reached the age of thirty. Franz Adenauer's two young children were brought up by their stepmother Eva in very straitened circumstances. After leaving elementary school at the age of fourteen (like 90 per cent of children at that time) Johann Konrad worked for four years as a farm labourer, bricklayer and domestic servant before joining the Prussian Army. Ten years later he was a sergeant in the Seventh Westphalian Regiment. In 1864 his Regiment was sent to Cologne, an important military base, and it was there that he met his future wife, Helena Scharfenberg. In 1866, Johann Konrad was promoted Second Lieutenant after the battle of Königgrätz in the Austro-Prussian War. This unusual distinction was a reward for outstanding bravery in the field. Two years later Johann Konrad left the army with a view to getting married. He could only have remained a soldier if his wife had been able to provide a large enough dowry for the couple to live at the standard considered appropriate for Prussian officers. Johann Konrad found a job as a secretary in the law courts in Cologne, where he worked as a junior civil servant in the Court of Appeal until his death in 1906. As a reservist he was recalled to the colours briefly during the Franco-Prussian War of 1870–71.

No sooner had that war ended than Johann Konrad married Helena Scharfenberg, he being thirty-nine and she twenty-three. The Adenauers bought 6 Balduinstrasse, Cologne, a two-storey, terraced house with a small back garden. They rented out the first floor, and Helena took in sewing to supplement the family income further. Although both Adenauers were devout Catholics, Helena came from a partially Protestant background. Her father, August Scharfenberg, an army musician from Thuringia and subsequently a clerk in Cologne, was a Protestant. But his wife, Anna Maria Schell, was a Catholic, and Helena was brought up a Catholic. We are inclined to think of Konrad Adenauer as essentially a Catholic Rhinelander, which of course he was, but it is interesting to note that his maternal ancestors came from Thuringia, a strongly Protestant part of Germany. Much later, as leader of the Christian Democratic Union (CDU), Adenauer was to play an important part in bringing together Catholics and Protestants in the interconfessional, albeit predominantly Catholic, CDU.[2] Although Adenauer had a strong personal faith, it should be emphasized that he was never a religious bigot. Perhaps this was because of his awareness of his biconfessional background, even although it was Catholicism which permeated his early life. Indeed, Johann Konrad conducted family prayers every morning and evening, and the Adenauers attended mass every Sunday and then spent Sunday afternoons in prayer and meditation. Throughout his long life Konrad Adenauer was to go to mass regularly and to insist that grace be said before each meal.

The young Konrad seems to have been a shy, stoical, well-mannered child. He inherited his parents' religious devotion, his mother's staying power (*Ausdauer*) and his father's self-discipline, patriotism and ambition – also his quick temper, for throughout his life Adenauer never suffered fools gladly. He was to bring up his children as he himself had been brought up – strictly and devoutly: on Sundays Adenauer's children were forbidden to have friends in the house, were not allowed out except to go to church, and were expected to spend the afternoons reading morally uplifting books (with Adenauer deciding what was, and was not, 'morally uplifting'!). It is difficult for secular Europeans at the beginning of the twenty-first century to comprehend our nineteenth-century ancestors who had such strong beliefs in a personal God – a God who would more-over punish people ruthlessly for their sins. Adenauer's belief in this Old Testament type of God was only moderated in his early twenties when he read the works of Carl Hilty, a Swiss Protestant moral philosopher. Many years later Adenauer told his biographer, Paul Weymar, that Hilty had widened his religious views but had not undermined his Christian faith.[3] Two of Hilty's books, *Happiness* and *What is Faith?*, first read and marked by Adenauer at the turn of the century, were found on his bedside table at the end of his life.[4] Hilty combined Christianity and Stoicism in his moral philosophy, and many of his ideas became part of Adenauer's own philosophy. Hilty, for example, argued that happiness was not something one could aim to achieve in this world: rather it was a by-product of hard work, modest living and service to others. In addition, Hilty emphasized something which appealed particularly to Adenauer – the value of communing quietly with nature; certainly Adenauer always loved both hill walking, especially in the Eifel Mountains and Black Forest, and gardening. His childhood dream of becoming a professional gardener was in a sense fulfilled later in life among his beloved roses at Rhöndorf near Bonn.

Adenauer was no theologian, and his Christianity was always practical rather than theoretical. As a young administrator, and later as Mayor, he took a considerable interest in Cologne's social problems. The Catholic Church in the Cologne of Adenauer's youth was essentially ultramontane – in line with the anti-liberal, anti-modern stance of the Papacy in the late nineteenth century. But Cologne was also a centre of the Catholic social movement. In particular Adolf Kolping, a vicar at Cologne Cathedral, emphasized that it was essential for the Church to reach out to the working classes who, uprooted from rural security, had flocked into the industrial cities of Germany. Kolping argued that these rootless people would turn to Socialism if the Church did not address their problems. Inspired by Kolping, Social Catholicism made significant progress. By 1887 the Cologne Catholic Workers Association had 3,500 members, and by 1913 it had 11,000. Adenauer joined the Centre Party (*Zentrum*), which had been set up to defend the interests of the Catholic Church when it came under attack from Bismarck in the *Kulturkampf* of the 1870s. By the decade before the First World War the Cologne Centre Party was still essentially conservative, but it had a significant progressive ('social Catholic') wing. Overall, the Catholic Church to which Adenauer belonged was a force for stability. On the one hand, it was firmly opposed to atheistic, revolutionary Socialism; on the other, it was trying to implement the social teaching of the Church. Adenauer himself was always a conservative Catholic, but he also had a strong sense of social responsibility. This was later to be shown when, as Mayor of Cologne in the 1920s, he carried out a huge programme of slum clearance and created the city's green belt; and of course after the Second World War, when he was chairman of the Christian Democratic Union (CDU), a party which combined capitalist economic thinking with Catholic social teaching.[5]

If Adenauer was greatly influenced by his Catholic upbringing, by the ethics of Carl Hilty and by the practical attitudes and values of the Church in Cologne, he was also much influenced by his father's patriotism and ambition for his sons. Johann Konrad's strong patriotism doubtless owed much to his seventeen years in the Army. Although Konrad Adenauer never served in the Army owing to ill health, he was well aware of his father's patriotic views, the *Kulturkampf* notwithstanding. Indeed, Johann

Konrad was a strong admirer of Bismarck, and in 1894 he managed to get the Iron Chancellor to sign a photograph of himself, adding the words: 'To the young Konrad Adenauer'.[6] Moreover, Adenauer often recalled later in life that his proudest moment as a child had been when he was taken to see Kaiser Wilhelm I when the Emperor came to Cologne for the opening of the new Cathedral in 1880.[7] The idea that Adenauer was an 'unpatriotic' Rhinelander (see next chapter) or a 'cosmopolitan European' in the style of Metternich rather than a loyal and patriotic German simply does not square with his upbringing or his devotion to his country and respect for his father.[8] However, Adenauer was never militaristic or chauvinistic. He never forgot what his father had told him about the battle of Königgrätz (1866), after which thousands of men had been left to die in agony from their wounds. Given his father's personal experience of war – and even more in the light of Germany's appalling casualties in the First and Second World Wars – it was not surprising that Adenauer became a strong supporter of European reconciliation and integration after 1945. He was nevertheless a firm believer in the concept of the 'just war'. Certainly if a war had to be fought against an atheistic, totalitarian regime like the USSR, Adenauer had no doubt that democratic Germans should be prepared to fight. Hence, his strong commitment to the Atlantic Alliance and NATO as Chancellor of the Federal Republic in the 1950s. Adenauer thus came to believe both in European reconciliation and in the concept of the 'just war'.[9]

Adenauer's father, then, imbued his family with the values of Catholicism and patriotism. But above all he wanted his sons to achieve respectable middle-class jobs. In order to aspire to these Johann Konrad's three sons needed the best education he could afford. This was why he let out rooms in the house in Balduinstrasse. Indeed, one lodger, Karl Tonger, repaid the family handsomely, for on his death he left the Adenauers 30,000 Marks in shares to help pay for the boys' education. When the value of this legacy declined during the industrial recession of the 1880s, Johann Konrad had to sell the terraced house in Balduinstrasse and move into rented accommodation in Schaafenstrasse in order to continue to pay the boys' fees at the Aposteln Gymnasium in Cologne. Johann Konrad himself had taught the boys to read from the age of five, and in due course all three passed their *Abitur* (University entrance examination) at the Aposteln Gymnasium. August became a successful lawyer (dying in 1952), Hans became a canon of Cologne Cathedral (dying in 1937), and of course

Konrad went on to become Chancellor of the Federal Republic of Germany. Konrad Adenauer himself passed his *Abitur* in 1894. He was not one of the most distinguished scholars of his year, but he passed out in the top quarter. His best subject was singing, but he also achieved good reports for History, German and Latin. His overall grade was 'satisfactory'. Interestingly (although it was not uncommon at that time) he never learnt any English at school. Indeed, Anneliese Poppinga recalled many years later having to teach Adenauer a few English phrases so that he could converse with Queen Elizabeth when he visited London in 1959 aged eighty-three.[10]

Konrad Adenauer, then, came from a relatively humble background. He himself claimed that he had had to share a bed with his brother, Hans, until he was seventeen, although his sister Lilli later maintained that this was merely Konrad exaggerating the deprivation of his childhood.[11] It is certainly true that he was a somewhat sickly child: he had tuberculosis in a leg and had to wear a brace for a year, and he was troubled with bronchitis which later prevented him from doing military service; he also seems to have suffered from diabetes as a young man; and much later, when he was forty, he had a minor heart attack. He nevertheless went on to live to the age of ninety-one. The Adenauer family certainly seems to have been chronically short of money. In winter only the kitchen was properly heated, and in December each year the family stopped eating meat at Sunday lunch to save up for a Christmas tree. Their only holidays were to Lessenich, a hamlet near Bonn, where they occasionally stayed in a guesthouse. Like many from such a background, Konrad Adenauer retained simple tastes in food and drink throughout his life, and he was always very thrifty. Even when he was the highly paid Mayor of Cologne, he always insisted on the reimbursement of any official expenses incurred by him. And many years later, as Chancellor, he despised extravagant receptions and cocktail parties, preferring to give even distinguished guests a few sandwiches and a glass of wine when they visited him at Rhöndorf. He was always more interested in taking them round his beautiful garden than he was in satisfying their appetites.

Education

In a sense the biggest scholastic achievement of Konrad Adenauer and his brothers was to get into the Aposteln Gymnasium, a Catholic grammar school in Cologne which specialized in classics. Once they had gained places at this grammar school and, assuming the fees could continue to be paid, they were extremely likely to go on to university. Johann Konrad had spent many hours teaching his boys to read, and their skill at reading enabled them to miss the first year of elementary school. It should be remembered that in the 1880s fewer than 10 per cent of German children received an education beyond elementary school, and of the 8 per cent who went to gymnasia, only about a third made it into the élite classical gymnasia. The headmaster in Adenauer's time laid great emphasis on Catholic devotion and German patriotism, but the boys spent nearly half their time studying Latin and Greek, with the remainder being spent on German, History, Geography, Maths, Singing and Gymnastics. Much of the teaching was done by rote, and even in his old age Adenauer, like Harold Macmillan, could recite lengthy passages from Homer, Virgil and Horace.

After nine years of hard work at the Aposteln Gymnasium, university was a fairly relaxed time for Adenauer. Having more or less run out of money, Johann Konrad had wanted the young Konrad to go straight into paid employment. But after only two weeks at the Seligmann Bank, Adenauer persuaded his father to allow him to study law (as his eldest brother August had done). This decision was made possible thanks to a grant from a Cologne educational foundation. Adenauer followed the university programme common to many young Cologne law students. He spent one term at Freiburg University in Baden (1894), two terms at Munich University (1894–95) and six terms at Bonn University (1895–97). Not a great deal is known about his student days, but there is little doubt that they broadened his outlook and that for the first time in his life he had a little independence. Unlike many students of his time he seems to have attended lectures conscientiously, but with only 90 Marks to spend each month he was in no position to lead an extravagant life, even if he had wanted to do so. Adenauer enjoyed visiting the countryside, and he walked regularly in the Black Forest region around Freiburg, in the Bavarian Hills to the south of Munich, and in his final university year at Bonn in the Eifel Mountains and Siebengebirge. He had one particular friend as a student, Raimund Schlüter, and they remained on the best of terms right up to Schlüter's early death in 1901. Adenauer and Schlüter seem to have enjoyed not only walking but also music and art. Adenauer went to the opera for the first time as a student in Munich, and he remained a devotee of opera for the rest of his life. Apart from opera, his taste in music was generally conservative – Haydn, Mozart, Schubert and Beethoven. He also enjoyed poetry – again his tastes were conservative, notably Goethe, Heine, Mörike and Schiller, and again they remained life-long interests. Years later, as Chancellor of the Federal Republic, he liked to read poetry every night before falling asleep. When he was ninety, his former secretary Anneliese Poppinga organized an anthology of his favourite poems as a special present.[12]

Although Adenauer was a relatively impoverished student, he man-aged to save enough money while at Munich University to go on holiday with his friend Raimund Schlüter in Bohemia, Switzerland and Italy. They travelled fourth class and often slept overnight in waiting rooms at rail-way stations. Adenauer never lost his love for Northern Italy and was to spend many holidays at Cadenabbia on Lake Como when Chancellor. However, when he returned from his only lengthy student holiday in 1895, he had to face the wrath of his father who accused him of being a spendthrift. Adenauer promised to 'waste' no more money on such trips and settled down to six terms of hard work at Bonn University. In any case he had to spend the last six terms of his training as a lawyer at a Prussian University, and as Bonn was one of the best Prussian universities, it was ideal to go to the local university to complete his studies. In 1897 Adenauer passed his law finals with the grade 'good'. This entitled him to read for a doctorate, but, lacking the necessary finance, he opted instead for the higher civil service exams: he could perhaps eventually take a doctorate in law if in the meantime he worked in the legal services of Cologne. He spent four and a half years working in the city's courts as an unpaid legal assistant (1897–1902), and three more as a paid junior advocate under the distinguished Cologne barrister Hermann Kausen (1903–6). In the course of these eight years of legal work, he passed the higher civil service exams in Berlin in 1901, but to his disappointment only with the grade 'satisfactory'.

Marriage and early career

The years 1901–2 were a minor watershed for Adenauer. Disappointed with his grade in the final examination for the higher civil service and rather bored with his job administering justice in Cologne, he seems to have thought of becoming a country solicitor, but failed to find a suitable job. 1901 was also a year of tragedy for Adenauer, for his great friend Raimund Schlüter, who had become a solicitor in the small Eifel town of Gmund, died suddenly a fortnight before he was due to get married. However, there was a much happier side to the year, because in the summer Adenauer became unofficially engaged to Emma Weyer, an engagement which became official in 1902, leading to his marriage in January 1904.

Adenauer's marriage to Emma Weyer was undoubtedly a significant step up in the world, especially when combined with his new job (from autumn 1903) as a temporary replacement for his sick boss, Hermann Kausen. This 'temporary' replacement lasted two years and gave Adenauer access to Cologne's Upper District Court. His marriage was no less import-ant than his promotion in the legal world. Sixty years later Adenauer told his secretary, Anneliese Poppinga, that prior to his marriage he had felt a sense of inferiority in what was still a very structured society.[13] Until 1902 he had been dependent on his father's allowance, because he received no pay during his four years' work in the administration of justice prior to his civil service examination in October 1901. But, quite apart from money, he seems to have been very conscious of the fact that he was the son of a junior civil servant, even although he himself was a fully qualified lawyer and administrator. His meeting with, and marriage to, Emma Weyer changed all that, for he married into an old and distinguished Cologne family.

Adenauer met Emma at the Klettenburg Tennis Club, a Catholic club also known as the 'Pudelnass' (Wet Racquet) Club because the members apparently played tennis three days a week whatever the weather. The game was less important than the opportunity to meet the opposite sex, because in those days tennis was a highly stylized game with the men dressed in jackets and ties and the women in long dresses and hats. It seems very likely that Adenauer, who was no sportsman (although a keen hill walker), had an 'eye for the main chance'. If so, he was not disap-pointed, because he had not been a member of the tennis club for very long before he fell in love with Emma Weyer, a love which was soon recip-rocated. Emma's father had died in 1884 aged only forty-four as a result of a hiking accident when Emma was only two; at the time of his death he was already a senior figure in the Cologne insurance industry. Emma's grandfather, Johann Peter Weyer, had been an even more prominent figure, having been a distinguished architect and town planner. In the 1840s he had left the profession of architecture to become a railway entrepreneur, had made a fortune, and opened an art gallery, the Weyer Gallery. By 1862 the gallery had nearly 600 paintings, including works by Dürer, Holbein, Rembrandt and Rubens. Not surprisingly Emma and her family inherited many fine paintings, including some Dutch Old Masters, which in due course were to be found hanging in the various Adenauer houses.

Emma Weyer's mother also came from a prominent family of Cologne lawyers called Berghaus. The Berghaus family was notorious for its religious devotion – not least Emma's mother, who, stunned by the unexpected death of her husband, became a virtual religious recluse from the mid-1880s until her death in 1911. Although Adenauer came from an 'inferior' social background, his strong Catholicism and moral earnestness appealed to Emma's mother. She not only gave permission for Adenauer and Emma to marry, but also helped them financially in the early years of their marriage, which took place in January 1904, when Adenauer was twenty-eight and Emma twenty-three. The newly married couple had a distinctly upper middle-class honeymoon, described in detail in a diary kept by Emma. Their first stop was Bonn (the Siebengebirge looked particularly beautiful to Emma); they then went to Lake Geneva and stayed in Montreux; and afterwards they travelled down the Rhône valley to Marseilles, where Emma admired the famous Cannebière and the open markets full of Mediterranean fruit. The Adenauers' next stop was Monte Carlo, where Emma had a brief flutter on the tables, an extravagance avoided by the austere Konrad. After Monte Carlo they visited northern Italy, taking lengthy walks in and around Rapallo, San Remo and Genoa. Finally, they returned to Cologne via Switzerland and southern Germany, stopping off to admire Freiburg, where of course Adenauer had been a student. Their first home in Cologne was a well-furnished flat in Klosterstrasse, to which Emma brought some fine paintings and furniture.

During the first two years of his marriage Adenauer seems to have passed through further uncertainty about his career. He once again considered becoming a country solicitor in a small Rhineland town and applied successfully for jobs in Rheinberg and Kempten in 1904 and 1905; however, in the end he decided not to accept them owing to their modest salaries and limited prospects. Nevertheless, there can be little doubt that the applications were serious, because Adenauer was fond of walking and gardening, and a rural practice would in some ways have suited him. The year 1906 was an important one for Adenauer. His father died at the age of seventy-three; his first son was born (and named Johann Konrad after his grandfather); and, most important of all, Adenauer was elected one of Cologne's twelve Deputy Mayors. This career change seems to have come about almost by chance, because one of the Deputy Mayors retired unexpectedly. Adenauer applied for this administrative job, and with the support of his former boss, Hermann Kausen, chairman of the Cologne Centre Party, and with the approval of the Mayor, Wilhelm Becker, the City Council elected Adenauer a Deputy Mayor in January 1906. He took up his new job as a full-time administrative official in March. Adenauer's father died of a stroke three days after his appointment, but had time to tell his son that he hoped he would go on to become Mayor; Johann Konrad's ambitions for his sons clearly lasted right to the end of his life and now seemed to be on the verge of fulfilment.

Having become a Deputy Mayor, good fortune again shone on Adenauer. Mayor Becker retired two years ahead of time in 1907, and Max Wallraf, an Independent, was elected Mayor by the Council. Wallraf was in fact Emma Adenauer's uncle. It did Adenauer no harm to be related to the Mayor, although advantage seems to have accrued less from nepotism than from the fact that Wallraf took a 'relaxed' view of his job – for much of the time he was as interested in hunting as in administering Cologne, and was content to leave the day-to-day running of the city to his deputies. Adenauer was further helped by the decision of Wilhelm Farwick, the First Deputy Mayor, to join the Schaafhausen Bank in 1909. Farwick had been the leader of the Centre Party group on the city council, and, as that group was the largest, it was able to propose his successor. The efficient young head of the taxation department, Konrad Adenauer, was duly elected First Deputy Mayor in 1909. At the age of thirty-three this was a very significant promotion, reflected in the large salary which went with the job (18,000 Marks per annum). As First Deputy Mayor Adenauer was responsible for financial and fiscal matters and for personnel, and, in line with his new status and wealth, he decided to build a substantial detached house in the Max-Bruch-Strasse, beside the city's main park.

While Adenauer's career prospered during the first five years of his marriage (1904–9), and was to continue to do so until the outbreak of war in 1914 – indeed thereafter too – his home life was not entirely happy. This had nothing to do with his choice of bride, for he and Emma complemented each other ideally. But sadly neither was fully fit. While Adenauer suffered from mild diabetes and bronchitis, Emma became seriously ill. She had taken a long time to recover from the birth of Johann Konrad in 1906. Soon afterwards it became apparent that she had a problem with curvature of the spine, and this led to the malfunctioning of her kidneys. Although a second son Max was born in 1910 and a daughter, Rhia, in 1912, Adenauer was told by medical specialists that his wife's condition would deteriorate and that her illness was terminal. Emma was in fact an invalid from 1912 until her death in 1916 aged thirty-five. Adenauer remained devoted to Emma to the end of her life, and at least they had the means to employ nurses and domestic staff to look after her. But the strain on him was considerable, and when Emma finally died in October 1916 Adenauer was deeply moved, remaining in mourning until December 1917.

By the time of Emma's death the Great War had been going on for two years and, when Adenauer ended his mourning, he was already Mayor of Cologne, having been elected to this key administrative post in October 1917. The war was of course a climacteric for all Germans, but Cologne was very much at the centre of that climacteric owing to its being an important railway junction, industrial city and garrison town.[14]

Interestingly, no documents survive which indicate exactly what Adenauer thought about German foreign policy in the years prior to 1914, or indeed about his views when the war started in August of that year. However, there seems no doubt that Adenauer was a conventional patriotic German. Many years later his view was that the war had been a momentous mistake brought about by human stupidity. But there is no reason to doubt that at the time Adenauer watched with pride as the Cologne regiments marched to war; and that he admired the efficiency of Germany's war-machine – during the mobilization of August 1914 a troop train passed over Cologne's Hohenzollern Bridge every ten minutes. Adenauer was an administrator, a trained bureaucrat, not a politician – and certainly not a critic of the war. He agreed with the majority of Germans who considered that they must resist the 'encirclement' of Germany and Austria-Hungary by the Franco-Russian alliance. There was a job to be done. Adenauer's was to organize food and provisions for the huge garrison city of Cologne. He was in charge of the Provisions Office while he remained First Deputy Mayor (till 1917), and on the whole he succeeded in keeping Cologne adequately provided with bread, meat and milk for the first half of the war. After 1916 things became more difficult owing to the success of the Allied naval blockade. Rationing and a variety of ersatz foods were introduced, one of the most famous (or infamous) being 'Cologne bread', consisting of wheat, rice and barley. By 1917–18, there were severe shortages in Cologne, as in all major German cities.

Moreover, Cologne, as a major railway junction and military base, had to cope with large numbers of soldiers on leave as well as with hospitals for the wounded. The Cologne administration succeeded as well as it did in part because there was a party political truce. Owing to the restricted franchise[15] there were no Social Democrats on the City Council prior to 1914, and during most of the war the Council consisted of 60 members (36 Centre Party and 24 Liberals). But Adenauer worked successfully not only with the Centre Party and Liberals but also with the Social Democrats, who were led by Wilhelm Sollmann, the Cologne editor of the *Rheinische Zeitung* and a prominent SPD moderate and patriot. Adenauer insisted that three Social Democrats should be co-opted onto the Cologne City Council in recognition of the support he received from Sollmann and from the local trade union leaders. Adenauer thus demonstrated in the war years what he was to show in the 1920s – and even more in the post-1945 period – that he was not a narrow 'party' man. Indeed, he was quite prepared to work with politicians from other parties, provided they were not the sort of people he considered as ideologues or extremists.

Notes and references

1 All the major biographies of Adenauer contain much useful information about his youth and upbringing. For Adenauer's own memories of his early days, see especially P. Weymar, *Konrad Adenauer: the authorised biography* (London, 1957) [henceforth Weymar, 1957] and A. Poppinga, *Meine Erinnerungen an Konrad Adenauer* (Stuttgart, 1970) [henceforth Poppinga, 1970]. Weymar's book was written by an admirer and is based on discussions/interviews with Adenauer. Poppinga's is full of excellent insights – it was written by Adenauer's devoted secretary (from 1958 until his death in 1967). Poppinga also played an important part in helping Adenauer to organize his own *Erinnerungen* (4 vols), which contain some early memories [henceforth Adenauer *Erinnerungen* 1, 2, 3 or 4]. For further information about Adenauer's youth, education, career and marriage, see the early chapters of the two most scholarly biographies – H.P. Schwarz, *Adenauer. Der Aufstieg 1876–1952* (Stuttgart, 1986) – English translation *Konrad Adenauer: From the German Empire to the Federal Republic* (Providence, RI, 1995) [henceforth Schwarz, 1995], and H. Köhler, *Adenauer. Eine politische Biographie* (Frankfurt-am-Main, 1994) [henceforth Köhler, 1994].

Also useful, although more journalistic, are P. Koch, *Konrad Adenauer. Eine politische Biographie* (Hamburg, 1985) [henceforth Koch, 1985], T. Prittie, *Konrad Adenauer 1867–1967: a study in fortitude* (London, 1972) [henceforth Prittie, 1972] and C. Williams, *Adenauer: the Father of the New Germany* (London, 2000).

2 See below, chapter 3, pp. 64–7.

3 Weymar, 1957, p. 57.

4 Poppinga, 1970, p. 188.

5 See below, chapter 3, pp. 60–8.

6 U. Frank-Planitz, *Konrad Adenauer. Eine Biographie in Bild und Wort* (Stuttgart, 1994), p.11.

7 Weymar, 1957, p. 18.

8 Poppinga, 1970, p. 13 (and many other pages), where she emphasizes Adenauer's frequently expressed affection for his Fatherland, not least in his farewell speech to the Bundestag as Chancellor on 15 October 1963.

9 On Adenauer's foreign policy, see below, chapter 4.

10 Schwarz, 1995, p. 57.

11 Koch, 1985, p. 22.

12 Poppinga, 1970, p. 190.

13 Poppinga, 1970, p. 247.

14 On Cologne in the First World War, including Adenauer's Mayorship from October 1917, see below, chapter 2, pp. 15–37.

15 On the restricted franchise, see below, chapter 2, p. 31.

Chapter Two

Adenauer:
Mayor of Cologne in War and Peace

The Great War and its aftermath

The year 1917 – like 1906 – was a watershed in Adenauer's life. He spent almost the whole of 1917 in mourning for his wife Emma, who had died in October 1916; he was involved in a serious car accident in March 1917; and he became Mayor of Cologne in October of that year.[1]

In 1916 Adenauer had considered standing for the post of Mayor of Aachen, but had finally decided to stay on as Deputy Mayor of Cologne in the hope of succeeding Max Wallraf as Mayor in 1919. However, in August 1917 Wallraf was asked to join the Government in Berlin as Under Secretary of State at the Ministry of the Interior. At the time Adenauer was still convalescing in the Black Forest after his car accident, which had been caused by his chauffeur falling asleep and driving into a tram car. In spite of serious injuries, Adenauer had managed to stagger from the wreckage and reach the nearest hospital. But the accident damaged his face permanently, giving him the features which were said to make him look rather like a Red Indian Chief. On Wallraf's departure for Berlin the first question which had to be answered was whether Adenauer was fit enough to stand for the Mayorship. The Centre Party leaders, Hugo Mönnig and Johannes Rings, decided to give their full support to Adenauer after visiting him at his convalescent home in the Black Forest. They considered that in spite of his new physiognomy he had suffered no brain damage, and were apparently reassured when Adenauer remarked, 'I'm only abnormal on the outside!'[2]

It was also essential to obtain the support of the Liberal group, the second largest on the City Council. After some hesitation their leaders, Louis Hagen and Bernhard Falk, endorsed Adenauer, and he was duly elected Mayor by the City Council by 52–0 (with 2 abstentions) on 18 September 1917, being sworn in a month later. Thus at the age of forty-one Adenauer became the Mayor of Prussia's second largest city. The importance of the post was reflected in his substantial salary of 42,000 Marks. He was elected because he was considered to be 'a first-class administrator ... a tireless worker ... and an excellent speaker'.[3] Not surprisingly, in his inaugural speech as Mayor Adenauer emphasized his total support for the Kaiser and the German Empire, but more prosaically he also stressed his determination to keep Cologne's finances on a sound footing, to maintain its trade and industry, and to resolve its social problems.[4] By 1917–18 Adenauer was in fact faced with huge problems in relation to these three objectives. One hundred thousand of Cologne's young men were in the armed forces, and the city was beginning to run short of food and medicines. At the same time, it was striving to keep its armaments industry at full production, to maintain its hospitals for the wounded, and to cater for the thousands of soldiers who passed through the city on the way to the Front or spent their leave there.

As regards the overall war situation, by the beginning of 1918 the chances of Germany winning the war were evenly balanced. On the positive side (from Germany's point of view) Russia had collapsed after the revolutions of March and October 1917. The latter was followed by the Bolshevik Government's request for an armistice, and the Treaty of Brest-Litovsk (March 1918) left Germany in control of Finland, the Baltic provinces, Poland and the Ukraine. Ludendorff and Hindenburg, who had in effect run the German Government as a military dictatorship since August 1916, ignoring the views of the Kaiser and of Chancellors Bethmann-Hollweg, Michaelis and Hertling, could now redeploy Germany's Eastern armies on the Western Front. Another positive factor was that the unrestricted U-boat campaign, which had been pursued vigorously in the Atlantic since January 1917, had been relatively successful in spite of heavy U-boat losses. In the first three months after the United States entered the war (April 1917), 2 million tons of Allied shipping were sunk. Yet Ludendorff realized that the U-boat campaign alone would not win the war. He was also aware that the Allied sea blockade had led to severe food shortages and was causing great hardship in Germany. But, although the German High Seas Fleet had fared better than the British at the Battle of Jutland in 1916, since that time it had been confined to port, with Admiral Scheer judging that his fleet could not defeat the Royal Navy. The German Fleet had moreover been weakened by the large numbers of officers and men who had been transferred to submarines in 1917. Although the U-boat campaign was going well, the cost to Germany was huge: by the end of the war 180 of Germany's 350 submarines had been sunk, and in almost all sinkings the whole crew was lost.

Meanwhile, in Germany itself the Independent Social Democratic Party (USPD) had been set up in 1916 to demand a negotiated peace; and there had been strikes in Leipzig and Berlin with demands for better rations as well as peace without annexations. There had also been naval mutinies in June–July 1917 (long before the well-known Kiel mutiny of October 1918), with mutineers demanding better conditions on the lower deck and a negotiated peace. Then in July 1917 Matthias Erzberger of the Centre Party put forward a resolution in the Reichstag in favour of 'peace without annexations or indemnities'. The resolution was carried by a two-to-one majority, with not only the Social Democrats, Centre Party and Left Liberals voting for it but also a section of the right-wing National Liberal Party. Chancellor Michaelis 'accepted' the motion, but in practice could do nothing about it with Ludendorff in effective charge of the Government. After the replacement of Michaelis by Hertling in August 1917, the Government was widened to include more peace advocates, but Ludendorff and the High Command paid no attention to their views. In any case the Reichstag undermined its own position by endorsing the annexationist terms of the Treaty of Brest-Litovsk (March 1918), and even the Social Democrats did no more than abstain in the ratification vote.

Ludendorff realized that the war would have to be won in 1918. As time passed, the manpower and industrial strength of the USA would be bound to alter the balance in favour of the Entente countries. In fact, the *military* significance of the entrance of the United States into the war was relatively small, but the *psychological* effect of the USA's declaration of war was considerable. It boosted morale in France and Britain, particularly in France, which had experienced serious military mutinies in 1917. At the same time, the Germans, already short of food and fuel, realized that the naval blockade would be tightened and that shortages would increase the longer the war lasted. By early 1918 Ludendorff had only two options: either to try to negotiate peace from a position of military superiorty (momentarily the case owing to the collapse of Russia) or to win a decisive military victory in the West before the USA's manpower and munitions could alter the balance on the Western Front. Ludendorff opted for victory, and in March 1918 a major German offensive began along the Western Front. Huge advances were made against both the French and the British, but the Allies, under the supreme command of Marshal Foch, prevented a decisive breakthrough. Ludendorff had now used up all his reserves, and in August 1918 the Allies began their counter-attack, rolling back the Germans in three major attacks which gained ground week after week until the Armistice was signed in November 1918. Indeed, by late September, Ludendorff had come to the conclusion that the war was lost. He decided that a 'democratic' government would have a better chance of negotiating reasonable terms with the Entente; hence the appointment of the liberal-minded Prince Max of Baden as Chancellor. However, before an armistice could be negotiated, revolution had broken out in Germany and the Kaiser had abdicated. By the time of the signing of the Armistice, Friedrich Ebert, leader of the SPD, was Chancellor and Germany was a Republic.

The 1914–18 war had cost Germany 6 million casualties (1.8 million killed and 4.2 million wounded). But the final collapse was as much domestic as military. When Adenauer became Mayor of Cologne in October 1917, he seems to have been still relatively optimistic about the outcome of the war. Even in March 1918 he told the City Council that, although there were severe shortages, he hoped that a just peace could be achieved. However, according to his biographer Paul Weymar, he had told Max Wallraf early in 1918 that he thought the war was lost.[5] By June he must have known that it was. For by then Ludendorff's offensive had petered out, and both military and civilian morale had begun to collapse. In Cologne itself there were serious food shortages, and it was reckoned that there were about 17,000 deserters in the Cologne area. These men and other starving citizens were looting and stealing. In October a flu epidemic struck, crippling many factories. The situation was similar in cities throughout Germany, and at the end of the month sailors mutinied in Kiel (and shortly afterwards in Hamburg) on hearing the rumour that Admiral Scheer intended putting the High Seas Fleet to sea to fight the Royal Navy in a last desperate attempt to avoid an enforced armistice.

The naval mutineers were soon moving southwards, being joined by thousands more in Hamburg and Hanover. This was a real crisis for Cologne's young Mayor, but Adenauer rose to the occasion with courage and composure. The SPD leader in Cologne, Wilhelm Sollmann, Captain Otto Schwink, who had taken over the Cologne garrison when its commander General von Kruge fled, and the lawyer Josef Thedieck all attested to Adenauer's calm, decisive leadership during the dark days of October–November 1918.[6] As trainloads of mutineers arrived in Cologne early in November, Adenauer at first wanted to arrest them, but then realized that he had no alternative but to accede to some of their demands, especially as many of the troops in the Cologne garrison immediately joined the mutineers. Adenauer agreed to the setting up of a fifteen-man Soldiers and Workers Council (5 SPD, 5 USPD and 5 soldiers) to run the city. But in practice Adenauer and the city administration remained more important than the Soldiers and Workers Council. Adenauer agreed to wear a red armband, but refused to let the red flag fly over the City Hall. He worked closely with the Soldiers and Workers Council, but personally made many decisions which took the heat out of the situation, for example he ordered that meals be served to all hungry people, including deserters, mutineers and prisoners released from the city's gaols. He also set up a welfare committee consisting of representatives from the political parties and trade unions in addition to 'comrades' from the Soldiers and Workers Council. This committee oversaw, *inter alia*, the demobilization of troops, the issue of railway tickets to troops in transit, the organization of a curfew, the setting up of a special militia to patrol the streets, and the organization of basic food supplies.

Adenauer was undoubtedly an impressive figure throughout the November 'revolution'. Hitherto regarded as a highly competent administrator, he now emerged as a decisive leader in a time of crisis. He remained calm while working 16–18 hours a day, and showed fine judgement in dealing firmly with the 'revolutionaries' without antagonizing them. Indeed, Heinrich Schäfer, the chairman of the Soldiers and Workers Council and in theory Adenauer's political boss, thanked the Mayor on 21 November for staying at his post and 'for making every effort to reestablish law and order in association with the Soldiers and Workers Council'.[7] And the Cologne lawyer Josef Thedieck told his family that: 'The [revolutionary] conditions did not last long. Order was soon restored thanks to the diplomatic skills of Mayor Adenauer ... The Bolsheviks have been repelled in the meantime, and the city authorities are working normally under the supervision of the Soldiers Council.'[8] By the end of the month Adenauer and the city authorities were in full control again.

The 'revolution' of November 1918 was almost certainly less of a threat to the German bourgeoisie than it appeared at the time. Once the revolutionaries had secured the abdication of the Kaiser, the moderate Socialists of the SPD, who formed a majority in the national Government, gradually gained control of the situation. They were as imbued with the German love of order as the Liberals, the Centrists and the Mayors of the great cities. Those who wanted a Soviet-style revolution proved to be a tiny minority, and by early 1919 Ebert's (essentially) Social Democratic government had suppressed the Spartacists in Berlin and the extreme left regime in Bavaria.

Meanwhile in Cologne in late November 1918 there had been a dramatic transformation of the popular mood from quasi-revolution to old-fashioned patriotism. The transformation occurred partly because of the publication of the Armistice terms on 11 November. As far as Cologne was concerned, the key feature was that all of the left bank of the Rhine was to be occupied; buffer zones were to be established on the right bank; Cologne itself was to be occupied by the British Army; and all German Army units were to surrender or withdraw from the occupied areas by 3 December. If the revived 'patriotism' was a reaction to the apparently harsh terms of the Armistice, it was also occasioned by German pride in the half million soldiers of the Fifth and Sixth Armies (including the 65th Cologne Division) who had to retreat through Cologne to beyond the buffer zones on the right bank. The citizens of Cologne applauded the exhausted but superbly disciplined front-line troops with a sense of relief after the indiscipline of late October and the first half of November 1918. This was the spectacle which led Friedrich Ebert to make his unwise remarks about the German Army returning home 'unvanquished in battle',[9] words which were to be remembered in the 1920s by opponents of the Weimar Republic, who fostered the legend that undefeated German soldiers had been betrayed by democratic politicians. Adenauer seems to have been as impressed as his fellow citizens by the impeccable bearing of the retreating German Army. He ordered that church bells be rung (as in 1914), as the troops passed through the city, and he told the people of Cologne that they should welcome the 'courageous warriors' of the Fifth and Sixth Armies. His words of welcome could hardly have been more patriotic: 'Our brothers in field grey are coming home. They are coming home after four years of defending house and home with the greatest heroism the world has ever seen. Undefeated, they are coming home to us.

We will never forget them, nor what they have done for Germany and for the Rhineland.'[10]

Feeding and billeting the half million troops proved to be a huge administrative task, but one which Adenauer and the city administration tackled successfully between 20 October and 3 December 1918. Adenauer was now ready (or as ready as anyone could be) for the short-term uncertainties of occupation and long-term uncertainty about the peace treaty. The British occupying force under General Lawson arrived on 6 December 1918 and remained in Cologne for seven years, the final contingent not leaving until January 1926. The original occupation force consisted of 55,000 men. This number was halved in 1920, and reduced to 9,000 by 1925. On the whole, the discipline of the occupying troops was apparently excellent: the official statistics show that during the seven years of occupation only 18 murders, 81 accidental deaths (mainly in road accidents), 977 rapes and robberies and 4,000 cases of damaged property occurred, a remarkable record for an occupying army. In fact, after early problems over the curfew (soon relaxed) and over adults having to salute British officers (almost immediately abandoned), relations between the citizens of Cologne and the British Army were good. Moreover, this was apparent at the highest level. General Lawson, and later General Ferguson, both got on well with Adenauer. In spite of four years of war, Adenauer and the British commanders were united in their hatred of 'Bolshevism' and disorder; moreover, in the 1920s the British turned out to be much less anti-German than the French.

Remarriage and family life in the 1920s

Before discussing Adenauer's respective roles as Mayor of Cologne and national politician in the Weimar Republic it is appropriate to mention an important personal event which took place on 25 September 1919. For on that day Adenauer married Auguste (Gussie) Zinsser, the daughter of Dr Ferdinand Zinsser, an eminent Cologne dermatologist. The ceremony was performed by Adenauer's brother Hans, a Catholic priest. On the face of it the marriage seemed an unlikely one. The groom was an austere forty-three-year-old widower who was Mayor of one of Germany's greatest cities, while the bride was a lively, musical young woman of twenty-five with little experience of life or politics. He was a devout Catholic, while she had been brought up a Protestant. Moreover, Gussie's father was at first doubtful about the marriage, wondering how Adenauer's three children (then aged thirteen, nine and seven) would get on with their new 'mother', whom they had known throughout their lives almost as an older 'sister', for the Zinssers lived next door to the Adenauers in Max-Bruch-Strasse. When Adenauer asked for the hand of Gussie, Dr Zinsser sent her to Wiesbaden for six months to think things over. However, after three weeks, Gussie returned to Cologne, determined to marry Adenauer. Adenauer insisted only that Gussie should become a Catholic, which she willingly did. Despite the forebodings of the Zinsser parents the marriage was a successful and happy one, lasting almost thirty years. Sadly, the first-born child, Ferdinand, died after only three days, Gussie having given birth prematurely when suffering from eclampsia. Adenauer held the child in his arms throughout his last night, but he was too weak to survive. However, Gussie subsequently gave birth to four healthy children – Paul born in 1923; Lotte in 1925; Libeth in 1928; and Georg in 1931.

The marriage worked well for a variety of reasons. The fact that the two families lived next door to each other proved to be an advantage, as Adenauer's children (from his first marriage) knew the Zinsser girls – Gussie and her sister Lotte had helped to look after the young Adenauers after the death of their mother. Apparently, however, young Konrad made an early complaint that he found it difficult to call Gussie 'Mummy', because he still had clear memories of her as a schoolgirl setting off with her satchel each morning![11] In spite of such minor problems the Zinssers and Adenauers got on well, as did the seven Adenauer children from the two marriages. Gussie also helped the austere Adenauer to relax by organizing musical evenings in their house and by encouraging him to go out frequently to concerts. Gussie was herself an accomplished musician and, although Adenauer never played any instrument, he had enjoyed opera and classical music at university and continued to do so throughout his life.

Many years later some of Adenauer's children were to complain that their upbringing had been unduly strict.[12] It was certainly true that Adenauer lived a very regulated life and was a strict Christian father. And he expected his children to follow his ways – no friends were allowed to visit on Sundays, the whole family attended mass at 9.30 am, and the children's reading was carefully monitored by their father. During the week Adenauer was very punctilious. After breakfast with Gussie (but without the children) he walked his dog for a quarter of an hour. At 8.45 his chauffeur arrived to take him to the office. At midday he returned for lunch, and afterwards had a half-hour siesta – often in the garden, and woe betide any child who disturbed his sleep. Finally, the whole family was expected to be in bed at specific times, with Adenauer and Gussie retiring last at 10.30 pm. Despite this highly disciplined life, the Adenauers were a happy family. In particular, they remembered with great fondness their annual holidays in the Black Forest or at Chandolin in Switzerland, where Adenauer was at his most relaxed organizing daily walks and picnics.

The Rhineland problem

One of the first major post-war problems with which Adenauer had to deal arose directly out of France's policy towards Germany. France's determination to contain Germany was understandable. The French Government was acutely aware not only of France's loss of almost 2 million men in the Great War but also of the annexation of Alsace and Lorraine by Germany in 1871 and of France's general insecurity since that time. The first objective was of course to ensure the return of Alsace and Lorraine, which was accomplished in the Treaty of Versailles. The second was to exact a high price for the war, which the French blamed entirely on Germany. This too was written into the peace treaty. The third was to try to achieve the long-term security of France. This third objective was where the Rhineland came into the equation. The French Government realized that Louis XIV's dream of a Rhine frontier was still out of the question, or, as Adenauer put it at the time, a recipe for a future war.[13] But the idea, imprecisely defined, of a neutral – in practice Francophile – Rhineland buffer state was perhaps feasible. This objective, moreover, had some support among a small minority of Catholic Rhinelanders who had never fully accepted the 'takeover' (as they saw it) of the Rhineland by Protestant Prussia after the Treaty of Vienna (1815).[14]

In late 1918–early 1919 the political situation in Germany was as confused as the situation in Europe as a whole. Some things were, however, clear: Germany had lost the war, the Kaiser had fled to Holland, and Germany had become a Republic. However, the constitution of Germany had still not been drawn up. Nor had the future of Europe been decided. As regards the peace treaty, the Allies had decided that they were going to

lay down its terms at Versailles. Germany would not be involved in negotiating the Treaty: she would simply be told what its terms were, and, if
not acceptable, hostilities would be resumed (or at least that was the
implied threat). With the terms of the Treaty of Versailles unclear during
the first six months of 1919, and the new German constitution undecided
(it was being drafted at Weimar between February 1919 and May 1920),
there was plenty of room for speculation about the future of Germany,
even if it was accepted that the Allies could dictate Europe's international
frontiers.

As far as the Rhineland was concerned, a number of proposals were
being canvassed.[15] The first was that France should occupy all territory up
to the Rhine. Although this was not a serious option, as the British and
Americans were against it on the grounds that it would upset the balance
of power in Europe even more than Germany's annexation of Alsace and
Lorraine had in the previous fifty years, it was an option which had been
canvassed by the French Prime Minister Clemenceau. A second, much
more serious, proposal was that a buffer state, a 'Rhineland Republic',
should be created. This proposal was endorsed by a number of journalists
on the *Kölnische Zeitung*, by the Rhineland separatists led by Dr Josef
Dorten and by General Mangin, the Commanding Officer in the French
zone of occupation who was an enthusiastic protagonist of the 'Rhineland
Republic', which the French presumed would be a satellite state. The third
main option – and this was the one with which Adenauer was most associated (although at times he seemed to toy with the second option, namely
the 'Rhineland Republic') – was the proposal that in a new federal
Germany a new state (*Land*) should be created out of the Rhineland territories which had been part of Prussia since 1815. The final option was that
after the end of the allied occupation there would simply be a return to
the status quo of 1815-1918, i.e. the Rhineland would remain part of
Prussia within the German state, whose external boundaries were to be
decided at Versailles.

The German and Prussian governments not surprisingly favoured the
last option. Among the Germans of the Rhineland, however, views were
divided. The Social Democrats and Liberals supported the continuation of
the old Germany, as they both feared that a non-Prussian Rhineland would
become a 'confessional' (Catholic) state within Germany. However, the
most important party in the Catholic Rhineland was the Centre Party and,
although the Centre Party was not united in its views, Karl Trimborn

(1854–1921), the grand old man of the Party, to the surprise of many, came out in favour of a 'Rhineland Republic'.[16] He argued that after the abdication of the Kaiser there was no longer any reason for the Rhinelanders to maintain their century-long connection with Prussia; and, if the options were French annexation up to the Rhine or a semi-autonomous Rhineland Republic, the latter would be preferable. Moreover, the Rhineland would be returning to its Catholic roots by breaking with Protestant Prussia. But the majority in the Centre Party did not agree with Trimborn. Wilhelm Marx, a Cologne man and future Chancellor, stressed that a semi-autonomous Rhineland Republic would at the very least be strongly influenced by France. This view was also held by Louis Hagen, President of the Cologne Chamber of Commerce and a senior member of the Liberal Party. As a member of the Centre Party, Adenauer found himself in a difficult position. Two of his trusted friends, albeit in other parties, the Social Democratic leader, Wilhelm Sollmann, and the Liberal leader, Bernhard Falk, were strongly against any concessions to the 'separatists' or 'federalists'. But important members of the Centre Party were prepared to consider either a 'separatist' or a 'federal' solution. In these circumstances Adenauer unwisely held three meetings early in 1919 with Dr Dorten, the separatist leader. In the years to come Adenauer was to be accused of having been an unpatriotic German who had been prepared either to break up his country or to endorse a weak, confederal Germany.[17]

Adenauer's views were in fact clearly stated in a speech he made in Cologne on 1 February 1919 to the delegates from the occupied areas elected to the Constituent Assembly[18] (the Constituent Assembly began its deliberations a few days later in Weimar). Adenauer emphasized that he was totally against French annexation up to the Rhine, as this would create instability and doubtless lead to a future war. At the same time he stressed that he wanted to see genuine reconciliation with France. He understood France's fears about the strength of Germany, and not least her concern about the predominant position of Prussia within Germany (42 million of Germany's 65 million inhabitants being Prussian). Adenauer's favoured solution was the breakup of Prussia within a newly constituted federal Germany. He wanted to see the setting up of a 'West German state (*Land*)' within this new federal Germany, but he was against that state being a 'clerical' one; thus he wanted it to consist not only of the Prussian Rhineland but also of parts of Westphalia, the Ruhr and perhaps the Saarland. In addition, if the new state were to be created, it must be approved by all the main political parties in the Rhineland and within Germany as a whole. He realized that the new 'West German state' within a federal Germany would fall short of French aspirations, but he hoped it might receive the support of the British and Americans, who wanted to curb Prussian power but avoid arousing the enmity of the defeated Germans. The special assembly in Cologne – consisting, it should be stressed, of representatives of *all* the main political parties – agreed with Adenauer, and adopted the following resolution: 'Since the division of Prussia is being seriously considered, a Committee elected by this assembly is empowered to draw up plans for the establishment of a West German federal state within the framework of the German Reich and in conformity with the Reich Constitution which is to be drawn up by the German Constituent Assembly.'[19]

Soon afterwards it emerged that the British and American delegates at Versailles were opposed to French aspirations either for annexing German territory up to the Rhine or for setting up a Rhineland buffer state. In mid-May 1919, i.e. six weeks before the signing of the Treaty of Versailles, the German delegation in Paris was told that the Prussian Rhineland would remain within the boundaries of Germany, but that the occupied areas on both the left and right banks of the Rhine would remain under Allied control for fifteen years, after which they would remain demilitarized. When Adenauer heard about these conditions, he was very concerned. He summoned the Committee elected in February 1919 for its first and only meeting on 30 May, and told it that he feared that a fifteen-year occupation of the designated areas would in practice lead to the economic and political separation of the Rhineland from Germany. The Committee decided to send a delegation under Adenauer to see Count Brockdorff-Rantzau, Germany's Foreign Minister and the leader of the German delegation at Versailles, to try to persuade him that it would better for the long-term future of Germany if Prussia were to be dismantled by the setting up of a Rhineland state within a new federal Germany. Adenauer argued that this would satisfy French demands for security and prevent the proposed lengthy occupation of the Rhineland. Despite the strength of the Rhineland delegation – it included the Social Democratic leader Wilhelm Sollmann and the Liberal leader Louis Hagen as well as Adenauer – it achieved nothing. Brockdorff-Rantzau was against the proposal to break up Prussia. Moreover, he claimed that such an offer would be rejected by the Allies and would not lead to their ameliorating the terms of the Treaty.

Brockdorff-Rantzau, however, did pay a visit to Cologne on 7 June, the day after he had met the Rhineland delegation in Paris, to try to sound out local opinion. He was told by Cardinal von Hartmann, the leader of Cologne's Catholics, that what the Rhinelanders wanted above all was an end to uncertainty, i.e. they wanted the Treaty to be signed, even if its terms were harsh, adding that there was no popular support either for the break-up of Prussia or for the separation of the Rhineland from Germany.[20]

Nevertheless, at that very time, the separation of the Rhineland from Germany became, albeit briefly, a real possibility. For on 2 June 1919 Dr Dorten and the separatists, with the support of General Mangin, the commanding officer in the French occupation zone, announced in Wiesbaden that a separate 'Rhineland Republic' was now in existence. The German Government immediately condemned this move. Adenauer, with the support of General Clive, the commanding officer in the British occupation zone, did likewise, and within a few days the phantom 'Rhineland Republic' had collapsed. Meanwhile in Paris Brockdorff-Rantzau did nothing to support Adenauer's compromise proposal (as he saw it) for a Rhineland state within a new federal Germany, and on 28 June 1919 the Treaty of Versailles was duly signed. Under its terms Germany was forced to accept responsibility for the war and was condemned to pay massive reparations; her army was reduced to 100,000 men; Alsace and Lorraine were returned to France; Upper Silesia and the so-called Polish corridor were ceded to Poland; and any kind of union between Germany and Austria was forbidden. As far as the Rhineland was concerned, the occupation by the victorious powers would continue for fifteen years, and once the fifteen-year period was over, the occupied areas, together with a thirty-two mile (50 kilometre) strip of land to the east of the Rhine, would remain demilitarized in perpetuity; the whole bill for the occupation was to be paid for by Germany. In the event, Adenauer's fears proved unfounded, as the stiff terms of the Treaty of Versailles did not ruin the economy of the Rhineland; nor did they lead to the break-up of Germany, which Adenauer had predicted would be the consequence of a lengthy period of occupation.

Four years later there was another period of crisis in the Rhineland provoked by the French occupation of the Ruhr. The pretext for this occupation (January 1923–January 1924) was the failure of the Germans to pay reparations in full. But, as in 1919, one of the underlying purposes of the

French was to detach the Rhineland from Germany. In practice the occupation of the Ruhr was a complete failure. Condemned from the beginning by the British and Americans, its first consequence was a general strike in the Ruhr, followed by passive resistance and sabotage throughout the Rhineland. The occupation also had a disastrous effect on Germany's inflation, culminating in the total collapse of the Mark in 1923. Eventually, as a result of the skilful diplomacy of the German Chancellor, Gustav Stresemann, and the fall of Raymond Poincaré's government, which was replaced in January 1924 by the non-annexationist government of the radical Edouard Herriot, the occupation of the Ruhr ended.

As far as Adenauer was concerned, 1923 was a very difficult year. With the full encouragement of the French occupation forces, Dr Dorten and the separatists announced the inauguration of a 'Rhineland Republic' on 21 October 1923. This 'independent' state was to include all German territory west of the Rhine and the areas of Allied occupation to the east. It was to have its own currency, railways and postal service. The French occupation authorities encouraged the separatists in their attempts to 'occupy' Aachen, Trier, Mainz and Koblenz, but in practice they never gained full control of any of these cities. In the midst of the economic and political chaos of late 1923 Adenauer, with the support of Chancellor Stresemann, held a meeting with Henri Tirard, the French Head of the Inter-Allied Commission in Koblenz, on 14 November 1923. Tirard subsequently stated that Adenauer had 'agreed' to the detachment of the Rhineland from Germany. Adenauer denied this categorically on 27 November, emphasizing that, as he was only the Mayor of Cologne, he was in no position to 'agree' to any such thing. Moreover, while he was prepared – as in 1918-19 – to consider a Rhineland state detached from Prussia but *within* Germany, he was *not* prepared to consider separation.[21]

Although the separatist movement collapsed in February 1924, when Dr Dorten fled to France (subsequently he settled in Nice and became a French citizen), Adenauer was thereafter subjected to periodic attacks in the Nazi period and after the Second World War by those who claimed that he had been prepared to accept the break-up of the Fatherland. All the evidence goes against this. Adenauer was strongly opposed to the separatist movement. He judged that it was necessary in 1919 and again in 1923, i.e. at times of major economic and political crisis, to keep in touch with *all* sides – hence his willingness to consult with Dr Dorten in 1919 and with Henri Tirard in 1923. But he was far too patriotic a German by upbringing and attitude to consider the dismemberment of his country. As already emphasized, Adenauer regarded a separate 'Rhineland Republic' detached from Germany, and therefore under French influence, as a recipe for a future war. However, he did understand French fears about the power of Germany and the predominance of Prussia within Germany. He was therefore quite prepared to consider the break-up of Prussia *within* a newly constituted federal Germany.[22] He held this view in the period after the First World War, and was to hold it again after the Second, when the state of North Rhine Westphalia came into being as one of the new *Länder* of the Federal Republic of Germany.

The modernization of Cologne

One of Adenauer's greatest achievements as Mayor of Cologne was the modernization of his native city. He was greatly helped by the fact that the Treaty of Versailles laid down that all fortifications in the occupied zone of Germany were to be dismantled. This is precisely what Adenauer's two predecessors had wanted to do with Cologne's obsolete fortifications, but the Prussian Military Governors were able to resist any demolition until after the First World War. The fortified medieval wall had in fact been partially dismantled towards the end of the nineteenth century, but Cologne could not be fully modernized until the main fortifications were demolished. Adenauer was a conservative in many ways, but when it came to the modernization of Cologne he was certainly not. He was in fact well used to change in Cologne, for he had been brought up in a city which was in the throes of transformation thanks to the efforts of Wilhelm Becker, Mayor between 1886 and 1907. Adenauer wanted to complete the trans-formation Becker had begun with the partial demolition of the medieval walls in the 1880s and 1890s, followed by their replacement with a dual carriageway inner-ring road with a centre aisle of trees. Becker had also overseen the building of many new houses between the old wall and the sixteen outer fortresses. In addition to Adenauer's personal enthusiasm for urban renewal and the favourable post-war circumstances, he had considerable powers as the chief executive of one of Germany's great cities; indeed the Mayor and his 4,000 or so civil servants were for all practical purposes more powerful than the elected City Council. Finally, Adenauer never forgot his humble origins, and this strengthened his desire to improve the housing and recreational facilities of his fellow citizens. He was also a strong believer in advancement through education – hence his enthusiasm for the refoundation of Cologne University.

Cologne was of course one of Germany's great cities long before Adenauer became Mayor. Originally an important colonial city in Roman times (hence its name), Cologne had a long and proud history as one of the Holy Roman Empire's Imperial Cities, a status granted to it by Friedrich Barbarossa in the twelfth century. Its semi-independent status ended with its occupation by French revolutionary troops in 1794, and it remained in French hands until 1815 when the Rhineland became part of Prussia under the terms of the Treaty of Vienna. By the time of Adenauer's birth (1876) Cologne was already a major industrial city and railway junction with a population of approximately 170,000, which by 1914 had increased to 635,000. By the last quarter of the nineteenth century Cologne had become the most important railway junction in Germany as well as Prussia's second city. Karl Marx once remarked that the greatest revolution of the nineteenth century was the railway revolution, and his remark was certainly apposite with regard to Cologne. The railway entrepreneur, Gustav Mevissen, transformed Cologne into a major railway centre in the 1860s – the meeting place of Germany's two largest railway networks and the 'economic junction' between the Westphalia–Ruhr region to its east and Brussels and Antwerp to the west.

Cologne was not only a major commercial centre but also the headquarters of a number of powerful banks and finance houses. In the 1920s Adenauer was to be greatly helped in his modernization of Cologne by the directors of these institutions, notably Louis Hagen, whose family business was the finance house Levy, and Robert Pferdemenges, chairman of the Schaafhausen Bank. Indeed the latter was not only a close friend of Adenauer in his Mayoral days but also after the Second World War, when he helped to found the CDU and remained a trusted friend and adviser. By the beginning of the twentieth century Cologne was also a great industrial city, concentrating on engineering, textiles, sugar-refining, glass-making and armaments. So Adenauer grew to manhood in a Cologne which was vibrant and expanding, although it was also a city which had many slum dwellings. Finally, Cologne was an important garrison town with approximately 15,000 troops. The troops and citizens were well integrated, but the Military Governor was able to veto any plans which might impair

Cologne's effectiveness as a fortress city (despite the obsolescence of most of its fortifications). Lines of fire had to be kept open around the forts, preventing the development of parks and a green belt, both objectives dear to Adenauer's heart when he had the power to act in the 1920s.

Apart from the pre-1918 veto power of the Prussian Military Governors with regard to the fortresses, Cologne enjoyed a considerable degree of autonomy. Administratively it was a City within the Rhineland Province. The Rhineland Province, which was of course part of Prussia, had a provincial assembly (*Landtag*) which met in Düsseldorf, while Koblenz remained the chief military and administrative centre of the Province. However, the Mayor of Cologne was a powerful figure in his own right. Under a statute of 1856 Cologne had a Council elected by the Prussian three-class franchise. The first class consisted of very wealthy voters, one third of the Councillors being elected by them; the second class consisted of relatively well-to-do middle-class voters, one third being elected by them; and the third class were middle to lower middle-class householders who elected the remaining third of the Council. Only men could vote, and until 1918 fewer than one quarter of the male citizens were enfranchised. The Council then elected – though not from its own membership – the executive Mayor, who was formally appointed by the King of Prussia. The Council consisted of Liberals, Centrists and Independents until the First World War, but it was a relatively non-political – or at least non-interventionist – body, which tended to leave the governance of the city to the Mayor. In practice he had wide jurisdiction over building, housing, health, education, welfare, culture, libraries, markets, bridges and the harbour. Adenauer, like Mayor Wilhelm Becker (1886-1907), made full use of his powers.

It is also important to stress that the Prussian Government, both before and after the First World War, made a positive effort to give provinces such as the Rhineland a large degree of autonomy. Throughout the nineteenth century this had been the policy of the House of Hohenzollern. Kings Frederick William IV and Wilhelm I in particular strove to win over their Rhineland subjects by giving them as much autonomy as possible, and on the whole their policy succeeded. The most obvious exception to the non-interventionist policy was Bismarck's anti-Catholic *Kulturkampf* of the 1870s, which provoked the Centre Party into being to defend Catholic values and schools. But once that conflict had been resolved in the 1880s, leaving the Catholics with their own denominational schools, the Centre Party, like most Rhinelanders, became totally loyal to the Kaiser. The Catholics of the Centre Party admired Prussian efficiency and Prussian religious toler-ance, the *Kulturkampf* being seen as a short-lived aberration. Adenauer, like his father, had no difficulty in combining loyalty to Prussia with a strong Catholic faith. As Hans-Peter Schwarz put it: 'The idea that the Catholicism of the Rhineland and Cologne was anti-Prussian is a myth'.[23] Adenauer, then, was brought up in a city which was loyally Prussian, yet administratively largely independent of the Government in Berlin. After the First World War Prussia continued to pursue the same policy of administrative devolution, and this was a great help to Cologne's ambitious young Mayor.

The most significant of Adenauer's Mayoral achievements in the 1920s were the refoundation of the University of Cologne; the creation of many parks within the city boundaries; the construction of various sports stadia; the establishment of Cologne's world-famous trade exhibition halls; the expansion of the city's harbour facilities; the building of a municipal rail-way system; and the construction of a large new bridge across the Rhine.[24]

There had been a University in Cologne between 1388 and 1798. Indeed Cologne University was one of the four oldest in the Holy Roman Empire, but, when the French occupied the Rhineland in 1794, they closed the universities of Bonn, Trier, Mainz and Cologne. After the Treaty of Vienna (1815), only Bonn was reopened by the Prussian Government. Adenauer had shown an interest in reviving Cologne University before the First World War, and in January 1919 he went to Berlin to persuade the Prussian Government that a university should be reestablished in his native city. He used two arguments. Firstly, with Strasbourg University now in France, it was essential to have another university as well as Bonn in the western part of Germany; and secondly, with so much of the Rhineland in foreign hands, it was vital for Cologne to have a university to uphold German cultural values. The Prussian Government was per-suaded by these arguments, and Cologne University was refounded in 1920 with 150 staff and 4,000 students. In the decade after its refounda-tion approximately 25,000 students graduated, and Adenauer regarded the new university as one of his greatest achievements. It is interesting to note that as early as June 1919 Adenauer saw the university not just as a practical centre of higher learning and German culture but also as a means to promote reconciliation between the European nations:

> Whatever the shape of the peace treaty, over the coming decades German culture and the cultures of the western democracies will meet here on the Rhine, the old thoroughfare of the European nations. If there is no reconciliation, if the European peoples fail to recognize the elements common to all European cultures, as well as demanding the justifiable protection of their own identity, if they fail to bring the nations together through cultural rapprochement, and if they fail to avoid another European war, then Europe's preeminence in the world will be lost forever. It is the special task of the University of Cologne to promote the noble work of international reconciliation for the welfare of Europe . . . Above all, it should emphasise the universality of European culture; it should show that much more unites the European peoples than divides them.[25]

Adenauer could well have expressed these noble aspirations in the 1950s. But it is indeed remarkable that he used these words in June 1919, a fortnight before the signing of the Treaty of Versailles.

Adenauer was justifiably proud of other developments in Cologne in the decade after the First World War. With the help of Fritz Schumacher, an urban planner whom Adenauer recruited from Hamburg, he created the city's beautiful woodland parks after the demolition of the old fortifications. Remarkably, these fine parks remained almost untouched by the Second World War, although 80 per cent of Cologne's houses and factories were destroyed by bombing. Adenauer and Schumacher also oversaw the building of new housing estates and factories, the most notable of the latter being the Ford Motor Works. In his book about the modernization of Cologne Schumacher paid glowing tributes to Adenauer for his energy and vision:

> Adenauer was a man with qualities of inspiration which could only develop to the full outside normal conditions. Then the imagination of the tactician and the passion of a great chess player were aroused in him. I have often thought that the most powerful part of his personality might have lain fallow in normal times. If he had lived in previous centuries, he might well have been a great church dignitary, one of those men with two great qualities: the skill to pursue their objectives as resolute politicians in the cut-and-thrust of German politics, and the determination to translate their will into reality . . . The more difficult things became, the greater was the energy with which Adenauer pushed the work forward.[26]

The port of Cologne was also modernized in the 1920s, with the city's central harbour area being reconstructed. And the huge exhibition halls for international trade fairs (the *Messe*) were built at this time and opened by President Friedrich Ebert in May 1924. In addition, transport around the city was improved with the construction of the Gürtelbahn, the municipal railway running round the city's western crescent. Cologne Airport was opened in 1926, and Adenauer, with the full support of the Prussian Government, also encouraged the expansion of Germany's canal network. The Rhine–Herne canal and the Mittelstand canal were both built in the 1920s. The former provided a link between the Dortmund–Ems and Ems–Weser canals, and the latter enabled barges to go all the way from Cologne to Hamburg by river and canal. These improved communications helped to promote trade and commerce in Cologne itself and in the Rhineland generally. Finally, a new and somewhat controversial suspension bridge was built across the Rhine to the suburb of Mülheim. One of Adenauer's biographers claims that the building of this suspension bridge illustrates the deviousness which was part of Adenauer's character.[27] For the committee of experts set up by the City Council had voted for an arched bridge by 9 votes to 7, but Adenauer persuaded the Council to overturn this vote by 43 votes to 36 in favour of his preferred option, a suspension bridge. He argued that a suspension bridge would be aesthetically more attractive (a purely subjective view), and that an arched bridge would be dangerous, as it might sink into the sandy soil of the Rhine (a very weak argument, as there already was an arched bridge across the river!). But somehow Adenauer got his way, even although the suspension bridge was considerably more expensive.

Overall assessment of Adenauer as Mayor of Cologne

Even if Adenauer had not gone on to become Chancellor of the Federal Republic of Germany, he would have been remembered as one of Cologne's great Mayors during the one hundred and thirty years when the Rhineland was part of Prussia. However, despite all that Adenauer did to strengthen the economic infrastructure of Cologne and to improve its recreational and educational amenities, he was by no means universally popular. Indeed by 1929 he was so unpopular that he only just received the endorsement of the City Council for a second term as Mayor by 49 votes to 47.

Adenauer was criticized not only by the Social Democrats and Communists but also by Catholic trade unionists for his close links with big business. And it is certainly true that many of his closest friends were industrialists and bankers, men such as the coalowner Hugo Stinnes, the steel baron August Thyssen and the general industrialist Florian Klöckner. Two other close friends were Jewish financiers, Louis Hagen and the 'Europeanized' American Dannie Heineman. Hagen had many financial and industrial interests in the Cologne area; interestingly, although a Jew, he had left the Liberal Party in late 1919 to join the Centre Party as a city councillor. Heineman was based in Brussels, where he was chairman of the Sofina Corporation, but he had many commercial interests in Germany and throughout Western Europe. Adenauer's connections with such men aroused criticism and jealousy. By the late 1920s Adenauer was chairman of four Cologne companies – involved respectively with railways, construction, aircraft and the city's trade fairs. He was also on the board of Deutsche Bank, Lufthansa and a number of other large companies. In addition, he was said to be the highest paid Mayor in Germany and to be the beneficiary of a very large expense account. As the economic situation worsened in Cologne and throughout Germany in the late 1920s, Adenauer's political enemies became more vocal in their criticisms of his wealthy friends and his financial 'extravagance'.

And it is true that finance was Adenauer's Achilles heel both as Mayor of Cologne and later as Chancellor of West Germany. From 1924 to 1933 Cologne's budget was in deficit. Yet between 1924 and 1929 municipal expenditure almost doubled. Robert Görlinger, leader of the SPD group on the City Council, complained in 1927 about 'the excessive haste with which a number of projects have been pushed through by the Mayor'.[28] Görlinger emphasized in particular the lavish scale of the new exhibition halls. Johannes Rings, the leader of the Centre Party, also complained about the cost of some of the Mayor's projects. Adenauer was annoyed at this criticism from his own party, but he was unable to refute the figures with which Rings backed his claim. The German Government in Berlin also criticized Adenauer for his extravagance, notably Stresemann in 1927 and Brüning in 1931.[29] The problem was that Adenauer was much more interested in making Cologne into a great commercial and cultural centre than he was in balancing the City's budget. By 1927, 1928 and 1929 Cologne's expenditure was 50 per cent above its income, and the criticisms of the Government in Berlin were as valid as those of local politicians. Adenauer's response was to blame Berlin for not subsidizing cities such as Cologne while insisting that they pay out large sums in social security.

Meanwhile, in Cologne itself Adenauer favoured cutting back the social security budget so that payments would be made only to the most needy. This policy offended not only the Social Democrats but also the left wing of his own Centre Party. Cologne financed its great projects with loans in the hope that eventually the new developments would pay for themselves. This was a high-risk strategy and, when the economic recession began in 1929, Cologne, like many other German cities, suddenly found that its creditors were demanding back their loans. Adenauer can hardly be blamed for the world economic crisis. But he had embarked on a series of expensive developments for Cologne which depended entirely on continuing economic growth. However, by 1929 it was clear that he had been over-optimistic not only about Cologne's finances but about his own too.

In the late 1920s Adenauer made some serious personal financial miscalculations leading to his virtual bankruptcy. It has been reckoned that his wealth in late 1927 amounted to the substantial sum of over a million Marks, excluding his house in Max-Bruch-Strasse. His portfolio was managed by the Deutsche Bank. But in February 1928, on the advice of the German industrialist Fritz Blüthgen, and with the approval of Anton Brüning, his Deutsche Bank manager, he transferred much of his money into speculative American stocks at the height of the US economic boom. In October 1929 the American stock market collapsed, and by mid-1930 Adenauer owed the Deutsche Bank 1.4 million Marks. As he was on the board of that Bank, a rescue package was put together to avoid the public humiliation of the Mayor of Cologne. But Adenauer had lost his personal fortune. Moreover, his financial foolhardiness harmed him politically, because rumours of what had happened soon leaked out. Adenauer was then attacked remorselessly not only by the Nazis and Communists but also by the conservative nationalists of the Deutschnationale Volkspartei (DNVP). At the same time the City of Cologne's financial crisis worsened, and by the summer of 1932 the City was insolvent. To make matters worse, unemployment had risen from 60,000 to 100,000 between December 1930 and June 1932, and by the latter date Cologne was being constantly disrupted by hunger marches and violent street clashes between Nazis and Communists. In this crisis Adenauer tried to persuade Chancellor Heinrich Brüning to relax his deflationary policy. However, the Reich government had no money with which to help the great municipalities. Berlin blamed Cologne (and other cities) for their earlier extravagance, while the cities blamed the national government for doing nothing to alleviate their financial problems.

With Adenauer and Cologne both in major financial difficulties by the early 1930s, the personality of the Mayor did nothing to help. Not only was Adenauer regarded as a bad economist (which he was), he was also considered to be cold and aloof. One of his opponents on the City Council, Robert Görlinger, criticized him for his arrogance, claiming that the Mayor refused to discuss problems or listen to criticisms.[30] He cited the Mülheim Bridge as a typical example of Adenauer's brow-beating style – getting his own way without listening to the arguments of others, twisting the evidence to suit himself and spending far more money than was necessary. Politically it was not only the extreme right and extreme left who were now attacking Adenauer, but also the moderate left-wingers of the SPD and the progressive wing of his own Centre Party. In these circumstances it was not surprising that Adenauer was in a relatively weak position during his final years as Mayor of Cologne (1929–33).

After the City Council elections of 1929 the Centre Party held 35 seats (1924: 30), the Social Democrats 21 (11), the Communists 13 (16), the Liberals 14 (11), the Conservative National People's Party 4 (5), the Nazis 4 (0) and others 8 (15). However, only the Centre Party and Liberals were prepared to vote for the reelection of Adenauer as Mayor (the vote being 49–47 in his favour). Indeed, the Liberals, who had campaigned against Adenauer, only voted for him when he agreed to give up all honoraria paid to him by private companies. The Nazis and Communists naturally voted against him. But the key change was that the Social Democrats, who had generally supported Adenauer from 1919 to 1929, now went into opposition. Thus after 1929 Adenauer no longer had an effective coalition behind him, and his City's finances (as well as his own) were in deep trouble. In his running of Cologne Adenauer had been no more extravagant than many other Mayors of great German cities. Nor was he any more responsible than them for his country's economic and political crisis. But Adenauer's excessive financial optimism – indeed foolhardiness – blighted his Mayoral reputation during the final years of the Weimar Republic.

Adenauer's role in national politics in the Weimar Republic (1919–33)

Under the Prussian Constitution Adenauer, as a Mayor of a large city, sat in the State Council (*Staatsrat*), the second chamber of Prussia's

Parliament. In 1921 he became the President of the *Staatsrat,* retaining this post throughout the Weimar Republic. This entailed his spending three or four days a month in Berlin. Adenauer was thus very much at the geographical heart of Prussian and German national politics. Why, then, did a man of his experience, political skills and democratic commitment not play a more decisive part in national politics in the Weimar Republic? After all, many senior Mayors were involved in national politics. Indeed, during the fourteen years of the Weimar Republic eight Mayors (or ex-Mayors) held forty-four different Cabinet posts in the German Government. The best-known of these were Hans Luther, the former Mayor of Essen, who was Chancellor on two occasions, and Otto Gessler, the former Mayor of Nuremberg, who held fifteen Cabinet posts over the years.

Adenauer was in fact approached on two occasions about the possibility of standing for the Chancellorship, and one of his biographers has claimed that he might have saved the Weimar Republic if he had been prepared to commit himself decisively to national politics.[31] But the reality was that Adenauer was not one of those Mayors who was seriously interested in Ministerial jobs or the Chancellorship. There is no evidence to support the view that if Adenauer had been so interested, he might somehow have saved the Republic. To be frank, Adenauer, like most middle-class liberal democrats in the Weimar years, underestimated the Nazi threat. But, before coming to that, we must ask why Adenauer did not get more involved in national politics in the 1920s.

Some of the reasons emerged in May 1921 and May 1926 when Adenauer was approached about the possibility of becoming Chancellor. In 1921 he was asked by Otto Braun, the SPD Prime Minister of Prussia, and Adam Stegerwald, the Centre Party Minister of Labour in the German Government, if he would be prepared to stand for the Chancellorship. Adenauer said that he would, but only on certain conditions. President Ebert, together with Braun and Stegerwald, wanted a left-of-centre government based on the SPD, Centre Party and progressive Liberals. But Adenauer said he would only stand for the Chancellorship, if all proposals for the nationalization of industry were dropped; if the nine-hour working-day were reintroduced (instead of eight); if there were a move from direct to indirect taxation; and if he could choose his Cabinet with complete freedom. In effect Adenauer was saying that he would be prepared to head a centre-right government based on the Centre Party and two Liberal Parties but excluding the Social Democrats. This was unacceptable not only to the SPD but to the left wing of his own party. Adenauer thus placed himself clearly on the right of the Centre Party; indeed the SPD in Cologne never forgave him for his apparent 'betrayal' of the sacred eight-hour day introduced in 1919. In the end a Government based on the SPD and Centre Party was formed under Joseph Wirth, whose position in the Centre Party was well to the left of Adenauer's.

In May 1926, after the fall of Hans Luther's Government, Adenauer was again approached about the Chancellorship by Stegerwald. But, although he went to Berlin to discuss the possibility of leading a broad coalition of the centre-left and centre-right, the proposed coalition did not materialize. The SPD refused to participate in a government which would have included the conservative national DNVP, and the DNVP had strong reservations about going into a coalition with the SPD. Moreover, Adenauer did not get on personally with Gustav Stresemann, who was determined to remain Foreign Minister. Although Stresemann had only been Chancellor for three months in 1923, he was Foreign Minister from late 1923 until his death aged fifty-one in 1929. The years 1924-29 are often referred to as the 'Stresemann era'. Certainly Stresemann dominated German foreign policy in these years, working tirelessly for the revision of the Versailles Treaty, the reduction of reparations, close cooperation with the Western Allies and the entry of Germany into the League of Nations. In Germany he was also known as 'The Kingmaker' owing to the strength of his personality and the pivotal role held by the Deutsche Volkspartei (DVP), the conservative Liberal Party he founded in 1919 and led until his death. As regards foreign policy, Adenauer agreed with the main lines of Stresemann's policy, but was less Western-orientated than him. In complete contrast to his pro-Western foreign policy after the Second World War, Adenauer considered in the 1920s that Germany's interests would be best served by adopting a relatively neutral stance between East and West. The talks about Adenauer's possible Chancellorship lasted from 14 to 16 May 1926. Then Adenauer withdrew his candidature owing to foreign policy differences with Stresemann and his failure to persuade the SPD to consider serving in a coalition under him.

Adenauer returned to Cologne. The truth was that Cologne was where he wanted to be. The experience of other senior Mayors (or ex-Mayors) who participated actively in national politics in the Weimar Republic was that a choice had to be made between *national* and *local* politics. In Adenauer's case, he much preferred running Cologne to trying to run Germany. He was very much in command in his own city (or at least he was up to 1929). But as Chancellor of Germany he would have required acute political sensitivity to hold together a diverse coalition. Adenauer was not suited to such a task. He was too autocratic in style and too far to the right in his own party to run a Weimar coalition. Perhaps most important of all, in the 1920s Adenauer lacked the necessary *political motivation* for involvement in national politics at the highest level. In contrast, as we shall see, after 1945 he had that motivation in abundance.[32]

In order to understand Adenauer's somewhat detached attitude to national politics in the Weimar Republic, we must examine briefly the characteristics of that Republic, and in particular the dilemmas facing a man of Adenauer's background and political views in its final years of crisis. The problem facing any Chancellor or potential Chancellor was not so much the large number of parties in the Reichstag as the limited democratic base from which coalition governments could be formed. Moreover, this problem worsened as the Weimar Republic drew towards its fateful conclusion. The only parties which were firmly committed to the Republic were the SPD, the Centre Party (and its Bavarian ally, the Bavarian People's Party), and the two Liberal parties (Stresemann's conservative DVP and the more progressive DDP). The Communists and Nazis were of course determined to destroy the Republic, and the conservative nationalists of the DNVP oscillated between lukewarm support and outright opposition. After Field Marshal Hindenburg was elected President in 1925, the DNVP rallied briefly to the Republic, participating in coalitions in 1925–26 and again in 1927–28. But after the election of Alfred Hugenberg as chairman of the DNVP in 1928 the conservative nationalists joined Hitler in attacking Stresemann's policy of reconciliation, the 'Diktat' of Versailles and the 'weakness' of Weimar's political leaders. The joint campaign of Hitler and Hugenberg in the 1929 referendum against the Young Plan failed to overturn the Reichstag's endorsement of that Plan, but it gave the Nazis and Nationalists an opportunity to publicize their grievances nationwide.

The party situation in the Reichstag between 1920 and 1924 meant that only minority governments were possible – either centre-left coalitions based on the SPD, Centre Party and DDP or centre-right coalitions based on the Centre Party, DDP and DVP (see Table 1, p. 41). The 'revolutionary left' (Independent Socialists and Communists with up to 20 per

TABLE 1 Elections to the Reichstag during the Weimar Republic (1919–33)

	1919 Per cent	1919 Seats	1920 Per cent	1920 Seats	1924 (May) Per cent	1924 (May) Seats	1924 (Dec) Per cent	1924 (Dec) Seats	1928 Per cent	1928 Seats	1930 Per cent	1930 Seats	1932 (July) Per cent	1932 (July) Seats	1932 (Nov) Per cent	1932 (Nov) Seats	1933 (March) Per cent	1933 (March) Seats
Kommunistische Partei Deutschlands (KPD)	–	–	2.1	4	12.6	62	9.0	45	10.6	54	13.1	77	14.3	89	16.9	100	12.3	[81]*
Unhabhängige Sozialdemokratischepartie Deutschlands (USPD)	7.6	22	17.9	84	–	–	–	–	–	–	–	–	–	–	–	–	–	–
Sozialdemokratischepartei Deutschlands (SPD)	37.9	163	21.7	102	20.5	100	26.0	131	29.8	153	24.5	143	21.6	133	20.4	121	18.3	120
Zentrum (Z)	19.7	90	13.6	64	13.4	65	13.6	69	12.1	62	11.8	68	12.5	75	11.9	70	11.2	73
Bayerische Volkspartei (BVP)	–	–	4.2	18	3.2	16	3.8	19	3.1	16	3.0	19	3.2	22	3.1	20	2.7	19
Deutsche Demokratische Partei (DDP) (Deutsche Staatspartei from 1930)	18.6	75	8.3	39	5.7	28	6.3	32	4.9	25	3.8	20	1.0	4	1.0	2	0.9	5
Deutsche Volkspartie (DVP)	4.4	19	13.9	65	9.2	45	10.1	51	8.7	45	4.5	30	1.2	7	1.9	11	1.1	2
Deutschnationale Volkspartei (DNVP)	10.3	42	15.1	71	19.5	95	20.5	103	14.2	73	7.0	41	5.9	32	8.9	52	8.0	52
Nationalsozialistiche Deutsche Arbeiterpartei (NSDAP)	–	–	–	–	–	–	3.0	14	2.6	12	18.3	107	37.4	230	33.1	196	43.9	288
TOTAL SEATS (including other small parties not in Table)	–	418	–	459	–	472	–	493	–	491	–	577	–	608	–	584	–	566*
TURNOUT (%)	83.0		79.2		77.4		78.8		75.5		82.0		84.1		80.6		88.8	

*KPD excluded from Reichstag.

Source: H. Kaack, *Geschichte und Struktur des deutschen Parteiensysems* (Opladen, 1971).

Electoral Law. The Weimar Republic operated a system of straightforward national proportional representation (PR): every 60,000 votes cast nationally for a party gave it a seat in the Reichstag.

41

cent of the poll) would of course not join a 'bourgeois' government, and the 'traditional right' (conservative nationalists and allies with about 15 per cent of the poll) would have nothing to do with the Republic at this stage. Between the (two) general elections of 1924 and that of 1928 the democratic base widened somewhat when the DNVP went through its less anti-republican phase, but the party's brief flirtation with liberal democracy ended in 1928. Ironically, the general election of 1928 seemed to provide the Weimar Republic with its best chance of success, because the main democratic parties all polled relatively well, with the SPD reaching 30 per cent and the Centre and Liberal parties 30 per cent between them. After the 1928 election the Social Democrat Hermann Müller was able to form a coalition based on the SPD, Centre Party and two Liberal parties. The Müller Government had the support of 285 of the 491 members of the Reichstag, and at last the prospects for parliamentary democracy looked reasonable. But it was a false dawn. Soon the Weimar Republic's stability was undermined by the Hitler–Hugenberg 'pact' of 1929 (against the Young Plan, the Versailles Treaty and the Weimar system generally). Then, to make matters much worse, the Wall Street crash of October 1929 provoked a world economic slump.

The collapse of the American economy had drastic economic and political repercussions. By 1932 unemployment in the United States and Western Europe had reached 30 million. The economic crisis did not hit Germany any harder than Britain or the United States. But Germany's democratic roots were much weaker than those in the Anglo-Saxon countries. From the beginning of the Weimar Republic German nationalists, Prussian landowners and many military officers, civil servants and industrialists had opposed liberal democracy, which they considered to be alien to German culture and traditions. They could now claim that 'Western' free enterprise and the world economic slump were part and parcel of 'democracy'. There were too few committed democrats to sustain the Weimar Republic when it was confronted with economic collapse as well as relentless political attacks from the extreme left and extreme right. As the economic crisis worsened, German industrialists closed their eyes and ears to the Nazi Party's demagogic behaviour and violent language, preferring instead to see Hitler's movement as a bulwark against the 'red menace' of Communism. As one student of Fascism put it: 'The extension of Nazi influence through the Hugenberg alliance and the opportunities afforded by the economic depression allowed Nazism to appear as *both* revolutionary *and* safe', -a 'revolutionary' answer for the unemployed and 'safe' solution for the bourgeoisie.[33]

The Weimar Republic went through its final period of crisis between the general election of September 1930 and Hitler's nomination as Chancellor in January 1933. It is important to examine this period in some detail in order to understand Adenauer's rather detached behaviour during these critical years. It is probably true to say that nothing but a significant economic revival could have saved the Republic after 1930. However, such a revival did not occur until it was too late. In March 1930 Heinrich Brüning of the Centre Party became Chancellor, but, unable to command a majority in the Reichstag, he began to rule by Presidential decree under Article 48, which allowed the President to issue legally binding decrees so long as the Chancellor could not command a majority in the Reichstag. This was supposed to be a short-term political expedient. Hence Brüning asked President Hindenburg to call for an early election in September 1930. However, the beneficiaries of that fateful election were not Brüning's political allies but the opponents of the Weimar Republic, namely the Nationalists, Nazis and Communists, who between them won almost half the seats in the Reichstag (see Table 1, p. 41). Between 1928 and 1930 Nazi representation had thus risen from 12 seats (810,000 votes) to 107 seats (6 million), while Communist representation had increased from 54 seats (3.2 million) to 77 seats (4.6 million). The Nazis were now the second party in the Reichstag after the Social Democrats.

Brüning's Government lasted from September 1930 to May 1932. Brüning was an honourable man of conservative instincts who implemented a policy of financial orthodoxy. Fearful of the extreme solutions offered by the Nazis and Communists, the Social Democrats and Centre Party supported Brüning with great discipline, although unemployment rose from 4.5 million in late 1931 to 6 million by the end of 1932. Meanwhile, the Communists criticized the Government for doing nothing to help the unemployed, and the Nazis raged about the iniquities of the Treaty of Versailles and the weaknesses of Weimar democracy. In March 1932 Hindenburg was re-elected President. In the first ballot he polled 18.7 million, Hitler 11.3 million, Thälmann (Communist) 5 million and Düsterberg (Nationalist) 2.6 million. Düsterberg withdrew before the second ballot, and Hindenburg polled 19.4 million votes to Hitler's 13.4 million and Thälmann's 3.7 million. The democrats of the

SPD and Centre Party really had no option but to vote for the right-wing Hindenburg at the second ballot. Two months later Hindenburg was persuaded by the Defence Minister, General Schleicher, to dismiss Brüning, who was supported by the Catholics and Social Democrats (both of whom Hindenburg despised). Brüning, in spite of his innate conservatism, had proposed a modest redistribution of land in East Prussia to help unemployed farmers (the *Osthilfe* policy), but this was too much for the landowning President, who described Brüning's *Osthilfe* as 'communistic'. After this public humiliation by the President, Brüning resigned on 30 May 1932. This was precisely what Schleicher wanted, for he persuaded Hindenburg to appoint Franz von Papen Chancellor as a prelude to fresh elections and the formation of a right-wing government. Papen's Cabinet, consisting only of Nationalists (DNVP) and right-wing Liberals (DVP), was supported by only 70 out of the 577 Reichstag members. There was thus no course open to Papen but to ask Hindenburg to dissolve the Reichstag and hold a general election. Papen made two fatal moves in the summer of 1932. Firstly, he reversed Brüning's decree banning the *Sturmabteilung* (SA), Hitler's Brownshirts. Secondly, he deposed the SPD government of Prussia on the grounds that it was a minority administration which had been unable to govern effectively since the Prussian election of April 1932. This amounted to a *coup d'état*, as Papen took over as (temporary) Reich Commissioner of Prussia. Papen proceeded to govern Prussia, i.e. two-thirds of the population of Germany, by decree.

The general election of July 1932 took place in an atmosphere of crisis, with the Prussian government suspended, very high unemployment, and the extremists of Right and Left railing against the Weimar Republic. There was a turnout of 84 per cent. The Nazis polled 37.4 per cent (230 seats), the Social Democrats 21.6 per cent (133 seats), the Centre Party (including its Bavarian ally, the BVP) 15.7 per cent (97 seats) and the Communists 14.3 per cent (89 seats) (see Table 1, p. 41). The remaining parties polled under 5 per cent, and Germany became in effect 'ungovernable', or at least ungovernable by a coalition with majority support in the Reichstag. The parties which were opposed to the Weimar Republic, i.e. the Nazis, Communists and (most) Nationalists, now held 356 out of 608 seats in the Reichstag. Chancellor Papen's support had dwindled from 70 to 44. In theory a Nazi-led coalition could have been considered. But at this stage President Hindenburg, General Schleicher and indeed Papen himself were firmly against a Hitler-led government. So when Hindenburg held a meeting with Hitler (as leader of the largest party in the Reichstag) on 13 August, he refused to allow the 'Bohemian Corporal' to form a government. There thus appeared to be no solution to the constitutional crisis except to hold fresh elections.

These were duly held on 6 November 1932. Weary of voting, the German electorate abstained in larger numbers than in July, the turnout falling 4 points to 80 per cent. The Nazis lost 2 million votes and the Nationalists gained some ground, as did the Communists (see Table 1, p. 41). But the new Reichstag was no more capable of sustaining a democratic government than its predecessor. Hindenburg asked Papen to form another minority government but, when it became apparent that he could not do so, the President reluctantly accepted his resignation. Hindenburg was now prepared to consider Hitler as Chancellor, but only if he could form a government supported by a majority in the Reichstag. Hitler said he wanted to lead a 'Presidential Cabinet', i.e. a government like those formed previously by Brüning and Papen, ruling by decree with minority support in the Reichstag. Hindenburg rejected Hitler's proposal, contending that such a government was likely to worsen Germany's political and social crisis. Three months later Hindenburg was to reverse his decision and allow Hitler to form a government. But by the end of January 1933 the political situation had changed significantly.

In November 1932 Hindenburg would have liked Papen to form another minority administration, but by now General Schleicher, the Defence Minister, had persuaded a sufficient number of senior politicians to support him rather than Papen for the Chancellorship. Schleicher, who was an arch intriguer but not a very good judge of character, persuaded Hindenburg that a broad-based coalition led by him would be the best option. The President therefore asked Schleicher to form a government on 2 December 1932. Schleicher announced that he was a 'social General', whose government would bring together moderate members of the Right, the Centre Party and the SPD. He promised to tackle unemployment and the agricultural crisis in the East. In practice state help for farmers implied a return to the *Osthilfe* policy which had led to Brüning's fall. It was now that Hindenburg, abetted by Papen who had turned against Schleicher, began to show sympathy for Papen's plan to form a Nationalist-Nazi government. Papen's idea was that Hitler would be a figurehead Chancellor, the majority of his Cabinet being DNVP members. Papen argued that such a Cabinet would have popular appeal and be acceptable to his own Centre Party. Papen held a private meeting with Hitler in Cologne on 5 January 1933 at the home of the banker Kurt von Schröder. On the basis of this meeting Papen concluded that Hitler had moderated his political objectives and could be controlled in an essentially conservative government. Thus, on Papen's advice, Hindenburg finally overcame his aversion to the 'Bohemian Corporal'. On 30 January 1933 he asked Hitler to form a 'government of national unity'.

Within two months – after the Reichstag fire, the banning of the Communists, the institution of detention without trial and the Enabling Act (*Ermässigungsgesetz*) (23 March 1933) – the Weimar Republic was dead, and with it Germany's first attempt at parliamentary democracy. The Reichstag handed over power to Hitler's Government to legislate on its own authority under the Enabling Act, and in practice this meant that the constitution was suspended. To their eternal credit, 94 parliamentarians – all members of the SPD – voted against the Enabling Act. Most of these courageous Social Democrats were soon either in Dachau concentration camp or in exile.

What, one may well ask, was Adenauer's attitude to the momentous political developments which took place between 1930 and 1933? What in particular were his views on Brüning and Papen, who were after all both members of his own Centre Party? Why did a man like Adenauer, who disliked Hitler and the Nazis so intensely, not become more actively involved in the campaign to stop Hitler? Why in particular did Adenauer temporize in the crucial last six months of the Weimar Republic?

After the Second World War Adenauer's views on the collapse of Weimar were fairly orthodox. He blamed the economic crisis, the vacuum in authority after the collapse of Imperial Germany in 1918, the harshness of the Versailles Treaty, the strength of extremism (of both Left and Right) and the weakness of Weimar's democratic politicians. But he rejected the view that Hitler was a charismatic leader. Instead he saw the Nazi leaders – Hitler, Goebbels and Göring – as rootless social climbers who had succeeded in exploiting Germany's weaknesses to gain power and had then been impossible to oust.[34] There is a lack of precise evidence about Adenauer's attitude in the crucial years 1930–33. However, some things are clear. Firstly, Adenauer's main commitment was to Cologne, not to Germany. Adenauer remained an administrator rather than a politician throughout the Weimar Republic. Secondly, as a conservative, he was more concerned about the Communist than the Fascist threat, which is not to say that he welcomed either. Far from it, but he saw the latter as the lesser of two evils. He reluctantly came to the view that the Nazis could be controlled if given some responsibility in Prussia and/or Germany. This turned out to be a huge miscalculation. But Adenauer was by no means alone in coming to this conclusion. Indeed it was widely held not only by Nationalists (DNVP), Liberals and the majority of the Centre Party, but also by an increasing number of bankers and industrialists, the very group with whom Adenauer mixed in Cologne. Finally, he was so involved in dealing with Cologne's financial problems (as well as his own), that he had little time for national politics during the crucial final years of the Weimar Republic. Cologne's impending bankruptcy (from 1930 onwards) had one important political effect. It led to constant clashes between Adenauer and Heinrich Brüning, the Chancellor from 1930 to 1932. Adenauer originally supported Brüning for the Chancellorship. Both men were natural allies, being on the conservative wing of the Centre Party, but, as we have seen, Adenauer soon became very critical of Brüning's deflationary policy. In direct defiance of Brüning, Adenauer increased local taxes, which he saw as the only way to pay unemployment benefits and stave off social unrest and the bankruptcy of his city. But Adenauer's tax policy weakened his support amongst the middle classes and did little to alleviate the city's unemployment problem or its financial predicament. Between 1930 and 1933 Adenauer spent many hours negotiating with the German Government, the Prussian Ministry of Finance and private banks in fruitless attempts to defer his city's loan repayments. He was quite simply too busy trying to resolve Cologne's social and economic problems to have much time for national politics.

Adenauer's indecision vis-à-vis the Nazis reflected that of the Centre Party as a whole. His attitude towards the extreme right in the last years of the Weimar Republic was comparable to his attitude towards the extreme left at its beginning. In November 1918 he would have liked to have suppressed the left-wing extremists but, when this seemed inexpedient, he successfully 'contained' them by giving them responsibility. In 1932–33 he seems to have hoped that it would be possible to 'contain' the extreme right in the same way. It is true that at a Centre Party meeting in Frankfurt-am-Main in the spring of 1932 Adenauer told the delegates that it might be impossible to stop the Nazis by propaganda, as the only thing they seemed to understand was force.[35] He thus implied that he would support the use of force to defend democracy, a view he was to hold strongly after the Second World War with reference to the extreme left and right. However, with the exception of this one speech, Adenauer clearly preferred a more conciliatory approach to the extreme right in the early 1930s. When in 1932 the SPD-led Prussian Government proposed that 'organizations hostile to the state' (i.e. the Nazis and Communists) should be excluded from local government, Adenauer opposed this in spite of the fact that the anti-democratic element in Cologne had increased from one-third to two-fifths between the general elections of September 1930 and July 1932. Moreover, after the 'electoral disaster' of September 1930 Adenauer wrote a very complacent letter to his friend Dannie Heineman in Brussels. After remarking that there was now a large number of extremists in Germany – 'Here I include the Communists and National Socialists' – he commented 'I do not think, however, that the result of our election is as bad as it appears from outside.'[36] Adenauer clearly underestimated the threat to parliamentary democracy posed by the sort of politicians who had just been elected to the Reichstag.

After 1945 Adenauer criticized the Weimar democrats for their spine-less behaviour, but at the time his criticisms were distinctly muted. With the hindsight of history he saw Brüning as naïve and weak, and Papen as too unintelligent to realize what was happening – 'I have always taken account of mitigating circumstances in my judgement of Franz von Papen, who was a man of limited intelligence. Unfortunately many people allowed themselves to be deceived by his obliging manner and pious talk.'[37] This withering post-war attack does not square with Adenauer's attitude to Papen at the time. When Chancellor Papen suspended the Prussian Government in July 1932 and took over as Reich Commissioner on the grounds that Braun's SPD minority government could not govern Prussia effectively owing to the strength of the Nazis and Communists, Adenauer did not protest. Yet this was nothing less than a cynical 'coup' by Papen's Government, which was itself a minority administration governing Germany largely by means of Presidential decree (Article 48). Indeed, Adenauer went further by writing in August 1932 that, if a gov-ernment of Nationalists and Nazis were to be formed, the Centre Party should 'tolerate it and judge it purely on its deeds'.[38] This was at a time when President Hindenburg and Chancellor Papen were firmly opposed to the Nazis entering the government. Following the appointment of

General Schleicher as Chancellor (December 1932) and Papen's intrigues leading to his change of mind about Hitler becoming Chancellor, Adenauer accepted Papen's new line that the Nazis *could* be 'contained' if brought into the national government. Adenauer's view was perhaps not surprising, as one of his Cologne banking friends, Kurt von Schröder, played a key part in brokering the deal between Hitler and Papen on 5 January 1933. In December 1932 Adenauer had proposed that the Nazis should be given a trial run in the government of Prussia before their possible participation in the national government.[39] However, this was an extraordinarily naïve proposal, as it would have meant that Göring would have become Prime Minister of Prussia, because the Nazis were the largest party in the Prussian *Landtag* with two-fifths of the seats.

Adenauer knew from personal experience in Cologne that the Nazis were bullies and demagogues, whose objective was to destroy the Weimar Republic. Yet, like a lot of decent but naïve politicians of the centre and right, he came to the dangerous conclusion by late 1932–early 1933 that Hitler could be 'tamed' if given governmental responsibility. This colossal miscalculation by the politicians of the centre and right, including Adenauer, led to twelve years of totalitarianism in Germany and to appalling suffering for millions of Europeans.

Interlude: Adenauer in the Third Reich (1933–45)

A conservative Catholic gentleman like Adenauer despised the Nazis. Not surprisingly they returned the compliment. In the years 1933–37 the Nazis persecuted Adenauer by dismissing him summarily from office and by trying (unsuccessfully) to prove that he had been a corrupt Mayor. And in the months after the July 1944 Plot they arrested him and came near to ending his life. However, between 1937 and 1945, Adenauer, in spite of his strong distaste for the Nazi régime, retired into relative obscurity. Although he had brief contacts with active anti-Nazis such as Jakob Kaiser and Andreas Hermes (both of whom survived the war and became prominent Christian Democrats), Adenauer refused to risk actively resisting the Hitler régime. Once the Third Reich had developed into a police state, Adenauer did not believe it could be overthrown from within. Moreover, he was not a conspirator by nature. He did not have the blind courage of those who were prepared to face torture and death for their political beliefs. Above all, his family meant a great deal to Adenauer. The three children from his first marriage were adults by the 1930s, but in 1933 the four children from his second marriage were aged only ten (Paul), eight (Lotte), five (Libeth) and two (Georg). Finally, once war broke out in 1939, Adenauer found himself with three sons in the armed forces. In the circumstances, living in dangerous and difficult times – especially from 1939 onwards – who could blame Adenauer for not going beyond silent resistance? He was wholly opposed to the Hitler régime, but he was a non-Nazi (a tacit opponent of the régime) rather than an anti-Nazi (an active resister).

In February 1933 Adenauer did in fact carry out two acts of 'resistance', for which the Nazis never forgave him. When Hitler demanded not only a fresh Reichstag election (it took place on 5 March 1933) but also an election for a new Prussian parliament, he needed the agreement of three men for the dissolution of the latter, namely Franz von Papen, who was Reich Commissioner for Prussia (still standing in for Otto Braun, dismissed as Prime Minister of Prussia in the coup of July 1932), Hans Kerrl, the Nazi President of the Prussian Lower House (*Landtag*), and Adenauer, the President of the Upper House (*Staatsrat*). In Adenauer's opinion, fresh elections for a Prussian parliament were unconstitutional and unnecessary, as the elections of April 1932 had left the Nazis and Nationalists able to form a majority coalition now that they were prepared to work together. Adenauer was, however, overruled by Papen and Kerrl, and Hitler did not forget this act of defiance. Secondly, during the Reichstag election campaign of February–March 1933, Adenauer infuriated Hitler further. Hitler visited Cologne for a mass rally on 17 February, but as he was coming (in Adenauer's view) in his capacity as the leader of the Nazi Party and not as Chancellor of Germany, Adenauer did not meet Hitler at the airport. Moreover, he forbade the hanging of swastikas on municipal buildings, although he allowed them at the Cologne Exhibition Hall where Hitler was speaking. When some swastikas appeared on a bridge over the Rhine on the day before Hitler's arrival, Adenauer ordered their removal. The Nazis showed what they thought of this by surrounding Adenauer's house in Max-Bruch-Strasse with SA detachments to 'protect', i.e. intimidate, the Mayor. And on 10 March, three days before the municipal elections in Cologne, the Nazi-dominated Berlin Government forbade Adenauer's final speech to the Centre Party on the grounds that it would be 'a danger to public order'. In fact, if the speech had been allowed, it would have amounted to little more than a defence of his fifteen years as Mayor, with Adenauer refuting all charges of extravagance as well as rejecting the Nazi accusation that he had been a Rhineland separatist. It is certainly significant that it was the speech of a 'wronged' Mayor rather than a rallying cry in defence of democracy.[40]

For by this stage it was democracy itself which was in mortal danger. The Nazis had just 'won' the March 1933 general election after a violent campaign, from which the Communists had been banned on the (false) grounds that they had set fire to the Reichstag at the end of February 1933. Despite this ban on one of the main opposition parties and immense pressure on the electorate to vote for the Nazis, they polled only 44 per cent in March 1933, i.e. they never achieved a majority in a 'free' election. But with their allies, the Nationalists, the Nazis had a comfortable majority in the Reichstag and, as we have seen, they soon brought about the demise of parliamentary democracy in Germany.

Meanwhile, after a vicious anti-Adenauer campaign, the Nazis and their allies, the Nationalists, also 'won' the municipal elections in Cologne on 13 March 1933. The Nazis won 41 seats and the Nationalists 5. Strictly speaking they fell short of a majority, because the Centre won 27 seats, the SPD 13 and the officially banned Communists 10. The Nazi-dominated Government in Berlin, however, declared the Communist seats 'dormant'; hence, the Nazi–Nationalist coalition won control in Cologne. Adenauer, who, together with his family, had received threatening letters and phonecalls during the campaign, had in fact left Cologne the previous day and was on his way to Berlin to protest to Hermann Göring, the Prussian Prime Minister, about the behaviour of the SA in Cologne during the recent national and municipal elections. Göring kept Adenauer waiting for three days. When they finally met, Adenauer protested strongly about his illegal removal from office as well as about the violent behaviour of the Nazi storm troopers. He was abruptly told that he was under investigation for fraud and corruption, and that Hitler had been furious about the removal of the swastikas from the Rhine bridge in February. Shortly afterwards, when Adenauer protested in similar terms to his Nazi successor as Mayor of Cologne, Günther Riesen, the latter responded by branding him a criminal.

Adenauer's suspension from office was confirmed by Hitler's Government on 4 April 1933. The City of Cologne stopped paying his salary and the Deutsche Bank froze his account. In May 1933 a Nazi commission of inquiry began its investigation of the ex-Mayor on charges that he had been extravagant and corrupt in his management of the finances of Cologne. However, the Nazis failed to find incriminating evidence against Adenauer and, with the Third Reich in its early stages, decided not to proceed with false charges against one of the more famous Mayors of the Weimar Republic. The case was dropped in June 1934 after thirteen months of investigation. However, it was not until the summer of 1937 that a settlement was finally reached between Adenauer and the City of Cologne after much hard work by Adenauer's lawyer brother, August. Adenauer was also helped by the fact that Cologne's new Mayor (from 1937), Karl Schmidt, although a Nazi like Riesen, wanted to reach a settlement with Adenauer. The agreement was that Adenauer should forfeit his two houses in Cologne for a nominal sum, but henceforth be paid an annual pension of 12,000 Marks; Adenauer also received compensation of 150,000 Marks for loss of earnings between 1933 and 1937.

During these four years Adenauer had been given significant financial aid by his old friend Dannie Heineman, the Jewish industrialist who headed the Sofina Corporation in Brussels. He was further helped by Ildefons Herwegen, an old school friend who was now Abbot of the Benedictine Monastery of Maria Laach in the Eifel Mountains. Although Adenauer's family remained in Cologne, he spent a year from April 1933 as a guest at Maria Laach. As with Heineman, Adenauer never forgot his indebtedness to Herwegen and the monks of Maria Laach. The fact that Herwegen at first gave his qualified approval to Hitler's 'national revolution' may have helped Adenauer to avoid arrest or harassment. Herwegen, a committed royalist, seems to have held the improbable belief that a period of strong government under Hitler might be a prelude to the restoration of the monarchy. Moreover, like many Catholics – indeed Christians generally – he was attracted to the new government's support for the family and for law and order as well as its anti-Communism. Adenauer's whole family was able to stay at a small hotel near Maria Laach for Christmas 1933, but in the spring of 1934 Herwegen began to lose faith in fascism, at which point he was advised by the *Gauleiter* of the Rhineland that he should get rid of Adenauer. Herwegen rejected this request, but Adenauer decided it would be discreet to leave.

Somewhat surprisingly the Adenauer family moved to Berlin in March 1934, and rented a house in the suburb of Neubabelsberg near the Wannsee. In spite of their strong Rhenish connections the Adenauers seem to have settled down happily at Neubabelsberg, but the situation changed dramatically with the Röhm *putsch* of 30 June 1934. Ernst Röhm, leader of the 3 million members of the SA since 1931, a man who had distinguished himself by his bravery in the First World War and a fanatical supporter of Hitler from the earliest days of the Nazi movement, was unexpectedly and brutally murdered on the orders of the Führer, because Röhm wanted to move on to the next stage of the 'national revolution', i.e. to end the privileges of the old élites and to inaugurate a more egalitarian, quasi-socialist society. However, Hitler had by now decided to dispense with the 'socialist' part of the 'national revolution'. It was not only Röhm and his close associates who were murdered in the *putsch* but many others who were seen as a possible threat to the Nazi régime. General Schleicher and his wife were shot in Neubabelsberg near to where the Adenauers lived, and Adenauer himself was arrested by the Gestapo and held in Potsdam Gaol for two days. After his release and a letter from Herwegen telling him his life might be in danger if he returned to Maria Laach, Adenauer 'disappeared' for several weeks to the Black Forest. It seems that this was the point at which Adenauer and Herwegen, who had both believed (especially the latter) that the eccentric 'Bohemian Corporal' might be tempered by the responsibilities of power, realized that they were completely wrong. The events of 30 June 1934 had a huge impact on Adenauer. As he spent the months of August and September 1934 at a guest house in Kappel near Lenzkirch in the Black Forest, Adenauer seems to have concluded that Hitler was both serious and highly dangerous, and that sooner or later his foreign policy would lead to war, although in a letter to Rudolf Amelunxen soon after the Röhm *putsch* he optimistically suggested that a government which perpetrated such acts would probably not last more than two or three years.[41]

After spending the winter of 1934–35 in Neubabelsberg, the Adenauer family moved to Rhöndorf near Bonn in April 1935. Adenauer's brother August had found a suitable house there, and he and Heineman helped the family to pay the rent. But in September 1935 the Nazi *Gauleiter* banned Adenauer from living in the Cologne district, within which Rhöndorf lay. Adenauer returned to Maria Laach for a month, and then after a short period in the Black Forest spent ten months living in Unkel, only five miles from Rhöndorf but outside the Cologne district. There is some evidence that this petty persecution was getting Adenauer down and that his spirits were very low in the winter of 1935–36. But in August

1936 the ban against his living in the Cologne district was lifted, and Adenauer was able to buy some land in Rhöndorf, build a house, and begin a new and settled life as a reluctant pensioner. His four younger children were all still at school and Adenauer was able to take a close interest in their education. He also enjoyed walking, listening to music, reading and, above all, gardening. This was indeed a period of relative peace after the intermittent persecution of the years of 1933–37.

In spite of the Second World War breaking out in September 1939 with Hitler's invasion of Poland, this relative peace for Adenauer lasted until 20 July 1944. The failed attempt to assassinate Hitler on that day led to a period of terror for many in Germany. For Adenauer it inaugurated the most dangerous period of his life. After the Röhm *putsch* Adenauer had been in danger, but after the July Plot he was lucky to avoid summary execution or a slow death in a concentration camp. Four days after the July Plot, the Gestapo arrived at Adenauer's house in Rhöndorf, but, in spite of ransacking his study, failed to find any incriminating documents. A month later (23 August 1944) Adenauer was arrested in the course of Operation Gitter, a 'cleansing' operation against anyone considered to be (or have been) in any way critical of the régime. Among those arrested were former members of the Centre Party, the Social Democratic Party and the two Liberal Parties, as well as Christians of both confessions. Adenauer was interrogated at the Gestapo headquarters in Bonn and then sent to a detention camp in the Trade Fair Centre in Cologne. There he was warned by Eugen Zander, a Communist who had at one time been his gardener at Max-Bruch-Strasse, that he was on a list for deportation to a concentration camp. Zander advised him to feign illness, and, aided by the camp doctor, he was diagnosed with 'pernicious anaemia' and transferred to Hohenlind Hospital in Cologne. There he was given his own room and adequate food by an old friend, Dr Paul Uhlenbruch, the chief medical officer, and, with the connivance of Uhlenbruch and a Luftwaffe Major, Hans Schliebusch, he was 'spirited away' to Nister Mühle, a small hotel in the Westerwald forty miles south-east of Cologne. The proprietor, Josef Rüdig, knew Adenauer and allowed him to register as 'Dr Weber'. However, when the Gestapo discovered that Adenauer had disappeared from the Hohenlind Hospital, they went to his house in Rhöndorf and arrested his wife, Gussie. She was taken to Brauweiler Prison outside Cologne, and when the Gestapo threatened to torture her two teenage daughters, Gussie told the police where Adenauer was. Adenauer was then arrested at Nister Mühle and taken to Brauweiler Prison. In the course of the next ten days, when Adenauer and his wife were both in prison though in separate cells, Gussie tried to commit suicide by cutting her wrists and taking an overdose of sleeping pills. She damaged her arm badly, but was then released. Of the 67 Germans in Brauweiler Prison when Adenauer was taken there, 27 were hanged and one was shot. A similar fate almost certainly awaited Adenauer. But he was saved by his son Max, who was then a lieutenant in the *Wehrmacht*. Fortunately Max's commanding officer gave him leave to visit his father. Max then took his life in his hands and went to Gestapo headquarters in Berlin to tell the Gestapo that if the fathers of loyal officers were detained without reason, morale at the Front would collapse. This argument proved decisive, and Adenauer was released on 26 November 1944. He rejoined his family at Rhöndorf and was fortunate that, when the Allied offensive began in the spring of 1945, the fighting in the Königsberg–Rhöndorf region was relatively light: there were a number of hospitals in that region, and the German Army withdrew without much resistance. Moreover, the main Allied offensive occurred north and south of Bonn: that city and Rhöndorf were both captured (liberated) by American troops in March 1945. Thus Adenauer, after various unpleasant experiences, survived the twelve years of the Third Reich.

Notes and references

1 Much of the information in this chapter naturally comes from the biographies and memoirs cited in chapter 1, note, above, p. 13.

2 Weymar, 1957, p. 60.

3 Schwarz, 1995, p. 111.

4 Schwarz, 1995, p. 112.

5 Weymar, 1957, p. 41.

6 Schwarz, 1995, pp. 124–5.

7 Schwarz 1995, p. 125.

8 Cited Schwarz, 1995, p. 125.

9 H. Vogt, *The Burden of Guilt: a short history of Germany, 1914–45* (Oxford, 1965), p. 61.

10 Schwarz, 1995, p. 127.

11 Weymar, 1957, p. 64.

12 Prittie, 1972, p. 60.

13 K.D. Erdmann, *Adenauer in der Rheinlandpolitik nach dem ersten Weltkrieg* (Stuttgart, 1966), p. 240 [henceforth Erdmann, 1966.]

14 Adenauer's attitude to, and involvement in, the Rhineland problem have been thoroughly analysed not only in Erdmann (above, n.13), but also in R. Morsey, *Die deutsche Zentrumspartei, 1917–23* (Düsseldorf, 1966), p. 122 and ff; H.F. Lehmann, 'Adenauer und der rheinische Separatismus', pp. 213–25 in R. Morsey and K. Repgen, *Adenauer Studien 5* (Mainz, 1986); R. Morsey, 'Die Rheinland, Preussen and das Reich, 1914–45', in *Rheinische Vierteljahresblätter*, 1965, vol. 30; G.Meinhardt, *Adenauer und der rheinische Separatismus* (Recklinghausen, 1962); and H. Köhler, *Adenauer und die rheinische Republik* (Opladen, 1986).

15 For literature on the Rhineland problem, see n.14 above.

16 R. Morsey, *Die deutsche Zentrumspartei, 1917–23* (Düsseldorf, 1966), p. 221.

17 See below, p. 28.

18 Full speech in K. Adenauer, *Reden 1917–67* (Stuttgart, 1975), pp. 25–38 [henceforth Adenauer *Reden,* 1975].

19 Adenauer *Reden*, 1975, p. 38.

20 Schwarz, 1995, p. 148.

21 Erdmann, 1966, p. 94.

22 Erdmann, 1966, p. 19.

23 Schwarz, 1995, p. 19.

24 The key book on all these achievements is H. Stehkamper (ed.), *Konrad Adenauer. Oberbürgermeister von Köln* (Cologne, 1976).

25 Adenauer *Reden*, 1975, p. 39.

26 F. Schumacher, *Stufen des Lebens. Erinnerungen eines Baumeisters* (Berlin, 1935), p. 369.

27 Prittie, 1972, p. 69.

28 Letter of 14 December 1927, quoted in Schwarz, 1995, p. 206.

29 W. Stresemann, *Mein Vater, Gustav Stresemann* (Munich, 1979), p. 494.

30 Schwarz, 1995, p. 208.

31 Prittie, 1972, p. 75.

32 See below, chapter 3, pp. 59–60, and Conclusion, pp. 204–5.

33 H.R. Kedward, *Fascism in Western Europe* (Glasgow, 1969), p. 64; on the failure of the Weimar Republic, see especially A.J. Nicholls and E.Matthias (eds), *German Democracy and the Triumph of Hitler* (London, 1971).

34 R. Morsey, 'Adenauer und der Nationalsozialismus', in Stehkamper (ed.), 1976, p. 460.

35 R. Strobel, *Adenauer und der Weg Deutschlands* (Frankfurt-am-Main, 1965), p. 29.

36 Adenauer to Heineman, 17 September 1930, cited Schwarz, 1995, p. 711, n.12.

37 K. Adenauer, *Briefe (1945–47)*, p.350.

38 R. Morsey, 'Adenauer und der Nazionalsozialismus', in H. Stehkamper (ed.), 1976, p. 455.

39 Letter to Ludwig Kaas, Chairman of the Centre Party, cited Schwarz, 1995, p. 225.

40 Adenauer *Reden*, 1975, pp. 68–75.

41 Letter to Amelunxen, quoted Schwarz, 1995, p. 260.

Chapter Three

Adenauer and the Christian Democratic Party, 1945–63

Adenauer in the immediate post-war period

No sooner had the war ended in May 1945 than Adenauer was asked by the Americans to resume his pre-1933 job as Mayor of Cologne. A large number of similar 'pre-Nazi' reappointments was made throughout occupied Germany. However, within five months Adenauer had been unceremoniously dismissed by the British. This apparently minor administrative decision had momentous consequences for Adenauer and Germany. For within a few months Adenauer was the leader of the newly founded Christian Democratic Union (*Christlich Demokratische Union*, CDU), and within four years he was Chancellor of the Federal Republic of Germany.

The Cologne to which Adenauer returned in 1945 was devastated by Allied bombing. Approximately three-quarters of the houses and factories had been destroyed, together with all the bridges over the Rhine. There were virtually no supplies of gas, electricity or water, and the sewage system lay in ruins. The population, eking out an existence amidst the rubble, had been reduced to about 35,000 from a pre-war total of 750,000. It was to take Cologne ten years to recover fully from the devastation of 1945. The first, almost impossible task for Adenauer and his team of officials, aided by the occupying forces, was to ensure that the survivors and returning soldiers and refugees were somehow fed, housed and clothed. The restored Mayor and his colleagues apparently worked very long hours trying to achieve the impossible. Adenauer seems to have got on reasonably well with the Americans, although he was critical of the indiscipline of the US Army. Remembering the post-First World War years, he was initially pleased when the British took over the occupation of Cologne from the Americans in June 1945. However, relations with the British Army soon deteriorated, and Adenauer was dismissed as Mayor by the local military commander, Brigadier Barraclough, in October. Adenauer later claimed that he had been dismissed because the British Labour Government disliked his 'anti-socialist' views;[1] Barraclough claimed that it was because Adenauer had failed in his responsibilities to the people of Cologne.[2] In fact his dismissal seems to have been the result of a clash of personalities and of frustration on the part of both men at the inevitably slow progress towards restoring Cologne to some semblance of normality. However, the consequences were immense for Germany. For Adenauer was freed from municipal responsibilities at a crucial moment in the history of his country: he was now able to participate (after a brief two-month ban) in the much more important task of rebuilding the German national political system, beginning with the vitally important task of establishing Germany's first genuinely democratic, centre-right political party, the CDU.

Even before he was dismissed as Mayor, Adenauer was involved in the developments which led to the founding of the CDU.[3] Leo Schwering, a former Centre Party (*Zentrum*) leader in Cologne, had already proposed to Adenauer and other Centre Party members that a new interconfessional 'Christian' party should replace the old *Zentrum*. Schwering and likeminded representatives from other parts of the Rhineland met in Cologne on 17 June 1945 and decided to found a Christian Democratic Party, which was formally constituted on 2 September. Until his dismissal as Mayor Adenauer did not participate directly in the meetings of the new party, but he was consulted about its organization and policies. From the outset Adenauer had clear views about the party's programme and principles.[4] Still banned from political activity, he was only an observer at the first national meeting of the CDU in Bad Godesberg in December 1945, but in January 1946 he was elected Chairman of the Rhineland CDU at a meeting in Herford. This was followed in March 1946 by his election as Chairman of the CDU for the British Zone, a significant step, as that Zone included not only the Ruhr and Rhineland but also all of north Germany except for the American enclave of Bremen.

One may well ask how Adenauer, a sacked Mayor, made this remarkable political progress. First of all, he was of course lucky in the timing of his dismissal. Secondly, he had the right credentials as a former Centre Party member who had been persecuted by the Nazis. He had also had administrative experience as Mayor of Cologne from 1917 to 1933, and he had participated in national politics in the Weimar Republic.[5] Yet, as we have seen, he had never been *fully* involved in *national* politics in the Weimar Republic. But in 1945 both the *political situation* and Adenauer's *attitude* were very different. Although Adenauer was almost seventy years old (no disadvantage in view of the large number of fanatical young men who had recently been part of the Nazi élite), he now had a strong desire to make German democracy work at the second attempt. After the failure of the Weimar Republic and the bitter and disastrous experiences of the Third Reich, Adenauer was determined that Germany should make a completely new start. Again and again between 1945 and 1949 he emphasized that Germans must put their past behind them. The rights of the individual must be put before those of the state. For far too long the Germans had exalted the state, the emperor or the leader above the individual, and the final nemesis had occurred under Hitler. In Adenauer's view, the Germans had abandoned Christian values before the end of the Kaiser's Empire, but in the Hitler period they had descended into a 'Dantean' inferno. Therefore there must be a return to the values of Christian civilization. The Germans would need to commit themselves as never before to liberal democracy – not just the minority of Germans who had subscribed to liberal democratic values under Weimar, but also the majority who had not. In the Weimar Republic *institutions* had been changed, but not the *minds* of the people. Democratic rights would have to be enshrined in due course in a constitution, but in the meantime they could be developed through education, by building democracy from the base upwards, and by decentralizing the German state in a federal structure.[6]

From very early after the war Adenauer was also determined to resist both the Soviet Union and all versions of Socialism. To Adenauer Communism was totalitarian, which meant that it was no better than Fascism. And Socialism – even Social Democracy – he hated, because he believed that through state planning and economic controls any form of Socialism would lead to an authoritarian type of state.[7] Adenauer also wanted to be rid of the Occupying Powers, especially the atheistic, totalitarian Russians. But once the Occupiers had gone, he was determined that Germany – both parts in due course – would make liberal democracy work at the second attempt. In other words, his *motivation* to achieve political power at the *national* level and to *change Germany's political culture* was undoubtedly very strong after the Second World War – in complete contrast to his rather temporizing attitude in the Weimar Republic.

Adenauer's new-found political vision and determination after 1945 were certainly remarkable for a man aged seventy. Eventually he had to trim some of his policies, but his long-term objectives remained clear: he was determined to build a new Germany committed to the liberal democratic values of the West.

The Christian Democratic Union (CDU): early development and characteristics

Adenauer played a key part in moulding and leading the CDU.[8] From 1945 he realized that a new party system, and especially a new centre-right party, would be essential for the development of liberal democracy in Germany, for it was going to be vital to win the support of the bourgeoisie if Germany's second attempt at democracy was going to work.

Christian Democracy was a new phenomenon in post-war Germany, the pre-war *Zentrum* having been essentially a 'confessional' party, whose main objective was to defend the Catholic Church and in particular its denominational schools. Adenauer was determined, like many others, to break the mould. Above all, he wanted to see the development of a broad-based, interconfessional, non-socialist party, committed to the values of Western democracy, free market economics and social welfare. By any standards German Christian Democracy has been a highly successful political movement. Certainly, in Adenauer's time, the Christian Democratic vote never dropped below 45 per cent at general elections, except at the first general election in 1949 (31 per cent) (see Table 2, p. 62). Indeed, at the general election of 1957 the Christian Democrats polled an absolute majority (50.2 per cent), the only time this has been achieved by one party in a free election in German history. But, perhaps even more important than the electoral achievements of Adenauer's Christian Democrats, was the role they played in integrating voters of conservative temperament into the liberal democratic system. As Professor Kurt Sontheimer once put it: 'The CDU was the first German party to gather a pluralist collection of social interests into one political organization.'[9] Some pre-war parties had *called* themselves *Volksparteien*, but Adenauer's CDU was the first *genuinely* biconfessional, interclass *Volkspartei* in German history.[10] And the establishment of such a party in the immediate post-war period was of fundamental importance for the future of German parliamentary democracy. The Christian Democrats may have impregnated the political culture of the Federal Republic with rather unexciting, materialistic, non-ideological values, and they may have been paranoid in their anti-Communism in Adenauer's time. But they were also staunchly committed to parliamentary democracy and human rights; to the achievement of a synthesis between economic liberalism and social justice; to close cooperation between the nations of Western Europe; and to the alliance of those nations with the United States.

In order to understand the nature of the party Adenauer helped to create and mould, we must examine the origins of the Christian Democratic Union. For the CDU was very much the child of the years 1945-49, and throughout the 'Adenauer era' (1949–63) it retained most of the characteristics and values acquired in its early years. Adenauer, like most former Centre Party leaders, was opposed to the revival of a 'confessional' party which could not appeal to Protestants; moreover a new Centre Party (whatever the cosmetic changes) would be vulnerable to attacks by the SPD on the grounds that it had voted for the Enabling Act in March 1933. In Adenauer's view, the failure of the two branches of the Christian Church to cooperate politically under Weimar was one of the key factors which had made possible the rise of Hitler.[11] At the same time Adenauer seems to have originally hoped that Christian Democracy would develop as a democratic *socio-political movement* and not just as a *political party*. He wanted democracy to become rooted in German political and social culture, and not merely to be a phenomenon associated with elections and governing élites. Thus, the early Christian Democrats deliberately avoided the word 'Party', choosing instead 'Union', which had the additional merit of appealing to Protestants. They hoped too that the new Union would subsume the old class divisions, which had contributed to the fragility of the Weimar party system. From the start the CDU contained Catholics and Protestants, trade unionists and businessmen, working and middle-class 'wings'. In addition, it was loosely structured, partly because the occupation authorities wanted democracy to 'grow' from the grassroots upwards: only *Land* and Zonal parties were licensed during the period of 'denazification', which lasted until 1947. The CDU thus developed as a confederal party in which the regional associations *(Landesverbände)* wielded considerable influence and, so long as the party continued to win elections, i.e. throughout the Adenauer era, it remained essentially an association for the election of the Chancellor (*Kanzlerwahlverein*). Obviously this development of the CDU as

Table 2   Bundestag Elections in the Federal Republic of Germany 1949–61

| | 1949 | | | 1953 | | | 1957 | | | 1961 | | |
| Electorate (millions)
Turnout (per cent) | 31.2
78.5 | | | 33.2
86.2 | | | 35.4
88.2 | | | 37.4
87.7 | | |
	Votes (million)	%	Seats	Votes (million)	%	Seats	Votes (million)	%	Seats	Votes (million)	%	Seats
Christian Democrats (CDU/CSU)	7.4	31.0	139	12.4	45.2	244‡	15.0	50.2	270	14.3	45.4	242
Social Democrats (SPD)	6.9	29.2	131	7.9	28.8	151	9.5	31.8	169	11.4	36.2	190
Liberals (FDP)	2.8	11.9	52	2.6	9.5	48	2.3	7.7	41	4.0	12.8	67
German Party* (DP)	0.9	4.0	17	0.9	3.2	15	1.0	2.8	17	0.9	2.8	–
Refugees* (GB/BHE)	0.7	2.9	12	1.6	5.9	27	1.4	4.6	–	–	–	–
Total Seats	.		402			487			497			499

*By 1961 the DP and GB/BHE had amalgamated and stood as one party, the Gesamtdeutsche Partei (GDP).

‡ includes one Centre Party deputy affiliated to CDU.

Notes:

1. The full names of the parties can be found in the List of Abbreviations.

2. This Table refers to second votes (PR votes), i.e. those which decide the final composition of the Bundestag. See below, Electoral Law.

3. Minor parties, which were important in 1949, have been omitted. Hence the apparent discrepancy between party seats and total seats in the Bundestag. In 1949 the Communist Party (KPD) won 5.7 per cent (15 seats); the Bavarian Party (BP) 4.2 per cent (17 seats); the Centre Party (Z) 3.1 per cent (10 seats) [it also won 3 seats in 1953 owing to having joint lists with the CDU].

Source: H. Kaack, *Geschichte und Struktur des deutschen Parteiensystems* (Opladen, 1971).

Electoral law for Bundestag elections

A simple definition is that the electoral law is *personalized proportional representation (PR) with a 5 per cent hurdle.*
Each voter has two votes. The first is for a constituency representative, elected by simple relative majority. The second is for a *Land* (state) party list (the PR vote). Half of the membership of the Bundestag represents constituencies (elected by first votes). The other half is drawn from the *Land* party lists in such a way that the overall composition of the Bundestag reflects the national strength of the parties as shown by the second (PR) votes cast for them. Thus proportional representation is the predominant element in the Federal Republic's electoral system. However, no party can be represented in the Bundestag unless it wins at least 3 'direct' constituency seats by first votes **or** at least 5 per cent of the national poll of the second (PR) votes.

Notes:

1. The 1949 electoral law differed slightly from the above. Firstly, in 1949 three-fifths of the members were elected from individual constituencies; secondly, the 5 per cent hurdle applied at the *Land* rather than the national level.

2. If a party gains more constituency seats in a *Land* than it is entitled to receive as a result of its national proportional vote, it retains the extra seats (*Überhangmandate*). Hence, the total membership of the Bundestag may vary somewhat from one election to another.

an 'electors' party' rather than a 'membership party' was not in line with the hopes of those founder members who wanted the Union to be a 'movement' rather than just a 'party'.[12] But in due course it suited Adenauer, who, as he became more autocratic, was quite content that the party should be relatively morbid except when it came to life to win elections for him. The price for the failure to build up an effective socio-political movement and party organization (except at elections in the case of the latter)[13] was not paid until the late 1960s–early 1970s, by which time Adenauer had retired from politics.

The geographical spread and pluralistic nature of the CDU were apparent from its earliest days, the party developing spontaneously and simultaneously in Berlin, Cologne, Hamburg, Hanover, Frankfurt, Stuttgart and elsewhere. From the outset the CDU was, then, diverse – politically, socially, religiously and geographically. But the most important early centres were in the Rhineland and Berlin. By coincidence these two major branches were established on the same day, 17 June 1945. More important than the timing of these early Christian Democratic meetings was the type of person who attended them. If Catholics predominated, there was a significant number of Protestants who were founding members. And if former Centre Party members and Catholic trade unionists were particularly prominent in the new inter-class, inter-confessional CDU, there were also former Liberals (DDP and DVP) and Conservative Nationalists (DNVP), who were prepared to put the past behind them and join a party which was committed to 'Christian principles' in politics. Although the epithet 'Christian principles' is vague, there was at the time a strong feeling, including among non-Christians, that after the barbarities of the Third Reich a real attempt must be made to return to the old 'Christian' values – truth, honesty, respect for the individual and so forth. In Adenauer's view, this also meant respect for people of different Christian faiths or none. For, although Adenauer was a practising Catholic throughout his life, he was determined that old 'confessional' issues, such as the defence of Catholic schools, should be downgraded in CDU programmes.[14] Otherwise his dream of a large inter-class, inter-denominational, anti-Socialist party would not come to fruition.

Adenauer became the leading figure in the CDU between 1946 and 1949, and in 1949 he was elected Chancellor of the Federal Republic. His progress towards the leadership of his party and country was indeed remarkable. By 1947 he was Chairman of the Interzonal CDU. In 1948 he was selected to be President of the Parliamentary Council, which drew up the German Constitution (*Grundgesetz*, Basic Law). Then in 1949 the Christian Democrats emerged from the first Federal general election as the leading party and Adenauer was able to form his first government. But neither Adenauer's rise to ascendancy in the CDU nor his election to the Chancellorship were achieved without overcoming considerable obstacles. Within the CDU his main battles were against the 'Social Christians' and the Berlin group, which to some extent overlapped. As regards the Chancellorship, Adenauer had to defeat those (including many in his own party) who favoured a grand coalition of national unity (essentially a CDU–SPD coalition), which would, many believed, be the best way to defend the Federal Republic's interests in the face of the Occupying Powers. Adenauer in contrast believed strongly in a government which excluded the Social Democrats.[15]

The first battle Adenauer had to win was with the Berlin CDU. The leading Berlin figures were Andreas Hermes, a former *Zentrum* leader who was awaiting execution by the Nazis when released by the Russians in 1945, and Jakob Kaiser, a former Catholic trade union leader, another resister who was lucky to survive the war. Kaiser soon became the dominant figure in the Berlin CDU, and, until forced out of his Eastern base by the Russians at the end of 1947, he was a serious rival to Adenauer. Kaiser's perspectives were very different from Adenauer's. Firstly, he was a strong advocate of 'Christian Socialism', i.e. he believed in centralized economic planning, nationalization of major industries and a strong welfare state. He was quite prepared to work with the SPD to achieve these objectives. He also had a very different attitude to the Soviet Union and reunification: he believed that if the CDU maintained its links with the Russians (even after the takeover of the SPD by the Communists in the Soviet Zone in 1947) and adopted 'socialist' policies, the Christian Democrats might somehow be able to bridge the gap between East and West, leading ultimately to a reunited Germany. Adenauer, in contrast, had come to the conclusion by early 1946 that the division of Germany was de facto if not yet *de jure*. He did not believe that compromises could be reached with the Soviet Communists. Therefore the only way to reunification would be through the achievement of economic prosperity and liberal democracy in the Western Zones, followed eventually by the Communists giving in to the democrats of the West and allowing German reunification.

The views of Adenauer and Kaiser about the likely future for Germany were thus very different. It was not long before Adenauer's judgement of the situation appeared to be more realistic. It was, however, ironic that by 'dismissing' Kaiser at the end of 1947 the Russians played into the hands of Adenauer, for within a few years Adenauer was to prove himself one of the Soviet Union's most implacable opponents. Adenauer meanwhile found himself in a much stronger position than Kaiser, who, having moved to the West, of course lost his powerful base in the East. Thus by 1948 Adenauer had achieved ascendancy in the CDU throughout the Western Zones. Moreover, he was well on the way to creating the type of party he wanted, even if between 1947 and 1949 he had a struggle to overcome the 'Social Christian' wing associated with the Catholic trade unionists, the social committees (*Sozialausschüsse*), and men such as Karl Arnold, Mayor of Düsseldorf and Minister President of North Rhine Westphalia (1947–56), and of course Jakob Kaiser, whose power in the CDU had been considerably reduced for the reasons mentioned above, but who nevertheless remained an influential Christian Democratic politician.

Before discussing the conflicts Adenauer had with the 'Social Christians' over the issue of 'socialism' within the CDU, it should be stressed that Adenauer was largely successful in achieving an inter-class, inter-confessional party in the Western Zones by the end of 1947. Given the confessional balance in the Rhineland and Ruhr, it was inevitable that Catholics predominated in the CDU. Many well-known Protestants, however, were founder members, men such as the former Conservatives (DNVP) Robert Lehr and Friedrich Holzapfel and Adenauer's long-term friend, the banker Robert Pferdemenges. As Mayor of Herford Holzapfel was able to travel fairly freely even in the early days of occupation, and he played an important role in liaising with the mainly Protestant CDU leaders of north Germany. Another Protestant who was prominent in the foundation of the Rhineland CDU was Gustav Heinemann, one of the leaders of the 'Confessing Church' which had resisted the Nazis with great courage.[16] The Protestant pastor Hans Encke also gave his full support to the proposal for a mixed Catholic–Protestant party at the foundation meeting of the Rhineland CDU in June 1945. Nevertheless, the leading figures in the Rhineland CDU in 1945–46 were nearly all left-wing Catholics of 'Social Christian' leanings. This makes it all the more surprising that Adenauer, a prominent member of the conservative wing of the new party, succeeded in emerging not only as the leader of the Rhineland CDU but also of the West German CDU. Although the men of the left were prominent early on, Adenauer, as we shall see, was to win his battle with them by 1948.[17]

In northern Germany Protestants and Conservatives predominated in the CDU. In Schleswig-Holstein Hans Schlange-Schöningen, formerly a DNVP leader in Pomerania and a Protestant, was suspicious of the domination of the CDU by Catholic Rhinelanders, especially before Adenauer won his battle with the 'Social Christians'. Although Schlange-Schöningen eventually agreed to the establishment of a new inter-confessional party, he at first wanted to set up a Protestant CDU in north Germany. If he had succeeded, his party would presumably have been comparable to the 'independent' Christian Democratic Party in Bavaria, the CSU. However, Schlange-Schöningen was prevailed upon by Theodor Steltzer, a conservative Protestant politician from Schleswig-Holstein, to participate fully in the CDU at the Bad Godesberg meeting in December 1945, which was attended by Christian Democrats from all parts of Germany except Bavaria. The CDU had some difficulty in establishing itself in largely Protestant Hamburg, Bremen and Lower Saxony, but by 1946 branches had been established in all three *Länder*.

In the central part of Western Germany the new party had an interesting mixture of left-wing Catholic intellectuals, Catholic trade unionists, and conservatives – both Catholics and Protestants. In Frankfurt-am-Main Catholic left-wingers predominated, led by Walter Dirks and Karl-Heinz Knappstein. They drew up the Frankfurt Programme of September 1945, which demanded, *inter alia*, that the CDU should develop as a 'Social Christian' party, basing its programme on 'Sozialismus aus christlicher Verantwortung' ('Socialism based on a Christian sense of responsibility'). In Wiesbaden, on the other hand, the more conservative elements predominated, led by the Catholic Heinrich von Brentano, later chairman of the Christian Democratic parliamentary group, Foreign Minister and close colleague of Adenauer, and the Protestant Erich Köhler, former member of the conservative DNVP and future president of the Frankfurt Economic Council.

Finally, in south-west Germany (the French Zone), the CDU developed more slowly, partly because the French were the most reluctant of the Western allies to license parties. Nevertheless, a comparable, pluralistic party gradually emerged. In Württemberg the majority of the early CDU members were conservatives. They were led by Kurt-Georg Kiesinger, one-time member of the Centre Party and later a nominal member of the Nazi

Party. Kiesinger was to go on to be a prominent member of the Bundestag from 1949 to 1957, Minister-President of Baden-Württemberg (1957–66), and finally Federal Chancellor (1966–69). However, there were also advocates of 'Christian Socialism' among the founder members in Baden and Württemberg, men such as Fridolin Heurich, a Catholic trade union leader from North Baden and close friend of Jakob Kaiser, and Wilhelm Simpfendörfer, who even after the 1949 general election continued to advocate a grand coalition between the CDU and SPD. In the Rhineland-Palatinate (the *Land* was not formally constituted until the end of 1946) former *Zentrum* supporters predominated in the northern part around Koblenz and Trier, and as some of them favoured the reconstitution of the *Zentrum*, the CDU had some difficulty in establishing itself. But by March 1946 there were CDU associations in the north and the south of the Rhineland-Palatinate, and in March 1947 they amalgamated to form a single *Land* association.

Thus, within two years of the end of the war, a completely new type of party had emerged: a genuine *Volkspartei*, which brought together Catholics and Protestants, former members of the Centre Party and of the Liberal and Conservative Parties, trade unionists and businessmen, and even a few former (nominal) Nazis. But the CDU was still very loosely organized compared with the SPD, and it was by no means clear whether it was more committed to progressive or to conservative political principles. During the years 1947–49 the crucial decisions were taken about what sort of a party the CDU would be, in terms both of organization and policy. There is no doubt that the key figure in welding the pluralistic *Land* associations of the CDU into a highly successful vote-winning machine was Konrad Adenauer.[18]

There was, however, one exception to this promising picture. A nominally Christian Democratic Party was founded in Bavaria in October 1945. However, during its first ten years the Christian Social Union (*Christlich-Soziale Union,* CSU) was not an inter-confessional, inter-class party like its counterparts elsewhere Germany. And, although the CSU formed a joint parliamentary group (*Fraktion*) with the CDU in 1949, the two parties had (and have) their own organizations, congresses, chairmen and political programmes. It was not until the mid-1950s that the CSU became a Christian Democratic Party in the accepted sense of that term. Under the chairmanship of Hans Seidel (1955–61), the CSU developed into an inter-class, inter-confessional party with a large number of members. It continued as such under Seidel's successor as chairman, Franz-Josef Strauss (Chairman 1961–76). Under Seidel and Strauss the CSU of course *did* differ from the CDU – it was, *inter alia*, more right-wing, more Catholic and more successful at elections. At times its relationship with the CDU was fraught, particularly in the 1970s. However the later history of the CSU is beyond the scope of this book. The point to note here is that the CSU was a very different type of party from the CDU in its early years.[19]

One may well ask why the CSU differed so greatly from the CDU during these formative years. The simple answer is that Bavaria was (and is) very different from the rest of Germany. The differences were to become blurred over the years, but even today Bavaria is a distinctive *Land*. In spite of being a state within the Federal Republic of Germany it still insists on calling itself *der Freistaat Bayern*. When the Federal Republic was established, Bavaria was the only *Land* to retain its old boundaries and culture. The CSU reflected (and continues to reflect) this Bavarian particularism. Paradoxically, the founding members of the CSU, Adam Stegerwald and Josef Müller, did not want the CSU to develop in this way. For Stegerwald, a former trade union leader and Minister-President of Prussia, and Josef Müller, a Munich lawyer and Nazi resister who had been lucky to survive the war, wanted to set up an 'Adenauer-type' party. That is to say they both favoured a broad-based, inter-class party, and they had no wish to see the CSU develop as a right-conservative (*rechtskonservative*) or confessional party (as the pre-war *Bayerische Volkspartei*, BVP, had been).

The CSU, however, did develop as such a party. Stegerwald died un-expectedly in December 1945. And, although the first two chairmen of the party – Müller (1945–49) and Hans Ehard (1949–55) – were moderates, the party was hijacked by Catholic conservatives led by Dr Alois Hundhammer, and they dominated it until the mid–1950s. Hundhammer, a pre-war BVP leader, was a brave man who had been imprisoned by the Nazis, but he was also a narrow-minded, Catholic traditionalist. Certainly by the early 1950s the CSU had become a confessional party with a declin-ing membership limited to rural, Catholic Bavaria. Over 90 per cent of CSU members were Catholics, although only 75 per cent of Bavarians were – it should not be forgotten that the three Franconian provinces of northern Bavaria were (and are) largely Protestant. The CSU was, there-fore, quite unlike the Christian Democratic *Volksparteien* in the other *Länder* of West Germany. However, after its electoral disappointment in

1949 (the CSU only polled 29 per cent to the *Bayernpartei*'s 21 per cent), and the death of Hundhammer in 1953, the CSU gradually transformed itself into a more conventional Christian Democratic party. It recruited a large membership, made a real effort to appeal to city dwellers and Protestants, and overall became a very successful party – still distinctively Bavarian yet recognizably Christian Democratic, unlike in the early years of its existence.

The CDU swings to the right

Before discussing the CDU's electoral achievements under Adenauer, it is important to show how he won the party over to his views, especially on the economy.[20] For Adenauer believed strongly in the free market, and was determined to avoid a coalition with the SPD, which still advocated a centrally planned economy in the immediate post-war period. Within the CDU Adenauer made full use of his political and organizational skills to achieve his ends. He was remarkably skilful at persuading both the left and the right of the party that he was acting in their interests, when in reality he was essentially a conservative. Like many successful politicians, he was also quite simply lucky. Not only had his great rival Jakob Kaiser been deprived of his Berlin power base by the Russians, but he was also fortunate in the way the political and economic situation developed in Germany and in Europe as a whole. However, he undoubtedly showed great skill in taking advantage of the opportunities presented to him. Within the party this was illustrated in the early years by the way he won control of its organization and manipulated its policy in the direction he wanted, especially in 1948–49.[21]

As we have seen, Adenauer became Chairman of the CDU in all three Western Zones in 1947. In 1947–48 he took advantage of his leading position in the CDU as Western Germany moved steadfastly towards the foundation of the Federal Republic in 1949. In February 1947 the CDU had set up an inter-*Land* working association (*Arbeitsgemeinschaft*). At the first meeting of this working association in Frankfurt, Adenauer and Holzapfel represented the British Zone, Müller and Köhler the American, Altmaier and Steiner the French, and Kaiser and Lemmer Berlin. Against the wishes of Adenauer the working association decided to have a rotating chairman. Friedrich von Baffron-Prittwitz was elected to this post, but when he made it clear that he preferred the 'Social Christian' views of Kaiser to the more conservative views of Adenauer, the latter simply boycotted the meetings of the working association. The secretariat of the working association did help the CDU *Land* parties to fight various local elections in 1947–48, and it did the same for the national party at the 1949 general election. But as from June 1948, the newly established Conference of CDU *Land* chairmen, presided over by Adenauer and without any Berlin representatives, became the key national coordinating body within the CDU, and remained as such until the establishment of the CDU as a Federal party at Goslar in October 1950. At the Goslar party conference Adenauer was to be elected chairman, with Kaiser and Holzapfel as vice-chairmen.

In policy matters Adenauer also succeeded between 1945 and 1949 in manoeuvring the CDU in the direction he wanted. The distinctly leftish ('Social Christian') positions adopted in the Cologne, Frankfurt and Ahlen programmes of 1945–47 were gradually abandoned in favour of the free market policies which constituted the essence of the Düsseldorf Programme of 1949. The Düsseldorf Programme was very much an Adenauer–Erhard Programme, and the CDU fought and won the first Federal general election on that Programme.[22]

In the immediate post-war period the 'Social Christian' ideas of Jakob Kaiser (Berlin), Karl Arnold (Düsseldorf) and Eugen Kogon (Frankfurt) had undoubtedly predominated in CDU thinking. The three basic demands of the 'Social Christians' were (i) national economic planning; (ii) nationalization of the key industries; and (iii) co-determination between workers and management in the running of industry. However, the Catholic Church soon made it clear that it was not prepared to go beyond the social teaching contained in the 1931 papal bull, *Quadragesimo Anno*, which had declared that 'Christian Socialism is a contradiction in itself. It is impossible to be simultaneously a good Catholic and a committed Socialist'.[23] Adenauer was in full agreement with the Church over this matter. In June 1946 he stated that 'The word Socialism is scientifically and semantically worn out ... If we use it, we may win five people, but twenty will run away.'[24] It was typical of Adenauer's political skill and judgement to criticize a party (the SPD) which claimed to have a monopoly (or even partial monopoly) of the truth, because *Weltanschauungen* were very much out of fashion in the immediate post-war period. Already by the time of the Neheim–Hüsten Programme of February 1946, in the preparation of which Adenauer played a key part, the CDU was watering down its hitherto clearcut commitment to economic dirigisme. Significantly that Programme stated that 'The question of nationalization of parts of the economy, which is being strongly pressed, is currently not practicable, since the German economy is not free.'[25] And from late 1947 it became even less practicable as British influence declined (the Labour Government favoured nationalized industries) vis-à-vis American influence (in favour of free enterprise) owing to Britain's increasing economic difficulties. Once again outside circumstances favoured the policies which Adenauer wanted.

The Ahlen Programme of 1947 used to be regarded as the high point of the CDU's commitment to 'Social Christian' ideas. But more recent scholarship suggests that this view needs modifying.[26] The Ahlen Programme was certainly outspoken in its criticism of traditional capitalism, which it saw as being incapable of satisfying the 'political and social needs of the German people'.[27] However, the Programme did not commit the CDU to a state-run economy. As Schwarz points out, it would indeed have been ironic if a programme drawn up in Robert Pferdemenges's bank in Cologne in the presence of Adenauer had made such a commitment.[28] Although this was ostensibly the CDU's most left-wing programme, it was so in *social* but not in *economic* policies. It was in fact a compromise between the views of Pferdemenges (business wing) and Albers (social wing). It *did* commit the Christian Democrats to a strong social welfare programme and to some form of industrial codetermination (*Mitbestimmung*[29]), but it did not commit the party to any form of nationalized or 'socialized' industry. While agreeing with the Social Democrats that large-scale capitalism had helped Hitler to power in the early 1930s, the Ahlen Programme went on to criticize the 'state capitalism' of the later Nazi period, i.e. the state control of industry by Albert Speer from 1942–1945. Instead of either 'private capitalism' or 'state capitalism', the Programme proposed a middle way, namely *Gemeinwirtschaft* (semi-public ownership), which was defined as a mixed system of ownership in which public bodies (such as *Land* governments and trade unions) would hold a majority of shares, but no single body would be allowed to hold more than 15 per cent of the shares in any given enterprise. Individuals would also be entitled to hold shares, but no single person would be able to hold more than 10 per cent. The Ahlen Programme was endorsed by Adenauer, but was to be implemented only in the British Zone. It was left-wing in its social commitments but imprecise in its economic proposals. The Programme may be regarded as a subtle Adenauer compromise, for, although it appeared to be 'left wing', there was nothing in it which could upset 'bourgeois' entrepreneurs such as farmers, small businessmen and tradesmen.

Within two years the (vague) economic commitments of the Ahlen Programme had been abandoned. For the CDU fought the 1949 general election on the basis of the sixteen points of the Düsseldorf Programme.[30] This committed the party decisively to Ludwig Erhard's 'social market economy' (*Sozialmarktwirtschaft*), a blend of free enterprise and social justice, with the main emphasis on the former. Erhard's view was that 'social goods' were a by-product of market success rather than a parallel development. His economic views, with which Adenauer was in complete agreement, lay at the heart of the Düsseldorf Programme. The social element was grafted on, with much less precise commitments to the welfare state and codetermination in industry. The Düsseldorf Programme, then, was very much an Adenauer–Erhard programme, not only in its powerful message about the merits of the social market economy, but also in its commitments to parliamentary democracy; to federalism; to the family; to small businesses and farming; and to cooperation between the 'social partners' i.e. business and trade union leaders.

1949: Adenauer a national leader and the CDU a national party

The Parliamentary Council (*Parlamentarische Rat*), which drew up the Federal Republic's Constitution, the Basic Law (*Grundgesetz*) between September 1948 and May 1949, provided an important opportunity for Adenauer to project himself to the public.[31] The Parliamentary Council consisted of 65 representatives from the *Länder* – 27 Christian Democrats, 27 Social Democrats, 5 Liberals, and 2 each from the Centre Party, the German Party and the Communist Party. Adenauer was elected Chairman of the Parliamentary Council thanks to a compromise with the SPD. That Party's leading constitutional expert, Carlo Schmid, was given the chairmanship of the main constitutional committee in exchange for Adenauer becoming Chairman of the Parliamentary Council, a deal which Schmid later admitted was a mistake.[32] Meanwhile, Kurt Schumacher, the chairman of the SPD, did not even become member of the Parliamentary

Council, relying on the traditional discipline of the SPD to control and criticize from outside. As it happened, Schumacher was seriously ill for much of the time the Parliamentary Council was meeting. The combination of Schumacher's absence and Adenauer's constant appearances as the Parliamentary Council's spokesman converted Adenauer from being a relatively unknown political figure – or at least unknown outside the Rhineland and the British Zone – into a national political figure. Indeed, he even became a person of some international standing as a result of interviews with the foreign press.

Thus by 1949 both Adenauer and the Christian Democratic Union were very much in the ascendant in the embryonic Federal Republic. The CDU had been successfully established as an inter-class, centre-right party. It was not a conservative party in the traditional German sense, being neither *rechtskonservative* nor *deutschnationale.* However, it was sufficiently conservative to be able to rally the opponents of 'socialism' and 'collectivism' in the broadest sense of these words. Moreover, in terms of long-term strategy – making Germany's second attempt at democracy work, and short-term tactics – making the party electable, Adenauer and his close allies were undoubtedly wise to keep the CDU's membership and appeal as wide as possible. Although he himself had suffered under the Third Reich, he was prepared to accept former nominal Nazis into the party, and this helped to prevent the rise of a significant extreme-right party. He was a Catholic, but he insisted that Protestants should be represented at all levels in the CDU. He despised Socialism, but he presided over a party with a strong trade union base. He was conservative in his political and economic views, but he accepted the tenets and requirements of the welfare state. The CDU thus developed very much as an 'Adenauer' party.

Adenauer's electoral record, 1949-61

As we have seen, Adenauer emerged from his Chairmanship of the Parliamentary Council with a greatly enhanced public image, and by 1949 the CDU was well established in all the West German *Länder* except Bavaria. The Parliamentary Council approved the Basic Law on 8 May 1949, and the Allied Governors endorsed it four days later. Adenauer's only real 'failure' with regard to the Basic Law was that he would have preferred a relatively weak upper house (*Bundesrat*) to represent the regions of Germany. But he had to agree to a constitutionally powerful, even though indirectly elected, *Bundesrat* which was nominated by the *Land* governments to reflect their own political complexion. Otherwise Adenauer's views prevailed – a federal system of government, an electoral law based on proportional representation (the SPD had wanted a simple relative majority system), and Bonn as the capital of the Federal Republic. Not only did Adenauer succeed in achieving the nomination of Bonn rather than Frankfurt (by 33 votes to 29), but he also united the Christian Democrats decisively behind him when Schumacher unwisely stated that if Frankfurt were not selected, this would amount to a defeat for the SPD.

So, when campaigning began in July 1949 for the first Bundestag (to be elected in August), Adenauer felt quietly confident. Although seventy-three years old he was remarkably fit, and with economic issues at the heart of the election campaign, he believed that the non-socialist parties were in a strong position to succeed. Adenauer and Erhard made a series of speeches (Adenauer averaging four a day) on the merits of the free market economy. After the Allied-instituted currency reform of June 1948, there was increasing evidence that the worst of the post-war hunger, unemployment and deprivation was over. The success of Erhard's policies as Economics Director of the Economic Council was becoming apparent by the summer of 1949. In June 1948 industrial production had been only 54 per cent of the 1936 level, but by February 1949 it was 84 per cent and by the end of the year over 100 per cent. Unemployment had declined from over 2 million in the summer of 1948 to 1.5 million by mid-1949. The 'great hunger' was almost over by the end of 1948. Admittedly there were still huge problems to be resolved – only a start had been made on the rebuilding of Germany's ravaged cities; 12 million refugees from the East were only beginning to be integrated into western society; and there were an estimated 1.2 million war widows who were still receiving minimal financial assistance from the state. Nevertheless, Adenauer and Erhard drove home the message that housing and employment prospects were improving, and that the non-interventionist economic policy of Erhard was beginning to work. The emphasis on the economy, then, benefited Adenauer's Christian Democrats. So too did the failings of the SPD. Schumacher was very critical of the Western Allies at the very time when their attitude to the West Germans was mellowing, e.g. they were slowing up the policy of industrial dismantling, reducing their economic controls, and emphasizing – as American influence increased – the very economic policies advocated by Adenauer and Erhard. The SPD was meanwhile still strongly committed to a planned economy and to the nationalization of major industries. Schumacher also at one point unwisely referred to the Catholic Church as a 'fifth occupying power',[33] thus driving all good Catholics into the arms of the CDU/CSU. In addition, the SPD had lost many of its pre-war strongholds, notably in Greater Berlin, Saxony and Thuringia. Its western strongholds were still considerable – Hamburg, Bremen and the industrial cities of the Ruhr – but these could hardly make up for the losses in the East.

From Adenauer's point of view the general election of August 1949 was a qualified success (see Table 2, p. 62). The CDU/CSU polled 7.4 million votes to the SPD's 6.9 million, winning 139 seats to the SPD's 131 (31 per cent to 29.2 per cent). The Liberals (FDP) won 52 seats (11.9 per cent) and the remaining seats were mainly won either by right-wing parties favourable to Adenauer such as the German Party (DP) and Bavarian Party (BP) (34 seats between them), or by outright opponents such as the Communist Party (KPD) (15 seats). Immediately after the election Adenauer summoned the leading members of the CDU/CSU to his house in Rhöndorf to tell them that he was ready to stand for the Chancellor-ship at the head of a right-of-centre coalition, although some left-wing Christian Democrats still favoured a grand coalition with the SPD. Adenauer emphasized that nearly 14 million Germans had voted for 'free market' parties, whereas only 8.5 million had voted for 'interventionist' parties. Adenauer's arguments carried the day, and on 15 September 1949 he was elected Chancellor by 202 votes out of 402 (there were 142 oppo-nents, 44 abstainers, 13 absentees and 1 invalid vote). If all those who had agreed to support an Adenauer-led coalition had voted for him (CDU, CSU, FDP and German Party), he should have received 408 votes. It seems that a small number of Christian Democrats, hankering after a grand coalition, abstained in the secret ballot. In the event Adenauer was elected Chancellor with only one vote to spare, as he needed an absolute majority of the membership of the Bundestag. That vote was his own. When asked if he had voted for himself to become Chancellor, he replied 'Naturally; anything else would have been hypocrisy'![34]

In spite of the fact that the Christian Democrats outdistanced the Social Democrats at the general election of 1949, emerging from it with Adenauer as Chancellor at the head of a coalition of CDU/CSU, FDP

(Liberals) and DP (German Party), the election was not exactly a triumph for Adenauer and the Christian Democrats. For their percentage of the poll (31) was down by almost 7 points from their average poll at the *Landtag* elections of 1946-47. The SPD vote (29.2) was also down by 6 points compared with these elections. As far as Adenauer's party was concerned, the main lesson was that Christian Democracy had still not established itself fully in the nation's political consciousness. Thus Adenauer needed allies if he was going to be an effective Chancellor. As a relatively new party the CDU/CSU had of course polled very creditably, but the 1949 result suggested that rapid growth might well be followed by rapid decline. Fragmentation of the party system, so apparent under the Weimar Republic, could still become a characteristic of the Bonn Republic. Adenauer, however, was determined that Bonn should not repeat the mistakes of Weimar. This was one of the reasons why he wanted to include the bourgeois (*bürgerlich*) parties such as the FDP, DP and later the Refugee Party, in his coalition. His strategy was to keep on good terms with these small centre-right parties with a view to 'absorbing' them in due course, and this strategy eventually paid handsome dividends.

The 1949 electoral setback for the Christian Democrats (insofar as it was one) was partly a result of the more flexible party licensing policy applied by the Western Allies after the 1946-47 *Landtag* elections. In Bavaria, for example, the CSU poll was only 29 per cent in 1949, a drop of 23 points compared with the 1946 *Landtag* election, and this collapse of the Christian Democratic vote was largely attributable to the intervention of the *Bayern Partei* (BP), which had been licensed in February 1948. Likewise, in north Germany the roughly equivalent particularist, conservative, but Protestant *Deutsche Partei* (DP) cut into the CDU vote in 1949 by winning 18 per cent in Bremen and Lower Saxony, 13 per cent in Hamburg and 12 per cent in Schleswig-Holstein. Although founded in 1945, the DP had only been licensed in October 1947. Other right-wing votes were siphoned off by the *Deutsche Rechtspartei* (DRP), which polled 8 per cent in Lower Saxony, although only 2 per cent overall (altogether the DRP won five seats), and by the Bavarian refugee party, the *Wirtschaftliche Aufbauvereinigung* (Union for Economic Reconstruction), which, under its demagogic leader Alfred Loritz, won twelve seats after polling 14.4 per cent in Bavaria. Despite these setbacks for the Christian Democrats Adenauer was certainly justified in standing for – and winning – the Chancellorship in 1949, because, as stressed above, the election had largely been fought on economic issues, and the 'free enterprise' parties had outdistanced their opponents by over 5 million votes. Moreover, the CDU/CSU had beaten its main rival, the SPD, by 400,000 votes (7.4 to 6.9 million) and by nearly 2 percentage points (31 to 29.2) at an election in which both parties made it clear that their main objective was to win control of the Economics Ministry.

The 1949 election had indicated the possibilities open to small parties with distinctive ideological views or particular clienteles, and the *Landtag* elections of 1949–52 seemed to confirm Adenauer's fears that Bonn might follow the party fragmentation of Weimar. For, with a rash of smaller parties appearing, the Christian Democratic vote at the *Landtag* elections of 1949–52 declined to an average of 25 per cent (compared with 37.7 per cent in 1946–47 and 31 per cent in 1949). The worst threat came from the refugees, who outside Bavaria had had no party specifically committed to representing their interests at the 1949 general election. But in January 1950 the *Bund der Heimatvertriebenen und Entrechteten*, BHE (Union of those expelled from their homelands and of the dispossessed) was founded in Schleswig-Holstein, and at the subsequent *Landtag* election (July 1950) the BHE polled 23.4 per cent, pushing the CDU, with 19.7 per cent, into third place (the SPD won 27.5 per cent). The BHE participated in eight *Landtag* elections between 1950 and 1952. Its average poll was 12 per cent, largely achieved at the expense of the CDU and FDP, which also both lost votes to the extreme right *Sozialistische Reichspartei* (SRP), which polled 7.7 per cent in Bremen and 11 per cent in Lower Saxony in 1951. Clearly Adenauer would be unwise to underestimate the political importance of the refugees, even if the extreme right vote could be more easily contained.[35]

Overall, the electoral prospects for the Christian Democrats did not look particularly favourable in the period leading up to the 1953 general election. Yet the CDU/CSU polled 45.2 per cent in September 1953, and with 244 seats out of 487 became the first party in German history to win an absolute majority in parliament at a free election.[36] Although in 1957 the Christian Democrats were to win an even higher percentage of the poll (50.2 per cent), the 1953 election result was of crucial importance for them and for West German democracy. For Adenauer's great objective of saving Bonn from the party fragmentation of Weimar was achieved in 1953. The 1957 election only consolidated the vital breakthrough of 1953. What was important in 1953 was not only that the CDU/CSU outdistanced its main rival the SPD so decisively (45.2 per cent to 28.8 per cent), but that the CDU/CSU's main allies, the FDP, Refugees (GB/BHE) and DP, were clearly shown to be minor parties compared with the Christian Democrats. Adenauer wanted the support of these lesser parties to give himself a solid majority. But all the signs were that, in complete contrast to the Weimar Republic, the Bonn Republic was moving towards an essentially two-party system, with the CDU/CSU and SPD as the two dominant parties, for three-quarters of all votes were cast for these two parties in 1953.

Why, after the Weimar-like fragmentation of the party system at the *Landtag* elections of 1950-52, were the Christian Democrats so unexpectedly successful in 1953? In the first place, they made full use of their position as the governing party to put forward their case. They unashamedly, labelled themselves 'The Chancellor's Party'.[37] Adenauer had emerged in the previous four years as a reliable, successful Chancellor, a safe pair of hands when East–West relations were tense and the economy was still reviving slowly in difficult conditions. Moreover, in contrast to the 1949 election, when foreign policy was excluded as an Allied prerogative, in 1953 much of the campaign focused on foreign policy. The Cold War was particularly bitter at that time, with the Red Army having just suppressed the East Berlin rising (17 June). In these circumstances Adenauer's decisively pro-Western, anti-Communist stance appealed to a large number of voters. Likewise, the Christian Democrats could emphasize their success in stabilizing prices since 1949. By 1953 Erhard's 'social market economy' was clearly working, and there seemed to be no case for the SPD's planned economy, even although the SPD had qualified its enthusiasm for economic controls at its Dortmund Congress in 1952. Nor did there seem to be any good reason to take a chance with the SPD's foreign policy of reunification *before* rearmament and commitment to the Western Alliance.

In terms of the actual voting in 1953, the Christian Democrats gained votes both from their coalition partners (the FDP fell back to 9.5 per cent from 11.9 per cent, and the DP lost 0.8 per cent to poll 3.2 per cent) and from the small parties generally. Moreover, the Refugees – in spite of the amalgamation of the BHE and WAV, did relatively badly. Having averaged almost 12 per cent in the *Landtag* elections of 1950-52, they won only 5.9 per cent (27 seats) in 1953 in spite of the fact that they had changed their name to GB/BHE with a view to widening their appeal (GB = *Gesamtdeutscher Block*, All-German Block). The party's leaders, Waldemar

Kraft and Theodor Oberländer, had a tendency to make contradictory statements on foreign policy. On the one hand, they were firmly committed to German reunification and the return of the lost territories in the East; on the other, they wanted to support Adenauer's pro-Western, anti-Communist policy. But already by the early 1950s (as the SPD pointed out) there was a contradiction between these two objectives. Above all, the GB/BHE did relatively badly because the refugees were already becoming integrated into the economic life of West Germany.

Other factors which helped the Christian Democrats in 1953 were firstly that the extreme right was weakened by the banning of the *Sozialistische Reichspartei* (SRP) by the Federal Constitutional Court in 1952 – indeed, although five extreme right parties stood in 1953, none polled as much as one per cent. Secondly, the Christian Social Union inflicted a severe defeat on the Bavarian Party (CSU 47.8 per cent, a gain of 18.6 points compared with 1949, and BP 9.2 per cent, a loss of 11.7 points since 1949). Bavarian conservatives had clearly decided that it was pointless to vote for the BP, whose declared objective was to join a Christian Democratic-led coalition. Finally, most Centre Party voters transferred to the CDU. Whereas in 1949 the Centre Party had polled 9 per cent in North Rhine Westphalia (the only *Land* where it had a serious following), in 1953 its poll there dropped to 2.7 per cent, and the party returned three deputies to the Bundestag only because one of its leaders, Johannes Brockmann, was directly elected on a joint CDU–Centre Party ticket in Oberhausen.[38]

The Christian Democrats could have formed a government on their own after the 1953 election. However, Adenauer, partly because he required a two-thirds majority to alter the constitution so that the Federal Republic could rearm, invited the Liberals, German Party and Refugee Party to re-join his coalition, giving him 328 votes out of 497. The Refugee leaders, Oberländer and Kraft, were appointed Ministers and soon mitigated their criticism of Adenauer's eastern policy – or rather lack of it in the eyes of the more extreme refugees, who still hoped to recover their lands beyond the Oder–Neisse line. As a result of the 'moderation' of their leaders the Refugee Party split in 1955, with eighteen deputies going into opposition, while Kraft, Oberländer and seven others joined the CDU. Once again Adenauer's policy of 'integrating' others into the Christian Democratic political family had paid off. To a lesser extent the same thing happened with the Liberals, for after the 'Young Turks' revolt of 1956, which resulted in the formation of an SPD–FDP coalition in North Rhine Westphalia in place of Karl Arnold's CDU–FDP coalition, the FDP parliamentary party split, with thirty-three deputies going into opposition and sixteen (including four Ministers) remaining loyal to Adenauer. The sixteen did not actually join the CDU, but formed their own *Freie Volkspartei*, FVP, which in January 1957 merged with the German Party. However, the fact that one third of the parliamentary Liberal Party had remained loyal to Adenauer augured well for the Christian Democrats at the general election of 1957. Some Liberals at least could be expected to vote for the Christian Democrats rather than for the FVP. The other promising development for the Christian Democrats was that at the *Landtag* elections of 1953–56 their poll was up on average by 4 points compared with the 1949–52 *Landtag* elections. As the SPD vote had increased exponentially, it seemed likely that the Federal Republic was moving from a multi-party system to one dominated by the two major parties.

As it turned out, the CDU/CSU emerged from the 1957 general election as *the* dominant party, with 50.2 per cent of the poll, well over half the seats (270 out of 497) and a clear advantage over their main rival, the SPD, whom they outdistanced by twenty points (50.2 per cent to 31.8; 270 seats to 169) (see Table 2, p. 62). This was the election at which Adenauer reached his apotheosis. The Christian Democratic slogan '*Keine Experimente*' ('no experiments') struck exactly the right chord with the electorate. The economy was booming and the Federal Republic had become a full member of the Western Alliance. The suppression of the Hungarian rising by the Red Army in October 1956 seemed to confirm the wisdom of Adenauer's decisively pro-Western stance and the unrealistic nature of the SPD's continuing opposition to rearmament. Thus the CDU won an absolute majority by retaining all its 1953 voters and attracting others from the minor parties. The Refugee Party failed to win any seats, most of its voters transferring to the Christian Democrats. Likewise the German Party polled badly. Stagnant at just under 3 per cent of the national poll, it gained representation in the Bundestag only thanks to the CDU, which had allowed the DP to win six directly elected seats by not standing against it. As a result the German Party became eligible for eleven proportional seats, giving it seventeen in all.[39] However, the manner of the German Party's entry into the Bundestag in 1957 meant that it was little more than a satellite of the CDU/CSU (the DP's slogan was '*Kanzlertreu mit Rechtsblick*' – 'loyal to the Chancellor but with a conservative outlook'). In view of the continuing success of the Christian Democrats' 'absorption' policy, it was not surprising that in 1960 nine of the German Party's deputies decided to join the CDU.

The CDU/CSU's very considerable success in 1957 owed a great deal to Chancellor Adenauer personally and to the absorption of the smaller parties.[40] Adenauer, however, was now eighty-one (and presumably not immortal, despite political gossip to the contrary!), and there were no other small parties to absorb. Moreover, in spite of its failure, the SPD had gained 3 points in polling 31.8 per cent. More threatening in the long term to the Christian Democrats were the series of Social Democratic decisions of 1957–60 – the Bad Godesberg Programme of 1959 being the chief symbol – by which the SPD brought itself more or less in line with the CDU/CSU over rearmament, European integration and the social market economy. Having opposed the CDU/CSU vigorously over foreign and economic policy until the death of Schumacher in 1952, and verbally, but with less conviction, under Erich Ollenhauer until 1957, the SPD had changed almost to a strategy of 'non opposition' by the time Willy Brandt took over the leadership of the party in 1959. The new strategy was master-minded by Herbert Wehner, chairman of the SPD parliamentary party. Wehner and Brandt hoped to show that the SPD was more con-cerned with social justice than the CDU, and that it was equally pro-European, anti-Communist and financially sound. They hoped that this strategy would appeal to enlightened middle-class voters as well as to their traditional working-class electorate. There was some opposition to this strategy in the SPD, but the leaders had concluded that it was the only way to break out of the '30 per cent class ghetto', to which the party had been confined since the war.

By the time of the 1961 general election the dominance of Adenauer and the Christian Democrats was under threat. The Christian Democrats and Social Democrats were more or less in agreement on both foreign and economic policy. Moreover, the SPD's Chancellor candidate (chosen in 1959) was Willy Brandt, the energetic young Mayor of West Berlin. Brandt appeared to be in a strong position to challenge the apparently ailing Adenauer, whose autocratic manner and quarrels with Erhard and the Christian Democratic parliamentary party were becoming increasingly overt.[41] However, in spite of a five-point decline since 1957, the CDU/CSU emerged from the 1961 election with 45.4 per cent of the poll, nine points ahead of the SPD (36.2 per cent). *Der Alte* (as Adenauer was known) had obviously not lost his appeal to a substantial part of the electorate. However, the Liberals had polled 12.8 per cent, a gain of 5 points since 1957. Clearly a significant number of centre-right voters *did* have doubts about the eighty-five-year-old Adenauer continuing as Chancellor. As we shall see when discussing 'Chancellor democracy', it was not only his age but his judgement which was being increasingly questioned.[42] The FDP's considerable advance showed that many voters agreed with the Liberal slogan: 'With the CDU, but without Adenauer.' Almost half of the FDP's new voters came from the CDU, with most of the remainder coming from the German Party (especially in Lower Saxony), the German Party having amalgamated with the Refugee Party in 1961 after the DP's parliamentary party had split in 1960. The new *Gesamtdeutsche Partei* (DP + BHE) neither appealed to the small, but hitherto loyal, north German Protestant conservative electorate of the German Party, nor to the 'special interest' electorate of the Refugees. Only 2.8 per cent voted for the GDP (the two separate parties having polled 5.7 per cent between them in 1957), and of the GDP's former voters just over half went to the CDU and the rest to the FDP.

As far as Adenauer was concerned, the 1961 general election marked a decisive setback. True, *der Alte* had 'won' again, but in contrast to 1957 his Coalition was now dependent on the Liberals for its parliamentary majority. Moreover, the Liberals only agreed (after considerable debate) to rejoin an Adenauer-led coalition when Adenauer promised to resign the Chancellorship within two years. True, Adenauer's *'Keine Experimente'* slogan had succeeded again, with the majority of the electorate endorsing the Chancellor's economic and foreign policies. True, many left-of-centre voters had still not appreciated the full extent of the changes in the SPD. However, the 1961 election marked a more severe setback for the Christian Democrats than was immediately apparent. For the electorate was at last beginning to change its views significantly. Opinion polls showed that the voters had lost their faith in Adenauer: even a majority of Christian Democrats thought it was time for him to hand over to Erhard. The polls also showed that most of the SPD's new voters were former Christian Democrats, while other Christian Democrats – annoyed at Adenauer's refusal to give way to Erhard – had opted for the FDP. So the *underlying* Christian Democratic decline in 1961 was in the region of seven points (approximately 4.6 to the SPD and 2.5 to the FDP), but the extent of the decline was concealed by the CDU/CSU's continuing ability to pick up votes from the declining small parties. However, the pool of small party votes was now so small that by the 1965 election the CDU/CSU would be unable to compensate for any further losses to the SPD and FDP.

By 1965 of course Adenauer was no longer Chancellor, although, to his surprise, the Christian Democrats under Erhard succeeded in increasing their poll from 45.3 per cent to 47.6 per cent. Adenauer may have had a low opinion of Erhard as a politician, but Erhard's brilliant record in running the economy and skill as an election campaigner gave him a decisive victory. Nevertheless, during the economic downturn of 1965–66 Erhard's reputation rapidly declined, and his Government was replaced by the CDU–SPD Grand Coalition (1966-69) under the Christian Democrat Kurt-Georg Kiesinger. However, that is beyond the scope of this book. What the 1965 general election did show was that the Christian Democrats could win without Adenauer. Indeed, even by 1961, Adenauer had become something of an electoral liability, although his party had emerged victorious.[43]

Conclusion

In the case of Adenauer and the CDU, it is impossible to reach precise conclusions about whether the man 'made' the party or vice versa. Clearly they both influenced each other. After the Second World War a significant proportion of the German electorate was ready to support a biconfessional, inter-class, moderate conservative party, a party which was committed to parliamentary democracy, free enterprise and social justice at home; and to an anti-Communist, pro-Western policy abroad. And it is certainly true that Adenauer was strongly committed to precisely these objectives, and that, when he became the leader of the CDU, he used all his power and influence to ensure that the party pursued policies in line with these objectives. Thus both the man and the party were in tune with the spirit of their times.

With regard to the foundation and leadership of the CDU, Adenauer was certainly lucky. It was a stroke of good fortune that he was sacked by the British as Mayor of Cologne – this freed him for national politics at exactly the right time. He was also fortunate to reside in the British Occupation Zone, for that Zone consisted of all of northern Germany (except Bremen), including the new *Land* of North Rhine Westphalia, which was not only the industrial heartland of West Germany but also its most populous state. Moreover, the British were the first Occupation Power (apart from the Russians) to license political parties: this gave Adenauer and the CDU a vital headstart as the new party system began to establish itself. In addition, he was lucky to have Kurt Schumacher of the SPD as his chief political opponent. Schumacher was a courageous man, but his apparently xenophobic, anti-Western, anti-Catholic attitudes made him look distinctly backward-looking compared with Adenauer. And when he chose the wrong economic option as well (a state-run economy), he played further into Adenauer's hands.[44] Fortune also favoured Adenauer in relation to the division of Germany. For, with the loss of so much territory in the East, the confessional balance in Western Germany (at approximately 50:50) was such that a joint Catholic–Protestant Party became possible for the first time in German history.

Adenauer may have been lucky, but, like all successful politicians, he knew how to exploit the opportunities offered to him. This was apparent not only in the part he played in moulding the CDU after his own image, but also in the electoral choices he made between 1949 and 1963. He made the right economic choice in 1949 (free enterprise); the right foreign policy choice in 1953 (commitment to the West); and found the right electoral slogans in 1957 and 1961 – 'Keine Experimente', in effect an ongoing commitment to the policy choices made in 1949 and 1953. Adenauer was thus in tune with the public mood, at least during the decade 1949–59. Moreover, he also acted skilfully at the level of micro-politics, in particular by accepting the small parties into his Coalition and by welcoming people from very different political backgrounds into his broad-based, umbrella party. As we shall see when discussing 'Chancellor democracy' in chapter 5, Adenauer was to make significant political mistakes in the final years of his 'era'. However, these later miscalculations cannot detract from the major contribution he made to the creation of Germany's first great democratic Volkspartei, the CDU, and to his successful leadership of that party at successive elections during his Chancellorship (1949–63).

Notes and references

1 Adenauer, *Erinnerungen 1*, p. 38.

2 Prittie, 1972, p. 108.

3 On Adenauer's role in founding and moulding the CDU, see Adenauer *Erinnerungen 1*, esp.

pp. 48–62; H.G. Wieck, *Die Entstehung der CDU und die Wiedergründung des Zentrum im Jahre 1945* (Düsseldorf, 1953); A.J. Heidenheimer, *Adenauer and the CDU: the rise of the leader and the integration of the party* (The Hague, 1960); L. Schwering, *Frühgeschichte der Christlich-Demokratischen Union* (Recklinghausen, 1963); R. Morsey, 'Der politische Aufstieg Konrad Adenauer, 1945–49', pp.20–57 in R. Morsey and K. Repgen (eds), *Adenauer Studien 1* (Mainz, 1971); H. Pütz (ed.), *Konrad Adenauer und die CDU in der britischen Besatzungszone* (Eichholz, 1975); W. Jäger, 'Adenauers Entwirkung auf die programmatische Entwicklung der CDU von 1945 bis 1949', pp. 427–52 in D. Blumenwitz *et al* (ed.), *Konrad Adenauer und seine Zeit* (Stuttgart, 1976), vol. 1 [henceforth, Blumenwitz *et al*. (eds.), *Konrad Adenauer und seine Zeit*, 1976, vol. 1 or vol. 2]; and R.E.M. Irving, *The Christian Democratic Parties of Western Europe* (London, 1979), chapter 4.

4 For Adenauer's views in 1945–46, see R. Morsey chapter cited in n. 3 above; Adenauer *Erinnerungen 1*, pp. 39–47; Weymar, 1957, p.184 & ff. and p.223 & ff.; and Adenauer's first major speech as Chancellor, Adenauer *Reden 1917–67*, pp. 153–69.

5 For Adenauer's reluctance to get involved in Weimar politics, see chapter 2 above, pp. 37–49.

6 See n. 4 above.

7 See especially Adenauer *Erinnerungen 1*, pp. 205–9; and W. Jäger article cited in n. 3 above.

8 See n. 3 above.

9 K. Sontheimer, *The Government and Politics of West Germany* (London, 1972), p. 85.

10 See below, next two paragraphs.

11 See K. Forster, 'Deutscher Katholismus in der Ära Adenauer', in Blumenwitz *et al*. (eds), *Konrad Adenauer und seine Zeit*, 1976, pp. 498–523.

12 On party typology, see M. Duverger, *Political Parties* (London, 1954).

13 For a full discussion of the CDU's organization in Adenauer's time, see below, chapter 5, pp. 159–61.

14 Cf. K. Forster article cited in n.11 above.

15 Adenauer *Erinnerungen 1*, p. 205.

16 Heinemann later clashed with Adenauer over rearmament: see below, chapter 5, pp. 165–7.

17 See below, pp. 70–73.

18 See below, pp. 74–84.

19 A. Mintzel, *Die CSU. Anatomie einer konservativen Partei, 1945–72* (Opladen, 1975).

20 Adenauer *Erinnerungen 1*, pp. 205–9.

21 See especially R. Morsey, n. 3 above.

22 See below, p. 75.

23 Pope Pius X1, *Über die gesellschaftliche Ordnung* (Freiburg, 1948), p. 156.

24 Quoted Heidenheimer, 1960, p. 120.

25 Neheim-Hüsten Programme in O.K. Flechtheim (ed.), *Dokumente zur parteipolitischen*

Entwicklung in Deutschland seit 1945 (Berlin, 1962), pp. 50–3 [henceforth Flechtheim *Dokumente*].

26 Schwarz, 1995, pp. 373–5.

27 Ahlen Programme in Flechtheim *Dokumente*, pp. 61–5.

28 Schwarz, 1995, p. 374.

29 On Adenauer's views about *Mitbestimmung*, see below, chapter 5, pp. 188–90.

30 Düsseldorf Programme in Flechtheim *Dokumente*, pp. 69–71.

31 Adenauer *Erinnerungen 1*, pp. 146-76; and see below, p. 189; on debates in Parliamentary Council, see D. Feldkamp, *Der Parlamentarische Rat, 1948-49. Die Entstehung des Grundgesetzes* (Göttingen, 1998).

32 C. Schmid, *Erinnerungen* (Munich, 1979), p. 319.

33 L.J. Edinger, *Kurt Schumacher* (Stanford, CA, 1965), p. 136.

34 Adenauer *Erinnerungen* **1**, p.182.

35 On the Refugee Party, see F. Neumann, *Der Block der Heimatvertriebenen und Entrechteten 1950–1960* (Meisenheim, 1968).

36 The 1953 general election is analysed thoroughly in H. Köhler, *Adenauer* (1994), pp. 775–85.

37 See below, chapter 5, pp. 167–75, for full discussion of 'Chancellor effect' at elections.

38 See p. 63 for Electoral Law.

39 See p. 63 for Electoral Law.

40 See below, chapter 5, pp. 158–61, for discussion of Adenauer's personal dominance of his party.

41 See below, chapter 5, pp. 163, 175–9; for a full discussion of the differences between Adenauer and Erhard; and see D. Koerfer, *Kampf ums Kanzleramt. Erhard und Adenauer* (Stuttgart, 1987).

42 See below, chapter 5, pp. 180–3.

43 See below, chapter 5, pp. 180–3 for further discussion of Adenauer's declining influence in the CDU by the early 1960s.

44 For further discussion of Adenauer–Schumacher differences, see below, chapter 5, pp. 168–72.

Chapter Four

Adenauer's Foreign Policy

SOVEREIGNTY AND COMMITMENT TO THE WEST

Introduction

The two German States are not régimes that created foreign policies, but foreign policies that created régimes.

Karl Kaiser, *German Foreign Policy in Transition*, 1968, p.1

In the beginning was Adenauer.

(title of Arnulf Baring's book on Adenauer's foreign policy, *Im Anfang war Adenauer. Die Entstehung der Kanzlerdemokratie*, 1982)

Kaiser's remark suggests that Adenauer's foreign policy was largely dictated by the Cold War, Baring's that he had considerable influence over the Federal Republic's foreign policy. In fact there is a large element of truth in both judgements. Adenauer brought the Federal Republic into the Western Alliance, even although he had little alternative, but the enthusiasm with which he committed his country to the American-led alliance was personal. He had rather more leeway with regard to developing a new relationship with his Western European neighbours. In this matter his determination to reconcile Germany with France and to work closely with the other countries of Western Europe owed something to personal choice and something to political necessity. The first part of this chapter is focused on the Federal Republic's achievement of sovereignty within the Atlantic Alliance, and the second to its reconciliation with France and to its commitment to Western European integration. This chapter is concerned largely with *foreign policy developments* in the Adenauer years. In the next chapter, when 'Chancellor democracy' is analysed, there is further discussion of Adenauer's *personal* influence on the foreign policy-making process.

From the time Adenauer became Chancellor in 1949 until his death in 1967 foreign policy was his preeminent concern.[1] Adenauer had clear foreign policy objectives throughout his fourteen years as Chancellor (indeed in the years before and after as well).[2] As a patriotic German, he was determined that his country – or at least the Western part of it – should become a sovereign state once again. He would have liked to have seen Germany reunited – ideally on the basis of its 1937 frontiers – but *not* at the price of concessions to Soviet Russia or its satellites. For he was resolute in his determination to resist totalitarian Communism, which he despised even more than Fascism. Finally, in order that the era of European civil wars (as he saw them) should finally come to an end, he was a strong advocate of reconciliation with France and of Western European integration.

Like all successful statesmen, Adenauer needed a little help from the goddess Fortuna to achieve his ends. Paradoxically the first piece of good fortune he had was that under the Occupation Statute of 1949 (a quid pro quo for the setting up of the Federal Republic), West Germany was at first not allowed to have a Foreign Ministry. Arnulf Baring has emphasized that this meant that Adenauer as Chancellor had considerable influence over foreign policy in the early years of the Federal Republic, because he was in constant personal contact with the Western High Commissioners, while no other politicians had this privileged access.[3] And, when in March 1951 the Federal Republic was granted the right to have a Foreign Ministry, Adenauer appointed himself Foreign Minister. Indeed, the Federal Republic did not have a separate Foreign Minister until May 1955, when full sovereignty was achieved and Heinrich von Brentano was appointed to that office. However, even after 1955, Adenauer continued to keep a firm grip on most aspects of foreign policy until the end of his Chancellorship in 1963. Moreover, he regarded defence as an adjunct of foreign policy, and he kept a close watch on his country's defence policy, including during the years 1956–62 when the formidable Franz-Josef Strauss was Minister of Defence.

The development of international relations in the early 1950s also worked in favour of Adenauer. For within a year of his becoming Chancellor the Korean War broke out. Coming soon after the Berlin

Blockade (1948–49), this development in the Cold War resulted in the Americans and British looking with increasing favour on Adenauer's desire to arm the Federal Republic. The Chancellor considered that a state could only regard itself as fully sovereign if it had the means to defend itself. Moreover, at the height of the Cold War he positively wanted West Germany to contribute to its own defence because of the threat posed by Soviet Communism. Adenauer was further helped by developments in Western Europe during the first half of his Chancellorship. France began to mellow its hard line towards Germany, especially after the setting up of the European Coal and Steel Community (ECSC) in 1951 and the resolution of the Saar problem in 1955. It should be emphasized that Adenauer always put *Westpolitik* before *Ostpolitik*, i.e. he considered that the achievement of West German sovereignty within the Atlantic Alliance was more important than reunification. His view, seemingly so unrealistic at the time, was that the Soviet Union would eventually agree to German reunification when faced by a strong West Germany firmly rooted in the Western Alliance. In fact, the Soviets were to do just that in 1989–90, but only after West Germany had made important concessions to the USSR, the German Democratic Republic and Poland in the 1970s. Adenauer's 'policy of strength', then, did eventually succeed, but only thanks to Willy Brandt's *Ostpolitik* in the post-Adenauer era.

Sovereignty, rearmament and the Western Alliance

In spite of Germany's total defeat in 1945 and the subsequent revelations about the atrocities committed by the Nazis, Adenauer saw the Third Reich as an aberration in German history, albeit an appalling one. He remained proud of his Fatherland – indeed his *Memoirs* were dedicated to it (each volume beginning with the words 'Meinem Vaterland'). He wanted to see Germany rise Phoenix-like from the ashes: not however the Germany of the Kaisers or Hitler, but a free and democratic Germany, a cultured and civilized Germany, a prosperous and caring Germany. He realized that his country would have to pay for the sins of the Third Reich, but in a sense he believed it had already done so. For in the Second World War approximately 2.5 million German soldiers had been killed and 4.5 million wounded. In addition, 1.5 million German women had been widowed and three-quarters of a million civilians had been killed in bombing raids. In his first speech to the Bundestag on 20 September 1949 Adenauer was not surprisingly contrite about Germany's recent past. However, he also made it clear that as Chancellor his chief objectives would be to restore German sovereignty; to develop good relations with Germany's neighbours and former enemies; to work closely with those countries which believed in freedom and democracy; to achieve economic prosperity and social justice; and to end all anti-Semitism and racism.[4]

Between 1949 and 1955 Adenauer considered that his single most important task was to create a sovereign, free and democratic Germany. If that entailed a Germany deprived of its Communist territories – the German Democratic Republic and the occupied Eastern Territories beyond the Oder–Neisse line – so be it. Germany might have to be truncated in the short term, but the new Germany must be free, democratic and committed to the West. If these objectives were achieved, Germany would have taken a vital step towards rescinding its past and opening the way to a worthwhile future – a *German* future certainly, but above all a *Western, liberal democratic* future. Adenauer never wavered from these objectives.

The first major step was achieved in 1949 with the setting up of the Federal Republic of Germany with its liberal democratic constitution enshrined in the Basic Law (*Grundgesetz*). The next stage in Germany's rehabilitation proved to be more difficult. For Adenauer and his Government had to obtain many concessions from the Western Allies before the Federal Republic could in any meaningful sense be regarded as a sovereign state. Although the occupying Military Governors changed their name to High Commissioners on the establishment of the Federal Republic, the High Commissioners retained overall control of foreign policy, defence policy and the industries of the Ruhr until 1955. In addition, the Germans still had to pay for the cost of their own occupation, which in the early years of the Federal Republic amounted to one-third of its budget.

Adenauer, however, did have certain advantages over his predecessors of 1919. No peace treaty had been made, as the Four Powers could not agree on the future of Germany. This at least meant that the German Government of 1949 could not be blamed for an imposed peace – in contrast to the 'Diktat' of Versailles (1919). Moreover, the surrender of 1945, unlike the armistice of 1918, was *unequivocal* and *unconditional*, and the guilty men were exposed to the world at the Nuremberg Trials in 1947. Adenauer's task was nevertheless difficult. He had somehow to exact major concessions from the Western Allies without conceding too much to them. Otherwise he risked being accused of colluding with the 'Occupiers' – as indeed he was by Kurt Schumacher, the chairman of the SPD, who on one occasion called him 'the Chancellor of the Allies'[5] (November 1949). Moreover, many West Europeans, in particular the French, remained very suspicious of the Germans for at least a decade after the war, and wanted to make minimal concessions to them. The Americans and British were determined not to repeat the mistakes of Versailles, in particular with regard to reparations, but they too had little sympathy for the Germans in the aftermath of Nazism. They also wanted to eradicate German aggression and militarism and make the Germans pay for their crimes. So it is quite wrong to imagine (as with the hindsight of history it is easy to do) that the journey from the creation of the Federal Republic in 1949 to its becoming a fully sovereign state within the Atlantic Alliance in 1955 was straightforward. Major problems were encountered, *inter alia* over rearmament, the European Defence Community and the Saar problem. Even the vital breakthrough marked by the setting up of the European Coal and Steel Community (1951) was not achieved without difficult negotiations.

Adenauer realized that if he was going to achieve his main foreign policy objectives, it was essential that the most powerful of the Western Allies, the United States, should support him.[6] Indeed, he remained remarkably consistent in his strong commitment to the United States throughout his fourteen years as Chancellor. As it happened, he was greatly helped by the way the Cold War developed. For the Berlin Blockade (1948–49), Korean War (1950–53) and Indochina War (1949–54) all boosted Adenauer's reputation as a pro-American, anti-Communist leader. By the mid-1950s Adenauer was sometimes labelled 'the Chancellor of the Americans', but in fact he was strongly anti-Communist out of *political conviction* and not merely because he wanted the Federal Republic to be closely allied to the United States. One of Adenauer's recurring worries during his Chancellorship was that the United States and Soviet Union might do a deal over Germany, resulting in a united but neutralized Germany under Soviet hegemony (or at least strongly influenced by the USSR). It was therefore not surprising that Adenauer was delighted when the Republican Dwight Eisenhower won the 1952 American Presidential

Election and appointed John Foster Dulles, an outspoken anti-Communist, as his Secretary of State. However it should be noted that Adenauer's anti-Communism led to his being committed to (West) German rearmament *before* the start of the Korean War in June 1950, i.e. before the Americans came to the conclusion that a German contribution to the defence of Western Europe was essential.[7]

With the High Commissioners in overall charge of foreign affairs, industrial affairs and the occupation, Adenauer had a difficult task. His relationship with the High Commissioners was not always easy, but in time both sides came to respect each other. France and the United States had new High Commissioners, André François-Poncet and John J. McCloy having replaced Generals König and Clay. General Brian Robertson changed into civilian clothes and became the British High Commissioner; then in 1950 Sir Ivone Kirkpatrick, a career diplomat, took over from Robertson. Adenauer found François-Poncet an awkward man. He had been France's ambassador to Germany in the 'appeasement' years (1933–39), which did nothing to endear him to Adenauer. He was very knowledgeable about German culture and history but an arrogant man. To some extent of course François-Poncet was an awkward High Commissioner (from Adenauer's point of view) simply because he reflected France's continuing paranoia about the security threat posed by Germany. Adenauer at first also had an uneasy relationship with John J. McCloy, an American banker with no first-hand knowledge of Germany. However, McCloy had to work closely with Dean Acheson, the US Secretary of State, and by 1950 Acheson had come to the conclusion that Adenauer was strongly committed to the West; moreover, difficult though Adenauer could be, Acheson considered that he was much easier to deal with than Schumacher.[8] Overall Adenauer got on well with Brian Robertson and Ivone Kirkpatrick. In spite of his general lack of respect for high-ranking military men, Adenauer soon came to the conclusion that Robertson, like General Lawson in the 1920s, was an able and fair-minded man. He also liked Kirkpatrick, a tough negotiator but a man who was determined not to repeat the mistakes of the inter-war years. In addition, as a practising Catholic and strong anti-Communist, Kirkpatrick had a natural affinity with Adenauer. But of course the key High Commissioner was John J. McCloy, and it was very important that McCloy and Adenauer soon developed a close working relationship, especially after the outbreak of the Korean War in June 1950, which drew these two anti-Communist statesmen together.[9]

The first real breakthrough between the Chancellor and the High Commissioners occurred at the end of November 1949 with the signing of the Petersberg Agreements, which marked a relaxation of the Occupation Statute. No concessions were made by the Allies over the powers of the Military Security Board. In particular it rejected Adenauer's request that nominal Nazi party members who had served in the *Wehrmacht* should be released. Nor could he persuade the Allies to change the Ruhr Statute, through which the economy of the Ruhr was run by an international body consisting of the United States, Britain, France and Benelux, and as a reluctant minor partner, the Federal Republic. However, with the Americans pushing for a relaxation of industrial controls in the Ruhr in line with Adenauer's demands, there was soon progress over industrial dismantling. When the Petersberg Agreements were signed, 400 of the 744 companies on the dismantling list were removed from it, and the dismantling of the remaining 344 was suspended (within a few months the postponement became cancellation). The High Commissioners, led by McCloy, had accepted Adenauer's argument that the Germans could never be converted to Western-style democracy with unemployment running at 10 per cent and industry still shackled by controls. Adenauer was very concerned about France's continued 'special status' in the Saarland (i.e. the policy of integrating it with France), and he had no wish to join the International Ruhr Authority. However, he agreed to postpone discussion of the Saarland and to join the Ruhr Authority in exchange for the economic and industrial concessions mentioned above. Thus the Petersberg Agreements of November 1949 marked an important first step towards closer understanding between the Federal Republic and its former (Western) enemies.[10]

Progress towards Rearmament and Sovereignty, 1950–55

Between 1950 and 1955 there were two main thrusts to Adenauer's foreign policy as he strove to achieve sovereignty for his country, namely the moves towards rearmament and towards European integration.[11] They did not appear to be obvious bedfellows, for rearmament looked like a reversion to Germany's nationalistic and militaristic past, while European integration appeared to be a rejection of that past. Adenauer's strong commitment to rearmament was on the face of it surprising. Yet well before the outbreak of the Korean War in June 1950, after which the Americans began to call for German rearmament, the Federal Republic's peace-loving, liberal democratic Chancellor was proposing just this. Why, one may well ask, was Adenauer advocating rearmament, albeit *sotto voce*, as early as 1948 and 1949, and then more vocally from 1950 onwards? For there can be no doubt that Adenauer's rearmament policy was dangerous and by no means wholly popular. It might have provoked a preventive strike from the Soviet Union; it could well have made the French even more anti-German than they already were; and it could have undermined the some-what limited popularity of the Adenauer Government in the early 1950s. At that time many Germans had had enough of patriotism and militarism, both of which were linked in their minds with the carnage on the Western Front in the Kaiser's time and on the Eastern Front in Hitler's. The policy of rearmament could therefore easily have backfired, leading to Adenauer losing the 1953 general election.

Although Schumacher and the SDP were strongly anti-Communist and rejected rearmament only because they wanted reunification *first*, they gave the impression that they agreed with the pacifist (*'Ohne Mich'*) cam-paign of the early 1950s. Many right-wing politicians in the German Party and the Refugee Party also had doubts about rearmament, not because they were against German armed forces, but because they believed that a rearmed West Germany would provide the Russians with a perfect excuse not to make any concessions over the Eastern Territories (beyond the Oder–Neisse Line) or over the reunification of East and West Germany. In addition, prominent Protestants like Gustav Heinemann, Adenauer's Minister of the Interior who was to lose his Cabinet post in October 1950 owing to the rearmament controversy,[12] and Martin Niemöller, formerly a courageous opponent of Hitler, were outspoken opponents of rearma-ment, arguing that it would fuel German nationalism and provoke the Soviet Communists. Moreover, Jakob Kaiser, the CDU Minister of All-German Affairs, would also have preferred German reunification to pre-cede rearmament.

Despite all the misgivings inside and outside Germany, Adenauer was an early convert to, and advocate of, rearmament. Even Hans-Peter Schwarz, a sympathetic biographer, finds it hard to understand why Adenauer was so committed to rearmament in 1948 and 1949, i.e. *before* the outbreak of the Korean War in 1950, from which point his policy became more under-standable.[13] In 1948–49 Adenauer seems to have considered that the Berlin

Blockade was not an isolated event, but a probe which would lead to Communist aggression against the West; the West Germans should therefore be able to help the Western Alliance if this happened. In late 1949 Adenauer told American and German journalists that the Federal Republic ought to be contributing to its own defence, even if at this stage only by means of an armed Federal police force which could repel any attacks by East Germany's 70,000 *Volkspolizei*. (At the time there were only *Land* police forces in West Germany.) Then on 6 June 1950, i.e. *before* the outbreak of the Korean War, Adenauer offered a defence contribution to High Commissioners Robertson, McCloy and François-Poncet. This offer was repeated twice in August 1950, two months after the invasion of South Korea by the North.[14]

So it is clear that Adenauer offered German rearmament *before* it was requested. Of course, Adenauer realized that without rearmament the Federal Republic could not be sovereign and would therefore not be treated as an equal by the other West European countries. He realized too that a rearmed Germany would be bound politically and defensively to the Atlantic Alliance, and above all to the United States, but that of course was precisely what Adenauer wanted. For in 1948 and 1949 he was very concerned about the security of his country. He seems to have considered that a Soviet attack was almost inevitable. He believed that Communist aggression might well begin with 'infiltration' by East Germany's national police force (the *Volkspolizei*); hence his initial proposal that a Federal police force should be set up to counter this 'infiltration'. By 1950 he would have liked the Federal Republic to join NATO, thus obtaining the American-led Alliance's defence guarantee against aggression from the East. Indeed, Adenauer would have been prepared to contribute whatever forces the Allies would have allowed to his country's defence. But at this stage any such 'autonomous' West German contribution – even if acceptable to the Americans and British – was completely unacceptable to the French. Hence, as we shall see, in October 1950 René Pleven, the French Prime Minister, put forward his plan for a European Defence Community (EDC), through which the Federal Republic could contribute to its defence by means of an 'integrated' European army.[15]

Adenauer's advocacy of German defence forces was a logical consequence of his strongly held view that the only way to respond to the threat of force from a totalitarian régime was by force (or the threat of it). For Adenauer was very critical of the West's appeasement of the Third Reich in the 1930s. He was adamant that the Soviet Union should not be similarly appeased in the 1950s. He believed in the concept of the just war, and for him resisting totalitarianism, whether of the Right or the Left, was wholly justifiable. The *Realpolitik* associated with Germany regaining its sovereignty was important for Adenauer, but for him it was less important than his strong *ideological* dislike of Soviet Communism. The man who had been such a pragmatist in Imperial and Weimar Germany had changed significantly as a result of his experience of Nazism. However, Adenauer's strong ideological commitment against Communism was to have unfortunate consequences in the early 1960s, when his rigid anti-Communism obstructed the possible improvement of relations with the East. Nevertheless, while Stalin was still alive (he died in 1953), it was certainly understandable. Adenauer's views about Communism and rearmament were encapsulated in a letter he wrote to Gustav Heinemann in September 1950:

> While you take the view that one must hold back and wait, even in the face of the threat from Soviet Russia, in the hope that God will guide everything towards peace, I take the view that we are obliged to use all our strength to defend and save peace. In my opinion a passive attitude towards Soviet Russia will virtually encourage that country not to keep the peace. From the experience we have had with National Socialism, I think it must be clear that a totalitarian state is never restrained from its goals of conquest by patient waiting, but only by the establishment of forces which show that it can only achieve its goals of conquest by endangering its own existence.[16]

When discussing Adenauer's strong advocacy of rearmament, it should be stressed that he was equally committed to strengthening the defence contributions of the main NATO countries, the United States, Britain and France. Above all, he was determined to emphasize his increasing commitment to an alliance with the United States. By 1950 Dean Acheson, the American Secretary of State, had come to the conclusion that West German rearmament was indeed essential, and when, after the outbreak of the Korean War, he judged that a German defence force must be set up, he realized that this would only be acceptable to America's European allies as part of an overall reinforcement of NATO forces.[17] Adenauer and Dean Acheson were clearly committed to both these objectives, German rearmament *and* the strengthening of NATO. In a security memorandum dated 29 August 1950 Adenauer offered a Federal 'police contingent' to NATO, with the quid pro quo that NATO would defend the Federal Republic in the event of a Soviet attack. And on Acheson's request the Western Allies (without the Federal Republic of course) met in Washington in October 1950 to discuss the Communist threat and German rearmament. Acheson – and by now the British Foreign Secretary Ernest Bevin – were agreed that the Federal Republic should be allowed to enter NATO and make a full defence contribution to the Alliance. However, as the French Government was still adamantly opposed to this, Acheson and Bevin deferred to the French view. Nevertheless, the French realized that German rearmament in one form or another was now almost inevitable.

The direct result of the Korean War and the stalled Allied Conference in Washington was the French proposal for the European Defence Community (EDC) in October 1950. The Western Allies considered that the invasion of South Korea was not a localized attack but a Communist probe to test the determination of the West globally. In these circumstances it seemed vital for Western Europe to organize its defences with the help of the Federal Republic. It should be remembered that in 1950 there were 170 mililtary divisions (albeit smaller ones) on the Soviet side of the Iron Curtain and only 10 on the Western side. When Schuman – who ten months previously had stated that 'Germany will never be rearmed or included in the Atlantic Pact'[18] – returned to Paris in October 1950, he was convinced that the Americans intended to rearm Germany with or without French approval. This was the reason for the Pleven Plan (24 October 1950), which proposed 'the creation, for the common defence of Europe, of a European army linked to the political institutions of a united Europe'. The plan for the European Defence Community (named after the French Prime Minister) was, then, a backhanded proposal to rearm West Germany without quite admitting it. The proposal for the EDC had the semantic advantage of substituting 'a German contribution to European defence' for 'German rearmament' and 'German divisions within a European Army' for 'a German Army'.

The European Defence Community was difficult to implement technically as well as politically, and this led to a delay of nineteen months between the original proposal and the signing of the Treaty in May 1952. In the first phase of negotiations between October and December 1950 no progress was made, because the Americans wanted German units of at least 5,000 men while the French refused to consider units of more than 1,000 men. In the second phase of negotiations between January and August 1951 there were two negotiating teams. The one in Bonn eventually agreed that there should be twelve German divisions in the European Army. The one in Paris failed to come to a decision about the appropriate institutional machinery for the EDC. The third phase of negotiations ran from September 1951 to May 1952, eventually producing the Treaty of Paris. Again there were difficult negotiations in both Bonn and Paris. In the former the so-called Contractual Agreements were worked out. On the ratification of the EDC the Occupation Statute and High Commissions were to be abolished, although the occupation troops were to remain in Germany as NATO forces. It had already been agreed at an Atlantic Council meeting in Lisbon in February 1952 that Germany would not join NATO in the first instance. In Paris the EDC Treaty had meanwhile been finally agreed. The basic national military unit was to be the division; integration would occur only at the corps level, i.e. there was to be 'high level' not 'low level' integration. There were to be 14 French, 12 German, 12 Italian and 5 Benelux divisions; the military headquarters would be fully integrated; member countries could withdraw troops for overseas duties with the permission of the Commissariat, which would in all normal circumstances grant it. The institutional machinery consisted of the Commissariat of nine members (two each from France, Germany and Italy, and one each from the three Benelux countries). The Commissariat was to be the 'supranational' body of the EDC, but in many cases it could act only with the consent of the national representatives in the Council of Ministers, the second main organ of the EDC. The EDC Assembly was to be the same body as the European Coal and Steel Community (ECSC) Assembly, except that France, Germany and Italy were to appoint three extra members each; the Assembly would receive an annual report from the Commissariat, and could force it to resign by a two-thirds majority. Finally, the ECSC Court would also become that of the EDC.

The Contractual Agreements were signed in Bonn on 26 May 1952 and the EDC Treaty in Paris on the following day. Immediately afterwards Acheson, Eden and Schuman signed a tripartite declaration to the effect that, if the Federal Republic attempted to secede from the EDC, the United States and Britain would intervene to prevent this. France was ostensibly satisfied. But the controversy over the EDC was by no means over. As Jacques Fauvet of *Le Monde* perceptively commented 'To sign is not to ratify'.[19] In the case of France this was all too true for, while all the other participants ratified the EDC Treaty, the French kept on prevaricating. The *principles* of the Treaty were debated on no less than five occasions in the National Assembly between June 1952 and August 1954, but there was never a ratification debate, and when the National Assembly voted on 30 August 1954 to postpone further discussion of the EDC, that was the end of the matter: the European Defence Community was dead.

The collapse of the EDC caused considerable consternation throughout Western Europe, not least in Germany, where Adenauer was very disappointed by the decision of the French National Assembly.[20] Yet the situation had changed significantly between 1950 and 1954 – in the Federal Republic, in Western Europe and internationally. And within a relatively short space of time Adenauer was able to achieve what he had set out to do in 1950, namely the ending of the Occupation Statute, together with the Federal Republic's entry into the Atlantic Alliance as a sovereign state and into NATO as an equal partner, all of which were achieved in May 1955.[21]

We must, however, return briefly to 1950 to see how the Federal Republic achieved sovereignty in 1955 in spite of the collapse of the EDC in 1954. It should be remembered that Adenauer's policy with regard to sovereignty was based on two fundamental aspects. One was his commitment to rearmament. The other consisted of his negotiations with the Allied High Commissioners to revise the Occupation Statute. These negotiations eventually led to the Bonn and Paris Agreements of May 1952, more commonly referred to as the General Treaty (or confusingly sometimes as the German Treaty).[22] The General Treaty was finally signed on the same weekend as the EDC Treaty, i.e. 26–27 May 1952.

From Adenauer's point of view the General Treaty was just as important as the EDC. For he had to persuade the Western Allies to revise or rescind the Occupation Statute in order to win German public opinion over to rearmament and to membership of the Atlantic Alliance. He realized that the key to success was support from the Americans. He had to get the Americans to apply pressure on the French to accept the EDC, and at the same time he had to persuade the Americans, British and French to ameliorate the Occupation Statute, even if they refused to rescind it at this stage. While carrying out this delicate balancing act, he had to ensure that the Four Powers (USA, USSR, Britain and France) did not come to an agreement about Germany, thus undermining his whole strategy of integration with the West *before* German reunification. And the risk of this happening was no chimera, as the Soviet Note campaign of November 1950 to April 1952 showed.[23]

Fortunately Adenauer had some important allies during the crucial years 1950–52. John J. McCloy, the US High Commissioner, and Dean Acheson, the US Secretary of State, gave their full support to the German Chancellor, whom they increasingly admired as a strong supporter of the West, even if an obstinate and difficult man.[24] It was helpful too that Churchill had become Prime Minister of Britain in 1951, for Anthony Eden, the new Foreign Secretary, was more sympathetic to Adenauer than Bevin had ever been. However, it would be wrong to imagine that Adenauer had an easy task in achieving what eventually became the General Treaty of May 1952. He not only had great difficulty in persuading the High Commissioners to make the concessions which were eventually made, but he also experienced considerable difficulty in persuading his own countrymen that the concessions made by the Allies were sufficient. It was indeed not until May 1953 that the General Treaty was finally ratified by the Bundestag. In addition, there was the problem of the Soviet 'Note Offensive'.

The Soviet Note offensive, 1950–52

The four Soviet Notes of 1950–52 offering German reunification undoubtedly impeded progress towards the EDC Treaty and the General Treaty. Adenauer himself regarded all these Notes as dangerous diversions, but both the West Germans and the Western Allies seemed at times to be seriously tempted by the Soviet offers. The first Soviet Note was sent in November 1950. It proposed a Four Power Conference, which would draw up a final peace treaty and establish an All-German government for a neutralized Germany. The government was to have had an equal number of East and West German representatives. Adenauer feared that the French, and perhaps the British, might be tempted by this offer; that his own countrymen might also go along with it – the pacifist campaign being at its height in 1950–51; and that even the Americans might consider relapsing into the isolationism which they had espoused in the interwar years. However, with war raging in Korea, the Americans and British stood firmly with Adenauer in rejecting the Soviet proposal.

Ten months later an even more tempting offer was made. This time it was made indirectly by the East German Government. Prime Minister Grotewohl, with Soviet approval, offered not only a reunited, neutral Germany but also 'free all-German elections with the aim of building a united, democratic and peace-loving Germany'.[25] The only initial condition was that the reunited, neutral Germany would have to guarantee that its policy would not be influenced by the United States. Adenauer regarded this offer as pure Soviet propaganda, and he was supported by most of the CDU/CSU and all of the FDP and DP. However, Jakob Kaiser, the CDU Minister for All-German Affairs, and some members of the CDU/CSU parliamentary party queried Adenauer's negative response to the East German/Soviet Note. The SPD, led in this case by Ernst Reuter, Mayor of West Berlin, and Kurt Schumacher, Chairman of the Party, were agreed that a positive response of some sort should be made. Fortunately for Adenauer, Reuter's proposal that a trial run of free elections should be held in the whole of Berlin was rejected by the Communists. Meanwhile, Adenauer responded to public and parliamentary opinion by accepting the proposal for .free elections, *provided* they were supervised throughout Germany by UN observers. At the same time Adenauer claimed that the Soviet Union could not be serious about free elections, for the Russians would then have to agree to similar elections in Poland, Czechoslovakia and Hungary, i.e. the Soviets would have to surrender their East European cordon sanitaire. Thus, in 1951 Adenauer successfully called the bluff of the Soviet Union and its satellite the German Democratic Republic, which rejected the proposal for free elections supervised by the UN.[26]

The final attempt by the Soviet Union to sabotage the European Defence Community and the General Treaty occurred with the Notes of 10 March and 2 April 1952. The March Note proposed that a neutral Germany should be reunited and permitted to have its own armed forces, although they would be limited to a purely defensive role. This time there was no reference to free elections. However, a month later, in the Note of 2 April 1952, the Soviet Union, responding to Western demands for free elections, agreed to them, but again rejected the request that they should be held under UN supervision. Adenauer's view was that the Communists were once again playing politics, i.e. trying to prevent the signing of the General Treaty and the EDC Treaty. A united, neutralized Germany, even with its own army, would effectively be within the Soviet sphere of influence and could be overrun by the USSR at any time. The Federal Republic, he stressed once more, should commit itself to the West, and *then* the question of a reunited Germany could be broached. However, political opinion in West Germany and among the Western Allies was against this purely negative response to the two Soviet Notes. The *Frankfurter Allgemeine Zeitung, Die Welt* and *Der Spiegel* all criticized Adenauer for his negative attitude.[27] Later in his *Memoirs* Adenauer rejected these criticisms, arguing that the Soviets would never have allowed free elections, because if they had, they would then have had to make the same offer to all their other satellites in the Eastern bloc, something which in Adenauer's opinion would have been inconceivable.[28]

Adenauer considered that the main task to be achieved in May 1952 was the signing of the EDC Treaty and of the General Treaty. Anything which delayed these signings was a diversion and a delusion. The view of the French High Commissioner, François-Poncet, was that the Soviet offer should be taken seriously, but of course his Government was still trying to delay the signing of the EDC Treaty. More surprisingly, Acheson insisted that the Western Powers should respond positively in order to find out exactly what the Russians meant by free elections. On 13 May the Western reply was sent to Moscow with the agreement of Adenauer. The reply accepted negotiations on the basis of the Soviet Notes, *provided* the Soviet Union would agree firstly to full sovereignty for Germany; secondly to Germany's right to make alliances with whomsoever it chose; and thirdly to free elections under the auspices of the UN. Acheson, Eden and Adenauer were not surprised when the Russians never replied to the Western Note of 13 May 1952. Adenauer had won: provided the EDC Treaty and the General Treaty were signed, the Federal Republic would be fully committed to the West *before* a decision was made about German reunification. We will never know whether a more positive response to the Soviet Notes might have produced a different outcome. On balance it seems highly unlikely: the Notes were almost certainly only an attempt to prevent the signing of the EDC Treaty and the General Treaty. If the USSR had been serious about its offers, it could have responded to the Western reply of 13 May 1952. The fact that it did not indicates that Adenauer was right in his unwavering rejection of the Soviet 'offers' of 1950–52.

The Treaty of Paris (1952) and the General Treaty (1952)

The way was now open for the signing of both the Treaty of Paris (the EDC Treaty) and the General Treaty. Part of the prelude to these Treaties was the admission of the Federal Republic into the Council of Europe in May 1951. However, in spite of a more friendly attitude by the Western Allies towards the Federal Government, the negotiations which led to the General Treaty were far from easy. Throughout the negotiations of 1950–52 Adenauer's right-hand man was Walter Hallstein. He was in charge of foreign policy in the Federal Chancellor's Office, through which, as we shall see, Adenauer controlled the whole governmental machine.[29] Adenauer and Hallstein constituted a formidable negotiating team – the former as obstinate as ever, the latter a master of technical detail. Not surprisingly, the High Commissioners found them a difficult pair, but soon came to respect their negotiating skills and determination. Moreover, they admired them as committed allies of the West and staunch opponents of Soviet/East European Communism, and this ideological affinity encouraged the Allies to make more concessions than they might otherwise have made.

The Federal Republic's original demands for the General Treaty had been laid down in the Bürgenstock Memorandum of August 1951. This Memorandum asked the Allies to recognize the Federal Republic as a sovereign state and allow it to enter NATO as a full member. The Germans also wanted the Western powers to guarantee the security of the Federal Republic in exchange for their being allowed to continue to station their forces in West Germany. In addition, they wanted the Allies to give a commitment to support German reunification on the basis of the 1937 frontiers, i.e. Germany would regain the Eastern Territories which had been incorporated de facto into Poland and the Soviet Union. The West Germans also made significant economic demands. In particular they wanted to see the winding up of the International Ruhr Authority and the end to all Allied intervention in the German economy. Finally, they wanted the Saarland to be returned to Germany.

Adenauer had two key advantages. Firstly, the Allies now wanted a rearmed Federal Republic on their side with the Cold War at its most bitter. Secondly, the Americans, led by High Commissioner John J. McCloy, were in favour of economic and political concessions, and the Americans held the whip hand on the Western side. In addition, both Adenauer and Hallstein exploited skilfully their special relationship with the High Commissioners. However, they fell well short of achieving their Bürgenstock demands. Full West German sovereignty was not recognized in the General Treaty. Nor was entry into NATO granted, although of course it would be achieved indirectly through the Federal Republic's impending participation in the European Army. The Western Allies moreover retained their right to station troops in West Germany at the Federal Government's expense. And they (together with the Soviet Union) retained their special occupation rights in Berlin. Moreover, they did not commit themselves to German reunification on the basis demanded by the Federal Republic, and a decision about the future of the Saarland was deferred. Nor did the Allies agree to give any precise commitment about a final peace treaty, although they considered that the General Treaty was in itself an important step towards such a treaty. Finally, the West Germans had to accept the much-disputed Article VII of the General Treaty, which implied that, even after reunification, the victors of the Second World War would retain unspecified occupation rights, including the possibility of rewriting parts of the General Treaty in accordance with these rights.[30]

When the General Treaty had been finalized, Adenauer had to 'sell' it to his Cabinet, the Christian Democratic parliamentary party and his coalition partners, the Liberals and German Party.[31] Adenauer's Cabinet was in almost continuous session from 10 to 23 May 1952 discussing the Treaty, and the Chancellor was criticized not only by the Cabinet but also by the Christian Democratic parliamentary party for having been too secretive during the Treaty negotiations. But Adenauer maintained, reasonably enough, that this was the only way to negotiate an international treaty. The other means used by Adenauer and Hallstein to persuade their colleagues that both the General Treaty and the EDC Treaty should be signed was to paint a broad picture of the European context only seven years after the end of the war. Adenauer repeatedly pointed out that Germany had lost the war, and that, despite the establishment of the Federal Republic as a semi-autonomous, economically successful State, the Germans were in a weak negotiating position compared with the Allies. However, at least (unlike at the time of the Versailles Treaty) the Germans had been allowed to *negotiate*, and they had done so as effectively as possible. Hallstein emphasized that the Allies had conceded to the German point of view on 130 occasions during the General Treaty negotiations, and Adenauer stressed that non-ratification would be disastrous, as the High Commissioners had told him that if the Bundestag rejected the Treaty there would be no opportunity to re-negotiate it. He considered that in these circumstances the Western Allies might possibly do a deal with the Russians, which would leave Germany neutralized and undefended. It was, Adenauer stated repeatedly, far better for the Federal Republic to be securely based in the non-Communist West than to be reunited and neutralized. If some concessions had to be made to achieve this secure base, then they were worth it. And economic concessions certainly were made, in particular the Federal Republic agreed to continue to pay the full cost of the Western forces stationed in their country. As it turned out, this payment proved less burdensome than it might have done owing to increasing German prosperity in the 1950s. Nevertheless, at the time it looked as if Adenauer had agreed to pay reparations under a new name.

Schumacher and the SPD criticized the Chancellor unmercifully not only for agreeing to take on this economic burden but also for agreeing to an alliance with the West before the achievement of reunification. Moreover, Schumacher claimed, it was an unequal alliance. For the Federal Republic had agreed to be a junior partner in the EDC and also to be subservient to the Western powers as a result of its failure to negotiate favourable terms in the General Treaty. With characteristic hyperbole, Schumacher stated that the General Treaty amounted to a victory for the Allies and the 'Clerical Coalition' over the German people. Just before the signing of the Treaty he said 'Whoever accepts this General Treaty ceases to be a good German.'[32] And until his death in August 1952 Schumacher did not cease to criticize Adenauer for committing the Federal Republic to rearmament and for signing the General Treaty. Schumacher's overreaction to both the European Defence Community and the General Treaty in fact helped Adenauer. Certainly, by the summer of 1952 over 50 per cent of the West German electorate said that they agreed with Adenauer's foreign policy. This figure was higher than any comparable one since Adenauer became Chancellor in 1949. And in his *Memoirs* Adenauer justifiably stated that the signing of the General Treaty and the Treaty of Paris (EDC) in May 1952 constituted one of his most important political achievements.[33]

The final stage, namely the Federal Republic's achievement of full sovereignty and entry into the Atlantic Alliance in 1955, occurred without any major hitches after the collapse of the EDC in August 1954.[34] The really difficult political battle had been fought and won between 1950 and 1952, for by 1954–55 the international situation had changed significantly. The world seemed a less dangerous place: Stalin had died in 1953, the Korean Armistice had been signed in the same year, and the Indochina Peace Treaty had been signed in 1954. The clumsy and complex European Defence Community hardly seemed necessary. Moreover, by 1955 the Federal Republic was no longer a pariah state: she could enter the Atlantic Alliance and NATO without upsetting France or risking a Soviet military attack. Adenauer's foreign policy of 1950–52 had been courageous and perhaps even dangerous. He himself had undoubtedly played a crucial part in setting the Federal Republic of Germany on the road to sovereignty and to full membership of the Atlantic Alliance. His unswerving commitment to the American alliance and rejection of all advances by the Soviet Union were central to this. By 1955 the West German public no longer had any serious concerns about their country entering NATO, and (whatever they might say) nor probably had the leaders of the Soviet Union. Thus the Federal Republic entered the Atlantic Alliance as a sovereign state in 1955, a step which five years previously would have seemed almost inconceivable.

FRANCO-GERMAN RECONCILIATION AND EUROPEAN INTEGRATION

The background

While Adenauer was guiding the Federal Republic towards rearmament and sovereignty between 1949 and 1955, he was also striving for Franco-German reconciliation and Western European integration. Franco-German reconciliation had been an objective of Adenauer's since immediately after the First World War, while European economic and political integration emerged almost in parentheses as a means to achieving better relations with France. Adenauer considered that a new and better relationship with France was essential for European peace, being well aware that France and Germany had fought two disastrous wars within his own lifetime.[35]

As far back as 1919 Adenauer had emphasized that if France and Germany could not resolve their differences peacefully, the future of European civilization would be endangered, perhaps irrevocably.[36] By 1945 he was convinced that what he had said in 1919 was even more true.

Another 'tribal' war centred on France and Germany would be fatal for European civilization. Franco-German reconciliation thus became one of the cornerstones of Adenauer's foreign policy. In 1949 he told the weekly newspaper *Die Zeit*: 'I must work for Franco-German understanding. Such a policy must not be misinterpreted as being pro-French, let alone anti-British.'[37] He went on to say that reconciliation with all Germany's former enemies was important, but that a new understanding with France was vital for the peace of Europe.

Adenauer realized that in the aftermath of the Second World War it would be extremely difficult to reach an understanding with France. He knew that the French did not trust the Germans, and that they were afraid of Germany's superior numbers, military prowess and industrial capacity. The French considered that they had failed to control Germany after the First World War, and were determined not to fail again after the Second. In November 1945 Georges Bidault, de Gaulle's Foreign Minister, stated that the French Government did not even want a central German government. The various states (Baden, Württemberg, Bavaria, etc.) should in due course be allowed to have their own governments, but no Reich government should ever again be permitted.[38] France continued to hold these 'Gaullist' theses after the departure of the General from government in January 1946, and in many ways France's attitude towards Germany did not change until the mid-1950s in spite of Robert Schuman's important initiative towards reconciliation, the European Coal and Steel Community (ECSC) in 1950. France's concerns about her own security and fears about the revival of German political and economic power were wholly understandable and frequently reiterated in the late 1940s. In 1946 Bidault told the National Assembly that although the United States and Britain were ready to revive German economic and political life, France, like the Soviet Union, wanted to keep Germany weak. The French Government, he said, was determined that Germany should be incapable of reviving her war potential. The Saar coalmines should be handed over to France; the Ruhr should be internationalized and its resources 'used for the benefit of mankind'; the Reich should be disarmed 'militarily, economically and financially'; and the Germans should pay reparations.[39] The French Government also approved the Soviet takeover of Germany's eastern territories. Later in 1946 Bidault told *Le Monde* that 'the new decentralized Germany' should be deprived of the Ruhr and Rhineland: 'Our view is that the Ruhr and Rhineland should be under international control, implying their complete separation from Germany.'[40] Four months later he said that 'The separation of the Ruhr and Rhineland from Germany is the only way to keep Germany from its national industry – war.'[41]

France's views about the Ruhr and Rhineland, and even more the Saarland, were to prove a major obstacle to Adenauer's objective of achieving Franco-German reconciliation. France did not obtain the separation of the Ruhr and Rhineland from Germany at the Paris Conference of the four victorious Allies in July 1946. That Conference broke up after failing to reach agreement on the future of Germany, and by time of the Moscow Conference (April 1947) there were signs that France was moving away from its more extreme remedies for the 'German problem'. Bidault conceded that some degree of economic centralization would be necessary if Germany were to recover from the starvation and dislocation caused by the war, but he continued to advocate political decentralization with a national 'coordinating body' (not a central government) consisting of four representatives from each German *Land* (state). Moreover he was still insistent that Germany should pay reparations; that steel production should be limited; that the Ruhr should be internationalized; and that the Saarland should be incorporated into France.[42]

The Russians agreed with the French in demanding reparations (which the Americans and British believed to be impractical, given the state of the German economy), but would only accept the full incorporation of the Saarland into France in exchange for a role in the international administration of the Ruhr. As the British and Americans were opposed to a Russian presence in the Ruhr, France came away from the Moscow Conference empty-handed. Indeed, the Conference ended once again in deadlock, with the Four Powers deciding to reconvene in London in December 1947. But before the London Conference could take place the situation changed dramatically as a result of the American offer of Marshall Aid (June 1947).[43] The Western Allies accepted Marshall Aid on behalf of their Zones, while the Russians refused it on behalf of theirs. France, then, was brought much closer to the Western Allies as a result of the failure of the Moscow Conference and the consequences of the Marshall Aid offer. Moreover, by mid-1947 France had a clearly Western-orientated Government after the eviction of the Communists from government in May of that year. Yet France's paranoia about Germany's political and economic power did not decline for many years. It is important to emphasize this, because France's continuing distrust of Germany undermined Adenauer's hopes for reconciliation before and after his election as Chancellor in 1949.

After the failure of the December 1947 London Conference of the Four to reach any agreement about Germany, the three Western Allies decided to implement their own plans for the Western Zones of Germany at a conference in London in March 1948. France was still determined to subjugate and control Germany as much as possible. Before leaving for London, Bidault told the National Assembly that although France had in effect joined the Western side, her attempt to act as a bridge between the Anglo-Saxons and Russians having failed, she would nevertheless continue to press for some kind of international control of the Ruhr and Rhineland, for French control of the Saarland, and for the establishment of a decentralized system of government in Germany.[44] International events, however, once again conspired to weaken the French position at the same time as they opened the door to Adenauer, who was still very keen to extend the hand of friendship to France.

The French were forced to give way over the Anglo-American proposal for the establishment of a West German state with a central government, although they refused to fuse their Zone economically with the Bizone until September 1948. At the London Conference of March 1948, however, the Americans and British accepted France's demands for the setting up of the International Ruhr Authority and for the continued incorporation of the Saarland into France prior to final agreement about Germany as a whole. The London Agreements were signed in June 1948, although another conference was held in December to institute the International Ruhr Authority, whose headquarters were established in Düsseldorf in April 1949. The International Ruhr Authority was a concession to the French; it was a response to their continuing suspicion of the Germans, as neither the Americans nor the British wanted an Authority which could intervene in the Ruhr economy after the setting up of the Federal Republic of Germany. The Anglo-American doubts about the Ruhr Authority proved to be justified, as the German Social Democrats attacked it from the beginning as an interfering body, and Adenauer and Erhard agreed that it was inhibiting the development of the German economy.[45] By the time of the establishment of the Federal Republic of Germany (May 1949) most of the tenets of France's German policy had in practice been rejected, at least by the Western Allies. A centralized, although federal, governmental system had been established. No special regime had been established for the Rhineland. The industry of the Ruhr remained essentially in German hands despite the International Ruhr Authority. The Saarland, however, remained a French enclave in German territory.

The replacement of Georges Bidault by Robert Schuman at the French Foreign Ministry in July 1948 (a post he held until December 1952) did not lead to any immediate change in French policy towards Germany. The anti-German language and policies continued at least until 1950, and in relation to rearmament and the Saar problem until the mid-1950s. In November 1948 Schuman protested at the Anglo-American decision to hand back the Ruhr industries to the Germans, especially as the decision had been announced without consulting France. And a week later, with uncharacteristic hyperbole, he remarked that 'The Reich, which has been reconstituted in London, will evolve, as ever, towards adventurism'.[46] Nevertheless, the arrival of Schuman at the Quai d'Orsay was important from the point of view of Adenauer's long-held desire for Franco-German reconciliation. For Schuman was temperamentally and culturally very different from Bidault. Schuman, like Adenauer, had the Rhinelander's cosmopolitan, pragmatic approach to politics. Born in Lorraine (then part of the German Empire) in 1886, Schuman had been educated at various German universities and only became a French citizen in 1919. Adenauer and Schuman soon came to respect each other and in due course became close friends, doubtless helped by Schuman's ability to speak German fluently. Schuman had been steeped far too long in German culture to be a Germanophobe. Like Adenauer, he had been an outspoken opponent of Nazism in the 1930s, and like Adenauer had lain low during the war years. Like Adenauer, too, Schuman was a devout Catholic. He was really very different from his nationalistic predecessor Bidault, who had been a leader of the French Resistance.

The change in personalities at the Quai d'Orsay, then, undoubtedly helped to give a new, less anti-German orientation to French foreign policy, which was exactly what Adenauer wanted. Nevertheless, France's less hostile attitude towards Germany between 1948 and 1950 owed as much to the evolution of the international situation as to Ministerial changes in Paris. The development of the Cold War, as we have seen, made France increasingly dependent on her more powerful Western allies, who in their German policy were determined not to repeat the errors of the inter-war years. Moreover, the Cold War changed French perspectives on security, with the Soviet Union rather than Germany increasingly appearing as the main threat. At the same time France's membership of the Atlantic Pact

(1949) made her feel more secure vis-à-vis Germany. Schuman told the National Assembly that the Atlantic Pact complemented the Dunkirk Treaty of 1947 and the Brussels Treaty Organization of 1948, and that France's security within NATO was greater than it had ever been in the inter-war years.[47]

France's new confidence was reflected in a more generous approach to the German problem. In the second half of 1949 both Schuman and Adenauer made very similar statements about the need for Franco-German reconciliation and European integration. In August 1949 Schuman said 'There can be no solution to the problems of Europe without the progressive integration of the new Germany into Europe. It is in the interests of France to reflect on how this may be done, and, when the time comes, to act decisively.'[48] And in November Adenauer said 'I hope with all my heart for a better *entente* with France.'[49] He went on to say that he believed improved relations should start with closer economic cooperation, 'perhaps with an Anglo-French-German customs union'. The way was clearly open for Schuman's famous Coal and Steel proposal of 9 May 1950.

The Schuman Plan: the European Coal and Steel Community (ECSC)

Both Adenauer and Schuman were convinced that traditional intergovernmental cooperation in Western Europe, such as that operating in the Organization for European Economic Cooperation (OEEC) or the Council of Europe, would be insufficient to bridge the gap between Germany and its former enemies, and in particular to bring to an end France's profound distrust of Germany. How, then, was the gap to be bridged, and the distrust to be ended? For, although the OEEC had distributed Marshall Aid and encouraged free trade, it had done nothing to draw the economies of Germany and France closer together, which was a key objective of both Adenauer and Schuman. The German Chancellor and French Foreign Minister were also sceptical about the chances of the Council of Europe being able to bring the European nations closer together politically. They considered that an intergovernmental organization of fifteen states would be incapable of making effective decisions. Schuman, for example, wrote: 'The Council of Europe is the headlamp lighting the road to a united

Europe, but it lacks the authority of a body which can take majority decisions.'[50]

As we have seen, Adenauer was determined to achieve a better economic and political relationship with France. He had made this clear at the first Congress of the European Movement at The Hague in May 1948. He then met Schuman for private discussions in October 1948, and reiterated his commitment to Franco-German cooperation while emphasizing that progress would be difficult so long as the French maintained their control of the Saarland.[51] And in March 1950 he told a senior American journalist Kingsbury Smith, the Head of the International News Service in Paris, that he would like to see the establishment of a Franco-German customs union comparable to the nineteenth-century German *Zollverein*. He talked about 'the gradual fusion' of the customs and excise systems of the two countries, leading eventually to much closer economic cooperation; the 'customs union' could, he suggested, be run by an 'economic parliament' chosen from the parliaments of the two countries. He added that he had held comparable ideas for twenty-five years and that, if such an economic union were to be established, it would also strengthen Western Europe against the Communist threat. He also envisaged that Britain and the Benelux countries might join this customs union.[52]

So, when Robert Schuman produced what he himself called his 'bomb' on 9 May 1950, namely his proposal for the European Coal and Steel Community (the Schuman Plan), he was speaking to the converted. The idea was Jean Monnet's, but Schuman and Adenauer immediately endorsed it.[53] The proposal was that 'all French and German coal and steel be placed under a common High Authority in an organization open to participation by other European countries'. Well aware that this was a revolutionary proposal, which might well arouse hostility, Schuman was determined to act decisively and quickly. He was proposing no less than an integrated economic and political organization with a supranational governing body, which went for beyond the parameters of traditional intergovernmental organizations. Schuman let certain key members of the French Cabinet know about his proposal on 3 May 1950, but the whole Cabinet was not told until 9 May, when it at once expressed its approval. Britain, Italy and the Benelux countries knew nothing about the proposal until 9 May.

Adenauer alone was consulted in advance about the Coal and Steel Community, for Schuman realized that Adenauer was the key to the success or failure of the whole project. He sent a confidential envoy to the

German Chancellor with a copy of his proposal on 7 May 1950. Adenauer, having discussed it with his close advisor Herbert Blankenhorn, immediately responded positively both in an official letter and in a private letter to Schuman.[54] Adenauer realized that Schuman's initiative really was a uniquely forward-looking proposal and was very much in line with what he himself wanted. For the ECSC would mark the beginning of an economic union (albeit covering only two industries initially) between France and Germany, and within the ECSC the two countries would be able to treat each other as equals. Above all, the pooling of coal and steel under one supranational body would make war between France and Germany almost inconceivable. If the ECSC worked, it would immediately help to resolve France's security concerns vis-à-vis Germany. It would be nothing short of the first step towards a European federation of some sort. At the same time, it would strengthen the Atlantic Alliance by modernizing two of Europe's basic industries and drawing two of her traditional enemies into close partnership. It would thus constitute a vital breakthrough towards Adenauer's objective of Franco-German reconciliation.

Schuman later wrote that Adenauer's immediate endorsement of the ECSC was of great importance to him as a prelude to the official announcement of his Plan on 9 May 1950.[55] *Le Monde* reported that the reactions in Bonn, Washington and London were respectively 'enthusiastic', 'favourable' and 'cold'.[56] Italy and the Benelux countries welcomed the proposal. Schuman, however, regarded Adenauer's enthusiastic reception of his proposal as the vital first step. In fact, Adenauer went through a short period of doubt after his initially warm response to the Schuman Plan. In particular he was concerned that there might be some ulterior motive behind it, when it emerged that the real author of the Plan was Jean Monnet. Adenauer wondered whether a central government planner like Monnet (who had run the French Planning Commissariat after the war) might not be hatching some sinister plot to undermine Germany's free market economy. However, after meeting Monnet on 23 May 1950, Adenauer was reassured. He was impressed by Monnet's economic expertise as well as by the breadth of his political vision.[57] Monnet stressed that the ECSC would eliminate Franco-German rivalry and strengthen Western European democracy. And in the short term it would also bring to an end the Ruhr Authority's hated interference in the German economy and promote free and fair competition in the coal and steel industries. It remained only for Adenauer to appoint a suitable delegate to negotiate the Treaty in

Paris, for Monnet had stressed that he wanted Schuman and Adenauer to be in overall charge of their respective delegations. Adenauer immediately chose Walter Hallstein, the Head of Foreign Policy at the Chancellor's Office. When Monnet left Bonn, Adenauer was able to make the following historic statement: 'Monsieur Monnet, I regard the implementation of the French proposal as the most important task before me. Should I succeed in handling it well, I will not have lived in vain.'[58]

The six countries which accepted the proposal for the Coal and Steel Community (France, Germany, Italy and the three Benelux countries) met in Paris in June 1950 to work out the details of the Treaty. It was signed in April 1951, and the Community began to operate in August 1952. The most revolutionary feature of the Coal and Steel Community was its High Authority, a supranational body of 'independent persons' chosen by member governments but responsible to the Community, not their Governments. The High Authority's task was to modernize coal and steel production, develop the internal and external markets of these products, and improve the standard of living of the workers concerned. A Court was established to ensure that the Treaty was not infringed, and an Assembly was nominated by the National Parliaments to watch over the High Authority and, if need be, to dismiss it by a two-thirds majority.

For Adenauer the summer of 1950 had indeed been a very significant time. A huge step had been taken towards Franco-German reconciliation and European integration as a result of Schuman's proposal for the European Coal and Steel Community. In addition, albeit against the wishes of Schumacher's SPD, the Federal Republic had joined the Council of Europe, even although the Saar problem, to which we shall now turn, remained unresolved.

The Saar problem

Before discussing the next major step towards European integration, namely the setting up of the European Economic Community (EEC), it is necessary to comment on the Saar problem, which continued to dog Franco-German relations until the mid-1950s. Between 1949 and 1955 the Saar problem was a constant irritant to Adenauer. Indeed at times the dispute over the Saarland came close to destroying his hopes for Franco-German reconciliation. Looking back, it seems strange that the status of the Saarland proved so contentious. After all, the million Saarlanders were indisputably Germans who lived in a relatively small area (about 1000 square miles) on the left (German) bank of the Rhine. The Saarland was of course of considerable economic interest to France owing to its coalmines and steel industry, but its history, culture and language were all German. Therefore it was not surprising that, when a referendum on the status of the Saarland was held in 1955, the result was a pro-German vote. The Saarland then returned to Germany, becoming the eleventh *Land* of the Federal Republic in January 1957. These stark facts give no indication of the Franco-German animosity caused by the dispute over the Saarland during the first six years of Adenauer's Chancellorship.[59]

Two of Adenauer's biographers refer to the Saar problem as his 'Achilles heel'.[60] And there is no doubt that this relatively unimportant territorial dispute (although this was not how it appeared at the time) came near to undermining Adenauer's credibility and his whole policy of Franco-German reconciliation. Indeed, in 1954 it looked as if the Saar problem might also delay the Federal Republic's attainment of sovereignty and its entry into the Atlantic Alliance. In addition, in the later stages of the dispute, Adenauer undoubtedly made a major political miscalculation about the Saarland, from which miscalculation he was only rescued by the unexpected decision of the Saarlanders in the referendum of October 1955.

Underlying France's attitude to the Saarland was her sense of insecurity vis-à-vis Germany. Thus, after the First World War, in response to French demands, the Saarland was placed under the mandate of the League of Nations, and its coalmines were put in French hands as part of the Versailles Treaty's reparations policy. This situation ended in 1935, when 90 per cent of the Saarlanders voted to return to Germany. After the Second World War France was determined to achieve full political and economic control of the Saarland. Coal and steel were still the sinews of military power. If France controlled the coal and steel industries of the Saar basin, her coal and steel output would be roughly the same as (West) Germany's; if she did not, German output would be roughly double that of France. So, not surprisingly, France was determined to assimilate, or at least control, the Saarland. A series of measures were undertaken by the French to achieve this, and between the end of the war and the setting up of the Federal Republic the Saarland became to all intents and purposes part of France.

In 1945 Johannes Hoffmann, a Saar separatist who had gone into exile before the war, was brought back to the Saarland by the French, who appointed him Prime Minister in 1946. He led the Christian People's Party, and the only other licensed party was the Socialist Party led by another Francophile. The Saarland was situated in the French Occupation Zone, but was immediately detached from it and given a special status. In January 1946 it was united with France in a customs union, and it received preferential treatment compared with the other occupied zones: there was no industrial dismantling in the Saarland, and in the late 1940s the French sent in special food supplies at a time when Germans in the Ruhr and Rhineland were starving. Moreover, the French 'expanded' the Saarland by 50 per cent, extending its boundaries to the Luxembourg frontier and almost up to the River Mosel. This 'expansion' was reduced to 30 per cent when the Americans and British protested at France's unilateral action. The Saarland in effect became a French protectorate between 1946 and 1949, for not only did France sequestrate the Saar coalmines, but she also took over the railways, made the franc the only official currency and insisted that French be taught in all schools. She allowed elections to take place in October 1947, but only pro-French parties were permitted to stand for the Assembly's fifty seats. Hoffmann's Christian People's Party won the election decisively, and he moved from 'appointed' to 'elected' Prime Minister, remaining in this post until after the 1955 referendum. In January 1948 the French Military Governor was replaced by a High Commissioner. The Saarland was thus a quasi province of France, except that, unlike Alsace or Lorraine, it had a devolved government, albeit a puppet one, and a High Commissioner. Arguably this made it comparable to a French Protectorate, the status of Morocco and Tunisia at that time.

While some Germans, led by Schumacher of the SPD, protested about the French 'takeover' of the Saarland between 1946 and 1949, Adenauer remained silent until he became Chancellor in 1949. Then he began to pursue the policy which he followed until late 1954. He protested publicly about what France had done and was doing in the Saarland, but in private, for example in negotiations with Schuman, he was prepared to make concessions as long as it was agreed that no final decision about the status of the Saarland would be made until the peace treaty, i.e. the final settlement of Germany's territorial boundaries.[61] Throughout the years 1949–55 Adenauer had to perform a difficult balancing act. He was trying hard to work out a new and friendly relationship with France, while the French were equally determined to maintain their control of the Saarland. At the same time Adenauer had to retain the support of his Coalition in the Federal Republic. If he conceded too much over the Saarland, he could lose control over his Coalition (the FDP and DP frequently threatened to bring down the government over the Saarland), but if he lost the support of his Coalition allies, all his mainstream policies – rearmament, reconciliation with France and the achievement of West German sovereignty within the Atlantic Alliance – would be in jeopardy. This was why the Saar problem was so delicate and important.

In his *Memoirs* (written ten years after the Saar problem had been resolved) Adenauer claimed that as early as October 1948 Schuman had assured him privately that the return of the Saarland to Germany would in due course be possible, *provided* France's economic and security interests were satisfied.[62] If Schuman did say this (and we only have Adenauer's word for it), it certainly was not the line taken by Schuman after Adenauer became Chancellor in 1949. Indeed, when the two men met in Bonn in January 1950, Schuman defended all the measures France had taken in the Saarland. Two months later (on 2 March) Adenauer was told that on the next day the French and Saar Governments would sign four Conventions drawn up by the French Foreign Ministry. These Conventions proclaimed the 'autonomy' of the Saarland and its 'economic union' with France, and they confirmed that its coalmines and railways would remain under French control. On 4 March 1950 Adenauer protested strongly against the Conventions, claiming that they meant that the Saarland had become 'a French colony', and that they amounted to 'a decision against Europe'.[63] Adenauer also protested to the American and British High Commissioners, McCloy and Kirkpatrick, about France's unilateral action. However, at this stage the High Commissioners refused to bring pressure to bear on the French, although they did assure Adenauer that France was no more than a 'trustee' in the Saarland and that its long-term status would depend upon the terms of the final peace treaty.[64] In a speech in the Bundestag Adenauer also demanded that 'democratic freedoms' should be restored to the Saarlanders.[65] In particular he wanted them to have the right to form political parties freely and to be able study at German universities (at this stage the French refused to allow students at Saarbrücken University to pursue their studies outside the Saarland). Nevertheless, Adenauer also told the Bundestag that some concessions might have to be made over the Saarland to achieve wider European objectives. He went on to say that, for him, Franco-German reconciliation was more important than the status of the Saarland, although he did not offer to abandon the Saarland at this stage.

For the next two months Franco-German relations remained frosty owing to the Saar Conventions. Then the impasse was partially broken by Schuman's historic declaration proposing the European Coal and Steel Community (9 May 1950), because the coal and steel of the Saarland would be included in the ECSC. The Schuman Plan thus created a more favourable atmosphere for the long-term resolution of the Saar problem. But outwardly there was little evidence of a change in French policy towards the Saarland from 1950 to 1954. Indeed, in some ways the French became more intransigent in the two years prior to the breakthrough. Nevertheless, when Adenauer went to Paris in April 1951 to discuss the Schuman Plan and the Saar problem, Schuman told him privately that 'The French Government acts in the name of the Saarland *on the basis of its present status* [my italics]. It does not, however, consider that the signing of the Schuman Plan by the Federal Government anticipates the final status of the Saar, which will only be settled by a Peace Treaty or by an agreement in place of a Peace Treaty.'[66] This was exactly what Adenauer wanted to hear. Thus in the ratification debate on the ECSC in the Bundestag in January 1952 (the Treaty was ratified by 232–143) Adenauer was able to stress that the Federal Republic would gain significant advantages by joining the Coal and Steel Community, notably 'industrial equality' with the other ECSC countries and the abolition of the International Ruhr Authority, but that the status of the Saarland was still 'provisional'.[67]

The Saar problem, however, was far from being resolved. The Saarland remained firmly under French control with pro-German newspapers and political parties still banned. At the elections of November 1952, with only pro-French parties standing, 60 per cent voted for these parties (with Hoffmann winning and continuing as Prime Minister), but 25 per cent of voters spoiled their ballot papers. The elections were condemned by Terence Prittie, then the *Manchester Guardian*'s German correspondent, as 'undemocratic', because pro-German parties were banned, and 'unfortunate', because the elections had 'embittered Franco-German relations and set back the process of European integration'.[68] These words reflected precisely Adenauer's view of the unfortunate effect of the Saar problem.

The problem continued to dog Franco-German relations throughout 1953 and 1954, and then quite suddenly a solution was found in 1955. The

French put forward two plans for the resolution of the Saar problem in 1954 – the first before and the second after the collapse of the EDC in August 1954. The first, the Van Naters Plan, proposed that the Saarland should become a 'European territory', i.e. the site of the proposed European 'federal capital' (rather like the District of Columbia in the USA). The idea was that the Saarland would become a second Luxembourg, except that unlike Luxembourg it would not be an independent state, but would remain under French control despite its vaguely defined 'European' status. One problem was that Saarbrücken, a traditional mining town, hardly seemed suitable as the capital of 'Europe'. Another objection was that after the collapse of the EDC there seemed little chance that a European federation would become a reality for many years. In these circumstances the Van Naters Plan was quietly dropped.

There the matter rested until the late autumn of 1954, by which time Pierre Mendès-France was Prime Minister of France (his Government lasted from June 1954 to February 1955). Mendès-France was determined to resolve several outstanding French political problems, and quickly. Peace had been achieved in Indochina in July 1954 and the EDC jettisoned in August. Mendès-France then decided to tackle the Saar problem. Under his proposed Saar Statute the Saarland would be 'Europeanized' in the sense of its being given independence guaranteed by all the Western powers. Since France's main objective was to prevent the return of the Saarland to the Federal Republic rather than to keep it under French control, Mendès-France decided that the Saarlanders should be given a free vote in a referendum on his proposal. The Saarlanders were, however, only given the choice between 'Europeanization' and the status quo. If a majority voted yes, the Saarland's new 'European' status would come about. If they voted no, the current 'French' régime would continue.

In October 1954 Adenauer had to make a momentous decision, for on 22 October Mendès-France told him that if the Chancellor did not endorse the Saar Statute, he would not sign the London Agreements (due for signature on 23 October), i.e. the Federal Republic would not achieve full sovereignty through the ending of the Occupation Statute and entry into NATO. Adenauer decided to defer to Mendès-France's threat on the grounds that, if he did not, his hopes for the achievement of German sovereignty, Franco-German reconciliation and European integration could all be postponed for several years. Moreover, if he did not endorse the Saar Statute, the Saarland would remain a French protectorate:

'Europeanization' seemed the lesser of two evils. Adenauer therefore decided to sacrifice the Saarland for Franco-German reconciliation and European integration. Thus Mendès-France successfully blackmailed Adenauer in late 1954. But his 'victory' was to backfire on both of them.[69]

Not surprisingly Adenauer's 'surrender' was strongly criticized in the Federal Republic not only by the SDP but also by his Coalition allies, the FDP and BHE (Refugee Party), as well as by a minority of Christian Democrats, among whom were Jakob Kaiser, the Minister for All-German Affairs, and Heinrich von Brentano, the normally loyal Chairman of the parliamentary party.[70] Adenauer was particularly annoyed with the FDP for voting against the Saar Statute in January 1955, although he won the vote by 264 to 204. From this moment he was determined to get rid of the FDP from his Coalition, and in particular he never forgave Thomas Dehler, the leader of its parliamentary party, for his opposition to the Saar Statute.[71]

Ten years later Adenauer was to claim that he acted as he did because he knew that he could rely on the Saarlanders as 'good Germans' to vote against the Saar Statute.[72] This was a classic case of rewriting history after the event, for during most of 1955 Johannes Hoffmann and the French Government seemed extremely likely to win the battle for the 'Europeanization' of the Saarland. The French had implicit trust in Hoffmann, who had been 'their' Prime Minister for almost ten years, and opinion polls in the summer of 1955 indicated that a clear majority of Saarlanders would vote for 'Europeanization'. Moreover, if the vote did not go as the French hoped, the status of the Saarland would remain unchanged. But it was not only the French who miscalculated. Adenauer completely misread the mood of the Saarlanders. He *positively* endorsed the 'Europeanization' of the Saarland, because he assumed that the Saarlanders would prefer 'Europeanization' to subservience to France, having himself concluded that a 'Europeanized' Saarland would be a small price to pay for German reconciliation with France.

By the time of the referendum in October 1955 the confidence of the French and of Adenauer that a yes vote would be achieved had been undermined, because for the first time in the post-war history of the Saarland pro-German political parties were allowed to campaign. Within three months there had been a huge swing to the *Heimatbundparteien* (homeland parties), who in the end won the referendum comfortably, with 68 per cent voting against the Saar Statute and 32 per cent for it (423,000 to 202,000). Although this result was a blow to French prestige, it discredited Adenauer even more. He had been prepared to sacrifice the Saarland, but by their own efforts the Saarlanders had refused to be detached from their native land. Their eventual 'return' to Germany owed nothing Adenauer.

In a strange way, however, what had been a defeat for both the French and German Governments turned out to be a victory for both. For the Saarland debacle did not affect adversely the improved relations between France and Germany. Ironically it might well have worsened them if Adenauer had, like so many German politicians, campaigned *against* the Saarland Statute, because this would have implied that he was 'anti-French'. Moreover, the French Government quickly accepted that, despite the wording of the question in the referendum, it had not been about whether the Saarland should be 'European' or French, but whether the Saarland should or should not be allowed to return to Germany. After the French Government's rapid acceptance of the reality of the situation, the subsequent negotiations between France and the Federal Republic were conducted relatively amicably in 1956, leading to the Saarland joining the Federal Republic as its eleventh *Land* in January 1957.

As with the collapse of his EDC policy, Adenauer was fortunate with the consequences of the collapse of his Saarland policy. In both cases he had staked a great deal on the wrong horse. Yet in both cases he came out on the winning side. The passage of time had in fact healed past wounds with regard to both of these great political controversies. For in 1950 the French would neither have accepted German rearmament within NATO nor the reintegration of the Saarland into Germany. But by 1955 Franco-German reconciliation and Western European integration had progressed to the point at which both rearmament and the return of the Saarland to Germany had become politically acceptable. Despite what Adenauer claimed in his *Memoirs* about his confidence in the Saarlanders voting no,[73] he had made a major political miscalculation and got away with it. He had been prepared to sacrifice the Saarland for the sake of Franco-German reconciliation and European integration, but the Saarlanders saved themselves by their vote of October 1955. And the irony was that Adenauer, having survived this miscalculation, brazenly told the Saarlanders on the day of reunification (1 January 1957) that he had worked hard for their reintegration with Germany and that: 'This is the most wonderful day of my life.'[74]

The European *Relance* of 1955–57

Adenauer's faith in the functional approach to European integration had been shaken, but not broken, by the collapse of the European Defence Community. The impetus for the next major step towards integration came from the Benelux countries, but Adenauer gave his full support to the European *relance* from the time of the Messina Conference (June 1955) to the signing of the Treaties of Rome establishing the European Economic Community (EEC or Common Market) and Euratom in May 1957.[75]

The establishment of the EEC and Euratom proved to be much less controversial than the European Defence Community. Nevertheless, significant differences arose between France and Germany during the negotiations. These differences centred on trade, social policy, agricultural policy, the relationship between the Community and its 'associated territories' and atomic policy. There were also major internal German differences, with Adenauer and Erhard quarrelling openly about the relationship between the proposed Community and the non-applicant OEEC countries (in particular Britain), the common external tariff and issues relating to free trade, competition policy and social policy. However, in spite of Franco-German differences and internal German conflicts, the European *relance* was achieved because the political will to move forward was strong. Adenauer was particularly well motivated from a *political* point of view. Indeed, Erhard's main criticism of Adenauer was that he was prepared to make unwise economic concessions to France for the sake of his long-term political aspirations.[76] In the end Adenauer won his battle with Erhard. But one result was that the EEC was tailored to French economic interests. Yet, in the long run, neither German industry nor agriculture were penalized by membership of the EEC. Indeed the opposite happened, with the Common Market soon proving economically beneficial to all its members. On the other hand, although Adenauer, the non-economist, triumphed over Erhard, the economic expert, his hopes for the political development of the EEC were to be disappointed. Adenauer saw economic integration as the catalyst which would produce further political integration. However, he soon decided that the Treaty of Rome had not provided the Community with sufficiently strong political institutions, perceptively remarking that the institutions would have to become more 'supranational' if the Community were to function effectively in the long run.[77] In spite of the overall optimism expressed by Adenauer at the time of the signing of the Treaties of Rome, the 1960s were to be a disappointing decade for federalists like himself. Economic progress within the Community was considerable, but political and institutional progress was minimal, not least, as we shall see, owing to Adenauer's increasing subservience to his new-found political ally, General Charles de Gaulle.

At the risk of over-simplifying, it can be said that from 1957 until the end of Adenauer's Chancellorship in 1963, the German Christian Democrats had three main objectives for the European Community. Firstly, they wanted it to succeed economically, thereby boosting German exports and industry. Secondly, they wanted to see the progressive strengthening of the Community's institutions, especially the Commission and Parliament. And thirdly, they wanted to see the Community expanded to include Britain and the other applicant countries, although Adenauer's personal commitment to the third of these objectives was to wither away, as the negotiations dragged on and as de Gaulle moved towards the rejection of Britain.

Progress in the economic area was certainly significant. The EEC soon dismantled its internal customs barriers and lowered its external tariffs, but little progress was made in the early years towards the dismantling of non-tariff barriers or the implementation of common social, regional and fiscal policies. However a Common Agricultural Policy (CAP), which suited both French and German farmers, was forged in the 1960s. Disappointingly for Adenauer, the Community's decision-making process remained heavily weighted in favour of the Council of Ministers and, after the Luxembourg Crisis of 1965, provoked by General de Gaulle, there was little to distinguish the Council from any other intergovernmental body, as unanimous agreement was required for virtually all decisions. Finally, the Community was not widened, de Gaulle rejecting Britain's applications to join in 1963 and 1967.

What was Adenauer's attitude during the European *relance* of 1955–57? And what were the main problems facing his government as the negotiations progressed towards the Treaties of Rome? The *relance* certainly occurred in much more favourable circumstances than those in which the Schuman and Pleven Plans (ECSC and EDC) had been launched. First of all, the precedent set by the Coal and Steel Community was very encouraging. German and French steel production had increased considerably between 1952 and 1957 (from 17 to 24 million tons and from 10 to 14 million tons respectively), and there were correspondingly large gains in productivity. By 1955 not only the majority of politicians, but also a majority of employers and trade unionists in both France and Germany, were in favour of extending the common market in coal and steel to other products.

It was in this favourable economic and political atmosphere, then, that the Foreign Ministers of the six ECSC countries met at Messina in Sicily in June 1955 to set in train the next steps towards European integration. Adenauer at once realized the importance of the Messina Conference and sent his most able foreign policy advisor, Walter Hallstein, to represent him. On 3 June 1955 the Six stated that: 'The time has come to enter a new phase in European integration. We must work towards the establishment of a united Europe through the development of common institutions, the gradual merger of national economies, the creation of a common market, and the increasing harmonization of social policies.'[78] These objectives could only be achieved by stages, as it would take time to remove quotas and tariffs and achieve free trade and fair competition within the proposed Common Market. The Foreign Ministers set up an intergovernmental committee to prepare the way for the Common Market and Euratom. This committee was chaired by Paul-Henri Spaak, the strongly federalist Belgian Foreign Minister, whose appointment received the full support of Adenauer. The Spaak Committee completed its report in July 1956. And in May 1957 the Treaties of Rome were signed, i.e. the treaties setting up the European Economic Community (henceforth referred to as the Community the EEC or Common Market) and the European Atomic Energy Community (henceforth Euratom). Strictly speaking there were two treaties signed at Rome, but as the Treaty of Rome is normally used in the singular to refer to the EEC Treaty, we shall follow that convention from now on.

Adenauer's personal role in the moves towards European integration between 1955 and 1957 was less obvious than it had been in the ECSC and EDC phases of integration, but he was decisively supportive throughout the *relance*.[79] His consistent line in the late 1950s was that European integration must be pursued for *political* reasons, even if in the short term this entailed making economic concessions to France. The Federal Republic of Germany and France were of course the main countries in the (future) Community. They had the largest populations and economies and were its principal trading partners. It was therefore essential that they should negotiate treaties (EEC and Euratom) which could be ratified by their respective parliaments. Adenauer's willingness to make economic concessions to France for the sake of achieving progress towards the long-term achievement of a federal Europe can be illustrated in a variety of areas, notably over Euratom, trade, agriculture and the associated territories (France's former colonies).

In March 1956 the Bundestag passed a resolution calling on Euratom 'to develop atomic energy exclusively for peaceful purposes'.[80] But when the French objected to this on the grounds they had already invested heavily in nuclear weapons research, the German Government agreed to a let-out clause for France, which in practice allowed her to continue research in this area, leading in due course to her independent nuclear deterrent. The Germans were also opposed to France's demand that Euratom should have a monopoly in the use of fissionable materials, as the German chemical industry considered it would be disadvantaged by this. However, in November 1956 Adenauer accepted France's demand. Finally, Germany, against the wishes of its industrialists, agreed to France's demand that Euratom should have exclusive control over the purchase and sale of fissionable materials.

There were also significant Franco-German differences over various economic aspects of the proposed Common Market, and these spilled over into the much-publicized dispute between Adenauer and his Minister of Economics, Ludwig Erhard. The dispute centred on their different priorities. Adenauer always put politics before economics in his dealings with the French, whereas Erhard, a commmitted free-marketeer, put economics first.

Overall, the French economy had improved significantly since 1952, but the main improvements had occurred in the areas covered by the Planning Commissariat and the ECSC, i.e. coal, steel, electricity, transport and agricultural mechanization. There were many areas of manufacturing industry where the French employers' association (CNPF) considered that France could not compete on the world market or against Germany. The French therefore wanted to protect manufacturing industry with a high common external tariff and low internal quotas, whereas the Germans wanted a low external tariff and minimal internal trade restrictions. The French were also determined to achieve what they regarded as a level playing field in the area of social policy, arguing that the Germans should increase their welfare benefits and reduce their working week in order to be in line with France. Erhard and the leaders of German industry were strongly opposed to such demands but, while rejecting French demands for common social policies and an equal working week, they did accept a considerably higher common external tariff than they would have liked. This tariff was based on the average external tariffs of the Six at the time of the signing of the Treaty of Rome.

Erhard continued to express doubts about the Treaty of Rome right up to the last minute. He was not, he insisted, against the principle of European integration, but he regretted all the economic concessions which were being made to the French: 'France considers the Common Market solely from the point of view of the protection of its economy and cares little for true freedom of trade. The result will not be a market for free competition, but an economic burden for Europe.' Erhard went on to say that he was against the proposed harmonization of social welfare, claiming that France would soon want all members of the Community to accept 'common fuel and energy prices ... This will mean not integration, but disintegration of the worst kind.'[81] He was equally worried that the high common external tariff would damage German exports. In 1955–56 over 25 per cent of all German exports went to countries outside the proposed EEC, mainly to the United Kingdom, Austria, Switzerland and Scandinavia, whereas only 16 per cent of French exports went to these countries. So Erhard pressed for a free trade agreement with those European countries which did not want to join the Community, while the French wanted the opposite, namely protection against competition from these countries. When Britain and the Scandinavian countries refused to join the EEC negotiations, the Organization for European Economic Cooperation (OEEC) proposed (July 1956) that the EEC and OEEC countries should be linked in a free trade area. Not surprisingly Erhard supported this proposal and the French opposed it.[82]

In all these matters Adenauer came out decisively and openly against Erhard. He considered that it was vital to bind France *politically* into the Community by making whatever *economic* concessions were necessary. Hence he made a special visit to Paris in November 1956 to discuss France's demands with the Prime Minister Guy Mollet, whom Adenauer considered to be a 'good European' and a friend of Germany.[83] Shortly afterwards the Germans accepted the common external tariff, which was detrimental to German manufacturing industry, as German tariffs were considerably lower than the agreed average tariff. However, whatever the short-term economic disadvantages might be, Adenauer was determined to overrule Erhard. Adenauer considered that his own criticisms of Mendès-France just before the failure of the EDC Treaty in August 1954 might have caused the French Prime Minister to have turned against that Treaty. He was insistent that the same thing should not happen with the EEC. He wanted to give positive help to the French Prime Minister, Guy Mollet, to ensure that the Treaty of Rome was approved by the National Assembly, even if in the short term this meant upsetting Erhard and German industry.

With regard to agriculture Adenauer pursued a similar line, that is to say the Germans conceded more to the French than they gained from them. As most aspects of the Common Agricultural Policy (CAP) were not worked out until after the signing of the Treaty of Rome, we shall discuss agriculture when analysing Franco-German relations in the early years of the Common Market.[84] But even *before* the Treaty was signed, the Germans had agreed that the CAP would be drawn up on the basis of high external tariffs, high internal prices (compared with world prices) and a restructuring policy. These agreements enabled the German Government to 'sell' the Treaty to its farmers while at the same time opening the German market to French agricultural produce.

Finally, the Germans also conceded to the French over the question of the associated territories (mainly former French African colonies). Needless to say, Erhard was extremely concerned about the cost of subsidizing these territories by giving preferential rates to their produce entering the Community and through financial aid. He pointed out that 27 per cent of French exports went to the associated territories in contrast to 1 per cent of German exports. Apart from the cost of subsidizing these territories, many Germans considered that the proposed special agreements amounted to neo-colonialism. The territories would be tied to their former colonial masters, while the other Community countries would be subsidizing French neo-colonialism. The German business journal *Handelsblatt* stated that: 'We want nothing to do with French colonialism.'[85] It went on to complain that the Common Market negotiations had been taken out of the hands of Erhard and the Ministry of Economics, which understood about commercial matters, and taken over by the Chancellor and Minister of Foreign Affairs, who did not. In the end, to the consternation of Erhard and the business community, Adenauer made a series of concessions to the French over the special treatment of the associated territories. As Roy Willis put it: 'The final attitude of Erhard and German industry was one of resignation to political necessity and to the tactical subordination of economic interests to foreign policy.'[86]

With the hindsight of history, we can say that Adenauer acted with the statesmanlike vision over the European *relance* of 1955–57. In economic terms he was proved right and Erhard wrong. German industry benefited greatly from the Common Market, especially as the EEC soon became less protectionist by raising its internal quotas and reducing its external tariffs. The agricultural deal undoubtedly benefited France most, but the in-built protectionism of the CAP helped German farmers too. And as overall prosperity increased in the Community, the cost of subsidizing the associated territories turned out to be an insignificant burden on the German taxpayer. In the short term Adenauer's economic concessions undoubtedly helped the pro-Europeans in the French National Assembly, where the Treaties of Rome were ratified comfortably in July 1957 (by 344 votes to 239). In the slightly longer term Adenauer's concessions persuaded General de Gaulle that the Community, which he had originally opposed, was in fact to France's advantage. Of course it soon became apparent that de Gaulle's vision of the European Community was very different from Adenauer's, but at least the General did not withdraw his country from the EEC. As for the Federal Republic, in the short term the ratification debate proved a triumph for Adenauer, with the Treaties being endorsed on a show of hands without a formal vote in the Bundestag (5 July 1957) and in the Bundesrat (19 July). A few Liberals spoke out against ratification owing to the high external tariff, but the Social Democrats now endorsed Adenauer's European integration policy (having opposed the ECSC and EDC).[87] Even Erhard, while criticizing some of the economic aspects of the Treaties, supported Adenauer and recommended ratification on political grounds. Adenauer's hope that a federal European Community would develop quickly out of the Common Market was of course to be disappointed. But his strong support for the European *relance* of 1955–57 showed once again his continuing commitment to both Franco-German reconciliation and European integration. The long-term significance of the policies Adenauer pursued is shown by the fact that all his successors as Chancellor in the twentieth century, whether Christian Democrats or Social Democrats, followed the main lines laid down by Adenauer in both his French and European policies.

From the Treaty of Rome (1957) to the
Franco-German Treaty (1963)

When General de Gaulle returned to power in France on 1 June 1958 in the wake of the Army's revolt in Algeria, most German politicians, including Adenauer, were distinctly worried, because the General was reputed to have no love either for Germany or for European integration. De Gaulle's initial remit was to draw up a new constitution for France and to resolve the Algerian problem, and the Germans were to some extent reassured by the General's insistence that he should be voted into power legally by the National Assembly. Moreover, when he received a decisive 329–224 vote in his favour on 1 June 1958, it was noted that many of those who voted for him were friends of Germany and of European integration, notably the Conservative Antoine Pinay, a personal friend of Adenauer, the Christian Democrat Pierre Pflimlin, de Gaulle's predecessor as Prime Minister, and the leaders of the Socialist and Radical Parties, Guy Mollet and Maurice Faure. Adenauer's first concern was that de Gaulle would be no more successful than his predecessors in stabilizing the French economy, for, if the French economy remained weak, France would be unable to fulfil her obligations under the Treaty of Rome. Thus Adenauer's hope that economic integration would lead to political integration would soon be disappointed.

De Gaulle's past record certainly seemed to suggest that he was unlikely to be a friend of Germany or of the European Community. When in power from August 1944 to January 1946 he had advocated a decentralized, deindustrialized Germany. And in the 1950s he had been very critical of the European Defence Community, in which Adenauer had invested so much time and effort, and he had also opposed the European Economic Community and Euratom. Moreover, he had been critical of the United States's dominant role in NATO. In addition, albeit back in 1944, he had signed the Franco-Soviet Pact with Stalin, and Adenauer always feared that one (or more) of the Western Allies might do a deal with the Soviet Union at the expense of Germany. Was there not a risk that de Gaulle might try to do just this? The General, then, was expected to be against all the key tenets of Adenauer's foreign policy: Franco-German reconciliation, Western European integration and friendship with the United States. Yet, within a few months, Adenauer had changed his mind about de Gaulle.

Two key meetings between the two men occurred before the end of 1958, the first in September at Colombey-les-Deux-Eglises, de Gaulle's country home in north-east France, and the second in November at Bad Kreuznach in the Rhineland-Palatinate. Adenauer tells us that he was apprehensive when he arrived at Colombey, but almost immediately he found that he had much in common with de Gaulle *personally;* and, even more important, *politically.*[88] Both were of course old men – de Gaulle almost seventy, Adenauer over eighty; both were practising Catholics; both were rather prim, old-fashioned gentlemen; and both were well aware of the disastrous wars their countries had fought during their life-time. Adenauer, then, found de Gaulle to be unexpectedly friendly and, above all, committed to Franco-German cooperation as well as to achieving political and economic stability in his own country. Nor, to Adenauer's surprise, did de Gaulle seem to be in any way critical of the Treaty of Rome. Adenauer concluded: 'I was glad to have met a totally different person from the one I had expected to meet. I was convinced that after all de Gaulle and I could have a worthwhile and trusting relationship.'[89] On his return to Bonn, Adenauer remarked that de Gaulle's political views had changed significantly during his twelve years out of power.[90]

In reality, prior to this meeting at Colombey, Adenauer and his advisers had misunderstood de Gaulle, whose ideas about Germany and Europe were much more complex than they had assumed. Even if in 1945 de Gaulle had wanted a weak and politically divided Germany, with the Saarland controlled by France and the Ruhr internationalized, he had moderated his views significantly by 1950. Almost alone among French politicians de Gaulle responded positively to Adenauer's proposal for a Franco-German customs union in March 1950, and in the same year he had written: 'I believe that the only sensible road for us to take is the one which leads to an entente between France and Germany.'[91] De Gaulle had in fact both criticized and praised Germany on various occasions for over thirty years. As a boy he had spent two holidays in the Black Forest. He began to learn German at that time, and as a prisoner-of-war between 1916 and 1918 he had read a good deal of German literature. In the two books he wrote in the inter-war period, de Gaulle had emphasized the threat Germany posed to France but had also extolled the military prowess and organizational skills of the Germans. He claimed that, if French flair could be allied to German discipline, these two great European powers could achieve much together.[92] After the war de Gaulle continued to stress that

France and Germany were *both* potentially *great* European powers, but their *true* greatness could only emerge when they were working together. So, curiously enough, these two elder statesmen had one vital thing in common: in the 1950s, as in the inter-war period, they saw the need for Franco-German cooperation if Europe were to have long-term peace. Hence, it was perhaps not surprising that Adenauer found de Gaulle to be much more sympathetic and pragmatic than he had expected.

De Gaulle's pragmatic realism became even more apparent when the two men met at Bad Kreuznach in November 1958. By now de Gaulle was in a strong position at home. The Constitution of the Fifth Republic had been decisively approved in a national referendum in September (17 million votes to 4 million), and he had just won a comfortable majority at the general election of November. Shortly afterwards (December 1958) he was elected the first President of the Fifth Republic by 80 per cent of the 80,000 voters at an indirect election.

What was really important at Bad Kreuznach was that de Gaulle told Adenauer that he was determined to stabilize the French economy (it had suffered from inflation and balance of payments problems since 1953) *and* that he was in favour of France remaining in the European Community. Already de Gaulle's Finance Minister, Antoine Pinay, had imposed a wage freeze in the public sector, and in December 1958 the franc was devalued by 20 per cent. Adenauer now knew that de Gaulle was determined that France would fulfil her economic obligations under the Treaty of Rome. Indeed, one of the Adenauer's biographers claims that the Bad Kreuznach meeting marked the beginning of the 'Franco-German axis,'[93] although this phrase was not used regularly until the early 1960s.

Certainly, by the end of 1958, Adenauer could feel reasonably assured about de Gaulle. An unexpected bond of friendship had developed between the two men at Colombey and Bad Kreuznach. More important, de Gaulle seemed to be firmly committed to Franco-German reconciliation and, to Adenauer's surprise, to the European Community. However, even in the early years of the *entente* between Adenauer and de Gaulle, there were significant differences between the two men. These were focused upon their attitude to the United States and their vision of the future of the European Community. As already emphasized, they both wanted Franco-German reconciliation, but that key objective had to be squared with their different priorities over the other two matters. For since the early 1950s Adenauer had tried to pursue a dual policy of friendship with the United States and reconciliation with France. But after de Gaulle came to power it became increasingly difficult to reconcile these two objectives. Adenauer strove to combine the two for the next five years, but, to some extent he failed. His foreign policy became increasingly French-orientated, to the annoyance of many of his colleagues in Germany as well as his friends in the United States and Britain. The German Christian Democrats gradually split into 'Gaullist' and 'Atlanticist' camps, and Adenauer's once-united party became increasingly divided as the Chancellor became more stubborn in his 'Gaullist' leanings.

The differences between the 'Gaullists' (essentially those who followed Adenauer) and the 'Atlanticists' (essentially those who followed Erhard) can certainly be exaggerated. They were nevertheless significant. Both sides were committed to the Western Alliance, and they both supported Franco-German reconciliation and Western European cooperation. Broadly speaking, the 'Gaullists' favoured the General's ideas about a loosely integrated Western Europe; supported his view that France and Germany should have predominance in the European Community; and criticized to a greater or lesser extent the power and influence of the United States in the Western Alliance. On the other hand, the German 'Gaullists', particularly Adenauer, did not endorse the General's views about détente with the East or his idea that Western Europe should develop as a 'third force' between the United States and the Soviet Union. The 'Atlanticists', in contrast, were generally more 'outward-looking'. They supported contacts with the Communist East, such as the first tentative steps towards *Ostpolitik* which began when Gerhard Schröder was Foreign Minister between 1961 and 1966. They were very determined to maintain good relations with the United States, and certainly if a choice had to be made between Washington and Paris, they would choose the former. Again, they were much more positive about widening the Common Market to include Britain and other applicant countries, and if a choice had to be made between 'Little Europe' (the 'closed' Community of the Six) and 'Big Europe' (an expanded and more 'supranational' Community), they favoured the latter.[94]

In the Federal Republic the 'Gaullists' were mainly Catholics and Southerners, e.g. Adenauer, Strauss, the leader of the Bavarian CSU, and Brentano, the chairman of the parliamentary party from 1961 to 1964 after six years as Foreign Minister. The 'Atlanticists', on the other hand, tended to be Protestants and often Northerners, men such as Erhard (although he was a Protestant Bavarian), Minister of Economics and Adenauer's successor as Chancellor, Foreign Minister Schröder, and von Hassel, Minister of Defence from 1962 to 1966. Adenauer was very much against Erhard succeeding him as Chancellor precisely because he was an 'Atlanticist', who advocated a European Community which would be open to new members and to the maximum level of free trade.[95] Erhard also rejected de Gaulle's anti-Americanism, in particular his determination to reduce the influence of the United States in the Western Alliance and to transform (or even dismantle) NATO. The 'Gaullist–Atlanticist' quarrel was to come to a head over the British application to join the EEC, vetoed by de Gaulle in January 1963, and the Franco-German Treaty signed in the same month. But before discussing these important events, it is appropriate to analyse the differing views of Adenauer and de Gaulle about the nature and development of the European Community. For such an analysis shows clearly the tensions which underlay the Franco-German relationship even before the climacteric of January 1963.

Adenauer, de Gaulle and the European Community

Adenauer and de Gaulle were in general agreement about the *economic* development of the European Community, but disagreed fundamentally about its *political* development, for de Gaulle's concept of a Europe of nation-states was quite different from Adenauer's vision of a suppranational, politically united Community.

As an economic organization, the European Economic Community soon proved to be a major success. Between 1958 and 1962 West Germany's industrial production rose by 35 per cent and France's by 23 per cent; German and French trade with the other EEC countries doubled; Franco-German trade trebled; and Franco-German industrial cooperation expanded considerably in textiles, chemicals and mechanical engineering. In addition, the EEC successfully repelled the threat posed by the European Free Trade Association (EFTA) by accelerating its own programme of economic integration.

In July 1959 EFTA had been established as a direct challenge to the EEC. Consisting of the 'outer seven' European countries (Britain, Denmark, Sweden, Norway, Austria, Switzerland and Portugal), EFTA agreed to reduce tariffs on industrial goods by 20 per cent on 1 July 1960 and to abolish all tariffs and quota restrictions within ten years, but there was to be no common external tariff nor any common social or fiscal policies. The EFTA Treaty was signed in November 1959, and in principle EFTA seemed attractive to a major exporting country like the Federal Republic, as its Economics Minister Erhard immediately stressed.[96]

The French-led response to EFTA's challenge, however, received the backing of Adenauer. The essence of the EEC's response was to accelerate its own economic integration in order to make EFTA less attractive to the Federal Republic and Benelux. So the French proposed that tariffs between the EEC countries be reduced by 20 per cent instead of 10 per cent in July 1960, and that a common external tariff be introduced in July 1960 instead of January 1962. In addition, all internal quotas on manufactured goods were to be abolished in December 1961. In Germany the Social Democrats and Liberals were critical of this acceleration on the grounds that it would increase the division between EFTA and the EEC by forcing Germany to raise its external tariffs in line with the common external tariff. Moreover, the acceleration towards a common market would entail progress towards a common agricultural policy, which would almost certainly damage German farmers, and it would also require the development of social and regional policies, which would be detrimental to the German economy. Erhard emphasized the above reservations, but Adenauer supported the French proposals. The differences between Adenauer and Erhard were widely reported in the Federal Republic, accelerating the growing rift between the Chancellor and his popular Economics Minister.[97]

At Luxembourg in May 1960 the Germans agreed to the tariff and quota restrictions proposed by the French, but the French conceded to the German/Benelux demand for a 20 per cent lower common external tariff than the French had originally wanted. In addition, the French agreed to the German/Benelux demand that negotiations be opened with EFTA. Overall, then, Adenauer could, and did, claim that France under de Gaulle had proved its 'European' credentials; that the acceleration decisions had deepened and strengthened the Community economically; and that he was right and Erhard wrong. He could even claim that the Franco-German compromise on the Common Agricultural Policy (CAP) was less unsatisfactory then Erhard had feared it would be.[98]

The difficult agricultural negotiations between 1959 and 1962 had one significant political effect: they brought Adenauer and de Gaulle closer together. Agriculture was of great *political* importance in *both* countries. In general French farmers – certainly those who ran large, mechanized farms in the northern half of the country – were more efficient than their German counterparts, and they were determined to open up the EEC to their produce. However, German agriculture had been assiduously protected since 1949, so the powerful *Deutscher Bauernverband* (farmers' union) was firmly opposed to opening the German market to French competition without appropriate guarantees. Moreover, most German farmers regularly voted for Adenauer's Christian Democrats. German agricultural prices were well above those on the world market and considerably above those in France and Benelux. Indeed, it was reckoned that German farmers were being subsidized by about DM3 billion annually in the late 1950s. If the EEC adopted a low price structure, not only would French agricultural produce be very competitive in the Federal Republic, but many German farmers would be driven out of business. The struggle over the CAP was thus very much a Franco-German one. Adenauer wanted to bind France into the Community by accepting her demand for an open internal market in agricultural produce. But at the same time he had to protect his own agricultural voters.

From 1959 to 1961 the Community institutions worked intensively on the Common Agricultural Policy (CAP), and agreement was finally reached in January 1962. In a nutshell, the Germans conceded more than the French did. The Germans had to agree to the abolition of internal tariffs in agricultural products by stages and the abolition of all quotas, but the common external tariff for agricultural products was set relatively high (depending on the product) in order to protect German farmers. Moreover, the restructuring policy envisaged in the Mansholt Plan was expected to be of particular benefit to small farmers, and the average size of a German farm was approximately two-thirds that of a French one. Thus, through the CAP the French gained an open market for their agricultural produce, while the Germans gained adequate protection for their less productive farmers.

There can be no question that the agreement on the CAP helped to cement the friendship between Adenauer and de Gaulle. After almost three years of negotiations both men could claim that they had achieved what they wanted for their farmers as well as demonstrating their commitment to the European Community. On 17 January 1962 Adenauer told the Bundestag (with not a little exaggeration) that the economic achievements of the Community, including the agreements on agriculture, constituted 'one of the most important events in European history in recent centuries, because they mark a major step towards the realization of political union'.[99] He may have been right in his economic analysis, but he was wrong in his statement about 'political union'. For Adenauer's and de Gaulle's concepts of 'political union' remained quite different, and to these we must now turn.

Well before January 1962 de Gaulle had emphasized that his objective was an 'Europe des Patries', i.e. a group of friendly states who would cooperate at the governmental level while retaining their traditional 'sovereignty', whereas Adenauer was, at least in principle, committed to a united federal Europe. This united Europe would grow out of economic integration, i.e. 'sectoral' integration would lead to an increasing number of decisions being made by the institutions of the Community, leading in due course to a federal European Community. This was also the objective of Jean Monnet's Action Committee for a United States of Europe, to which many leading European politicians belonged – men such as Adenauer, Schuman, De Gasperi, Spaak and Luns, all of whom had supported the political integration of Western Europe since 1950. De Gaulle's concept of a loose confederation of nation-states thus contrasted starkly with Adenauer's vision of a supranational Europe.

For all his enthusiasm for the economic advantages of the Common Market, de Gaulle never made a secret of his opposition to *political* integration. In January 1959 Michel Debré, his first Prime Minister, told the National Assembly that France's objective was 'une Europe des Patries'.[100] De Gaulle, he said, wanted the European Community to have 'regular and continuing consultations between *Heads of Government*' [my italics]. In October 1959 the French Government formally proposed that the Six should hold periodic consultations on political matters and that a Political Secretariat should be established in Paris for this purpose. Though the Italian and Benelux governments were rather suspicious of this 'intergovernmental' initiative, they – together with the German Government – agreed that quarterly meetings of Foreign Ministers should be held. However, in May 1960 the suspicions of Italy and the Benelux countries were confirmed when de Gaulle announced his 'confederal' proposal for the political future of the European Community. He said that such a confederation would require only 'the political association of the States, of the Nations, of the Fatherlands (*patries*) through governmental cooperation

... It is cooperation, not fusion, that will permit the creation of confederal ties amongst the nations of Europe.'[101] This was the famous speech in which he envisaged that one day the European confederation might stretch 'from the Atlantic to the Urals'.

Adenauer, like all European federalists, was very concerned about de Gaulle's use of epithets such as 'governmental cooperation' and 'confederal ties'. However, having been invited by de Gaulle to Rambouillet in July 1960, he seems to have been reassured that the General had positive ideas about the political development of the Community. He therefore agreed that as a first step a permanent Political Secretariat of the Six should be established in Paris. Meanwhile Adenauer was criticized at home for appearing to endorse de Gaulle's 'Europe des Patries'. Not only the Social Democrats, but also many Christian Democrats, saw the Paris Political Secretariat as no more than an intergovernmental body, whose establishment amounted to a rejection of the 'Community method' of integration. *Die Zeit* asked the pertinent question: 'Are we heading for a French Europe or a European France?',[102] concluding that de Gaulle's objective was clearly the former and that Adenauer now seemed to agree with him. In September 1960 de Gaulle again used the epithet 'Europe des Patries', going on to say that he was in favour of more frequent meetings of Heads of Government, but was opposed to any more power being given to the institutions of the Community.[103] Between February 1961 and May 1962 de Gaulle pursued his campaign for an intergovernmental European Community based on the Fouchet proposals, a French plan for regular intergovernmental meetings of the Six to discuss their policies, but excluding any idea of majority voting on these policies.

The first Fouchet Plan (November 1961) focused on cooperation in foreign and defence policy, while the second (January 1962) added economic cooperation. The problem was that, although Fouchet used the phrase 'political union of the states', the unanimity rule was to apply, i.e. the 'union' would be exactly like a traditional intergovernmental organization. Moreover, the French Government made it clear that, although defence would be within the union's remit, France's nuclear deterrent would be excluded from discussion. The Fouchet proposals were strongly criticized by federalists like Spaak of Belgium and Luns of the Netherlands, who saw them as a betrayal of the Community principle of supranational decision-making. However, Adenauer was prepared to support de Gaulle on the rather spurious grounds that Fouchet's 'confederal' proposals might lead in due course to a federal system. In May 1961 de Gaulle had visited Adenauer at Rhöndorf to win his support for the embryonic Fouchet Plan, and Adenauer had agreed to support the General. In July 1961 the Six met in Bonn and accepted the Fouchet Plan in principle, agreeing to hold regular meetings 'to compare their views, harmonize their policies, and reach common positions with a view to furthering the political union of Europe, thus strengthening the Atlantic Alliance'.[104] Adenauer was still prepared to support de Gaulle's 'Fouchet' view of the Community in early 1962, but on 5 February 1962 the General announced in one of his famous television broadcasts that an 'integrated nation' would be an 'eclipsed nation'.[105] Adenauer was annoyed about this further attack on Community Europe, but after meeting de Gaulle in Baden-Baden on 14 February, he seems to have been reassured once again. Or at least he refused to support Spaak when the latter made a powerful attack on de Gaulle's 'Europe des Patries' as a betrayal of the aspirations of the Community. Spaak and Luns then announced that they wanted the Fouchet Plan to be put on hold until after Britain had joined the Community (the discussions on entry were going on at this time). De Gaulle's response was to hold a press conference on 15 May 1962, at which he derided the notion of 'Community Europe': such a 'stateless Europe', he claimed, would be as ridiculous as a Europe which tried to speak 'esperanto or *volapuk*'.[106] De Gaulle's press conference of May 1962 marked the end of his attempt to accommodate the European federalists. The Fouchet Plan – which was in any case barely even a *confederal* proposal – was now dead. Henceforth, de Gaulle's strategy was to focus solely on the Franco-German axis and, as part of this strategy, he decided to exclude Britain from the European Community.

Britain's attempt to join the European Community: Adenauer opts for de Gaulle and the Franco-German Treaty

As regards Britain's first attempt to join the European Community, Harold Macmillan, the British Prime Minister, had announced in July 1961 that the UK had applied for membership. The announcement was greeted with enthusiasm by almost all political parties and pressure groups in the Community, not least by those in Germany, where exports to the EFTA countries amounted to over $3 billion in 1960. If the tariff barriers were removed, the Federal Republic could expect to benefit greatly from increased trade with Britain. It was also felt that Britain would strengthen the 'democratic' element within the Community owing to the long-term stability of its parliamentary system. Meanwhile, the Benelux countries were particularly enthusiastic about British entry, as they were concerned about the growing weight of the Paris–Bonn axis within the Community. Even the French Government at first gave no indication that it was opposed to British entry: de Gaulle stated in September 1961 that he had 'always desired that others, and Great Britain in particular, should accept the Treaty of Rome, assume its obligations, and reap its advantages'.[107] However, when the negotiations began in October 1961, it soon became apparent that there were major difficulties relating to the British Commonwealth and Britain's low food price policy. Moreover, if concessions were made (such as allowing Commonwealth produce into the EEC at preferential rates), these would be detrimental to France in particular. So the Six, led by France, were adamant that Britain must accept the common external tariff and end Commonwealth preference. By late 1962 the negotiations were bogged down. Yet almost no one was prepared for de Gaulle's 'bombshell' of 14 January 1963, when he announced unilaterally that the negotiations were to be suspended *sine die,* because Britain was 'too insular, maritime and set apart by habits and customs from the Continent to enter the Community'.[108] One day, he continued, Britain 'might be transformed to the point where it could join the European Community', but that time seemed far ahead. After a fortnight of protestations from the 'Europeans', the negotiations were formally abandoned at the end of January 1963.

What was Adenauer's attitude to Britain's attempt to join the Community? During the negotiations most commentators assumed that he was in favour of British entry. However, this was not really the case. One factor which influenced Adenauer was that he did not get on personally with Macmillan, whom he regarded as weak in his attitude to the Soviet Union. Adenauer did not trust Kennedy for the same reason. He suspected that Kennedy and/or Macmillan might be prepared to sacrifice West Berlin for a deal on Germany. However, the main reason for Adenauer's opposition, albeit muted, to British entry was that he actually agreed with de Gaulle – or at least if he had to choose between France and Britain, he would choose the former. When he met de Gaulle in December

1961, Adenauer emphasized that Britain should not be given any concessions on behalf of the Commonwealth. And, although he rejected the
General's contention that, if Britain joined the Community, her main
objective would be to promote the interests of the United States, he
accepted his view that Britain would weaken the political cohesion of the
Community (in practice France's dominant position within it). Adenauer
also concurred with de Gaulle's opinion that Britain was not strong
enough economically for membership of the Community.[109]

Throughout 1962 a clear pattern emerged with regard to French and
German attitudes to the British application to join the Community: de
Gaulle opposed it, while Adenauer did nothing to promote it. In January
1962 Macmillan visited Bonn to try to persuade Adenauer to support
Britain's case, but he left disappointed with no commitments from the
Chancellor. In July 1962 Adenauer made an official visit to France, and
de Gaulle returned the compliment in September. Both these state visits
amounted to de Gaulle and Adenauer stressing the significance of the
Franco-German axis, while at the same time the two men privately
boosted their opposition to British entry. In his *Memoirs* Adenauer
claimed that by mid-1962 he was in full agreement with de Gaulle that
sterling was too weak for Britain to enter the Community, and that British
entry would undermine Franco-German influence within it.[110] By the time
of de Gaulle's visit to Germany in September 1962 Adenauer's doubts
were stronger than ever. He feared that the Labour Party would win the
next British general election, and knew that Hugh Gaitskell, the Labour
leader, was against British entry. He also considered that the British were
asking for too many concessions, and he agreed with de Gaulle that the
British were too 'insular'. Meanwhile, the British assumed that the Federal
Government was supporting their case as the Benelux countries were.
Indeed, Gerhard Schröder, Adenauer's Foreign Minister, made a very positive speech in favour of British entry on 24 September 1962, only a fortnight after de Gaulle's visit to Germany.[111] It seems that Schröder did not
realize the extent to which Adenauer was in agreement with de Gaulle. By
this stage the Franco-German axis clearly meant considerably more to
Adenauer than did British entry into the Community.

When de Gaulle vetoed British entry on 14 January 1963, the
Governments of Italy, Belgium, the Netherlands and Luxembourg at
once protested at France's unilateral decision. But Adenauer said nothing.
When Schröder suggested protesting, Adenauer told him that if Britain

were to enter the Community, progress towards political union would come to a halt.[112] This was certainly a very weak argument, as progress towards political union had already ended thanks to the attitude of General de Gaulle. Adenauer's mind was by now firmly focused on the Franco-German Treaty (signed on 22 January 1963) rather than on British entry. He seems to have believed that this Treaty would set the seal on his key policy of Franco-German reconciliation. Yet it was signed shortly after a series of snubs by de Gaulle. Only two days after rejecting British entry de Gaulle announced that France would go ahead with an independent nuclear deterrent, the *force de frappe*. De Gaulle had already rejected the Franco-German-Italian plan for nuclear cooperation, which Adenauer had supported and which had been under discussion from 1956 to 1959. Then in December 1962 de Gaulle had rejected Kennedy's proposal that France should join the United States and Britain in a Multilateral Force (MLF), equipped with Polaris missiles, which were to be supplied by the United States but which would be carried in British and French submarines as well as American. De Gaulle's 'all round' (*tous azimuts*) defence policy and his independent *force de frappe* were in total contrast to Adenauer's long-held policy of strengthening the role of the United States in NATO. Yet, despite these snubs to Adenauer's European and NATO policies during the months of December 1962 and January 1963, Adenauer gave de Gaulle his full support over the Franco-German Treaty.[113]

After the Treaty had been signed, de Gaulle announced that: 'There is not a person in the world who will not recognize the supreme importance of this Treaty, which after a long and bloody history opens wide the doors for a new future for France, for Germany and for Europe.'[114] Adenauer endorsed de Gaulle's ringing pronouncement by saying that: 'Every one of your words corresponds precisely with my hopes.'[115] Soon after the signing of the Treaty the two leaders went to Rheims Cathedral to celebrate mass, giving an almost religious significance to it. Maurice Duverger considered that the Cathedral service was like 'the marriage of an old couple', and then remarked that 'le contenu du Traité est proche de zéro'.[116] *Symbolically* it was important that Adenauer and de Gaulle signed the Treaty of Franco-German Cooperation, even if its contents were insubstantial. It was agreed that the Heads of Government should meet at least twice a year, but de Gaulle and Adenauer had been meeting far more frequently during the past five years. They agreed to set up a Franco-German defence liaison committee – this at the very time when de Gaulle was flaunting his anti-NATO policies. They agreed to reciprocal educational exchanges, but these were already going on, although their frequency did increase after the signing of the Treaty. Edmond Jouve called the Franco-German Treaty 'an *ersatz* treaty'.[117] It had the name and appearance of a treaty – indeed it was Adenauer who insisted that it should be called a treaty rather an agreement – but not the *content* of a treaty, because no institutions were established and no precise agreements were made. Moreover, Adenauer soon had to defer to the majority in the Bundestag, which insisted on a preamble being written into the Treaty before it would ratify it in May 1963. This preamble undermined the whole point of the Treaty, as it emphasized that the Federal Republic would not give up its close association with the United States nor its desire to promote closer political cooperation within the European Community, including the expansion of the Community to include suitable applicants. In France there was a large Gaullist majority in the National Assembly, and the Treaty was ratified without difficulty. But de Gaulle was furious with the Bundestag for adding 'this unilateral preamble' ('cet horrible chapeau', as he called it), which had 'completely changed the meaning of the Treaty'.[118] The Bundestag, however, unlike Adenauer, was not prepared to accept de Gaulle's ideas about Europe.

Conclusion

The twin pillars of Adenauer's foreign policy were the alliance with the United States and Franco–German reconciliation. His Europearn integration policy was a corollary of the latter. De Gaulle influenced Adenauer's *European* policy considerably from 1960 to 1963. But he did not undermine the German Chancellor's long-term commitment to the *United States*, for example Adenauer rejected de Gaulle's criticisms of NATO and gave his full support to President Kennedy during the Cuban missile crisis (October 1962). De Gaulle's concept of an 'Europe des Patries' was quite different from Adenauer's idea of a federal Europe, but de Gaulle made Adenauer appreciate the continuing strength of nationalism. De Gaulle's Anglo-Saxon xenophobia, then, contrased sharply with Adenauer's pro-American, if not always pro-British, views. Yet, who is to say that Adenauer was mistaken to defer to de Gaulle for a few years, if this saved the Franco-German alliance? For without a strong

Franco–German alliance the European Community itself could have been jeopardized in the years after the General's return to power. Moreover, in spite of the lack of substance in the Franco-German Treaty, the Franco-German axis proved to be a key feature of European cooperation long after the demise of Adenauer and de Gaulle. The Treaty may have been a disappointing 'final achievement' for the Chancellor and a short-term political setback for the General. Yet in the long run it was beneficial to both countries, for it *symbolized* Franco-German reconciliation. Indeed, in the years ahead, the close political cooperation between President Giscard d'Estaing and Chancellor Schmidt, and later between President Mitterrand and Chancellor Kohl, may be seen as a direct consequence of the special relationship forged by de Gaulle and Adenauer. Despite all the criticism directed at Adenauer as a dupe of de Gaulle, he was perhaps wise after all. His original hope for a great leap forward to a supranational European Community in the 1960s was perhaps as unrealistic as his excessive faith in the abortive European Defence Community had been in the 1950s. But it is essential to stress once again that, in spite of his short-term deference to de Gaulle, Adenauer's strong commitment to the Western Alliance and to NATO never wavered. The foreign policy objectives and achievements discussed in the first part of this chapter – centred on West German sovereignty within the Atlantic Alliance – remained as important to Adenauer to the end of his Chancellorship as did Franco-German friendship and Western European integration.

Notes and references

1 There is an immense literature on foreign policy in the Adenauer era (1949–63), reflecting the importance of foreign policy at that time and of Adenauer's influence on it.

Among the most important books and articles are the following:

K. Adenauer, *Erinnerungen*. The majority of all 4 volumes is devoted to foreign policy. Adenauer, not surprisingly, emphasizes the consistency of his aims and the success of his policies. A. Poppinga, 1970, supports him. H.P. Schwarz, a more objective observer, points out the inconsistencies of Adenauer's Saar policy, the failure of his EDC policy and the damaging effect of his subservience to de Gaulle, but otherwise supports the main thrust of Adenauer's contentions about the consistency of his foreign policy (see Schwarz books in this note); A. Baring, *Im Anfang war Adenauer. Die Entstehung der Kanzlerdemokratie* (Munich, 1982) [henceforth Baring, *Im Anfang*, 1982] (this is the second, virtually unchanged edition of Baring's *Aussenpolitik in Adenauers Kanzlerdemokratie* (Munich, 1969). In spite of its title, Baring's *Im Anfang*, 1982, is focused almost entirely on foreign policy. Baring stresses the general consistency of Adenauer's foreign policy up to 1955, but he also emphasizes his good fortune, especially his special relationship with the High Commissioners, a relationship which he and Hallstein exploited skilfully. Baring also emphasizes the important role played by the Chancellor's Office in Adenauer's control of foreign policy – see chapter 5 below.

See also the following:

Dean Acheson, *Present at the Creation: My Years in the State Department* (London 1969); A. Baring (ed.), *Sehr verehrter Herr Bundeskanzler! Heinrich Brentano im Briefwechsel mit Konrad Adenauer, 1949–64* (Hamburg, 1974); D. Blumenwitz *et al.* (eds), *Konrad Adenauer und seine Zeit* (Stuttgart, 1976), 2 vols. [henceforth Blumenwitz *et al.* (eds), *Adenauer und seine Zeit*, vol. 1 or 2]; H. Buchheim, *Deutschlandpolitik, 1949–72* (Stuttgart, 1984); G. Craig, 'Adenauer and the United States', pp.1–13 in R. Pommerin (ed.), *The American Impact on Postwar Germany* (Providence, RI, 1997); A. Doering-Manteuffel, *Die Bundesrepublik Deutschland in der Ära Adenauer. Aussenpolitik und innere Entwicklung 1949–63* (Darmstadt, 1988); A. Eden, *Full Circle* (London, 1960); J. Foschepoth (ed.), *Adenauer und die deutsche Frage* (Göttingen, 1990); K. Gotto, H. Maier, R. Morsey and H.P. Schwarz, *Konrad Adenauer und seine Deutschland und Ostpolitik, 1945–64* (Munich, 1975); W. Grewe, *Deutsche Aussenpolitik in der Nachkriegzeit* (Stuttgart, 1966); C. Hacke, *Weltmacht wider Willen. Die Aussenpolitik der Bundesrepublik* (Stuttgart, 1988), especially part 2, 'Die Aussenpolitik in der Ära Adenauer'; C. Hacke, *Die Ost- und Deutschlandpolitik der CDU/CSU* (Cologne, 1975); W.F. Hanrieder, *West German Foreign Policy* (Stanford, CT, 1987); K. Kaiser and R. Morgan (eds), *Britain and West Germany: changing societies and the future of foreign policy* (Oxford, 1971); E. Kirchner and J. Sperling (eds), *The Federal Republic and NATO* (London, 1992); I. Kirkpatrick, *The Inner Circle* (London, 1959); K. Knipping and K.J. Müller (eds), *Aus der Ohnmacht zur Bundenismacht. Das Machtproblem in der Bundesrepublik Deutschland in der Ära Adenauer 1945–60* (Paderborn, 1995); K. Maier and B. Thoss (eds), *Westintegration, Sicherheit und deutsche Frage. Quellen zur Aussenpolitik in der Ära Adenauer 1949-63* (Darmstadt, 1994); R. Morsey, *Die Deutschlandpolitik Adenauers. Alte Thesen und neue Fakten* (Opladen 1991); W.E. Paterson, 'The Chancellor and Foreign Policy', in S. Padgett (ed.), *The Development of the German Chancellorship: Adenauer to Kohl* (London, 1994), pp. 127–56; H. Pünder, *Von Preussen nach Europa. Lebenserinnerungen* (Stuttgart, 1976); K. Schwabe (ed.), *Adenauer und die USA* (Bonn, 1994); H.P. Schwarz, both volumes of his biography of Adenauer [see Bibliography] contain many chapters on foreign policy, as do his 2 volumes *Die Ära Adenauer* (Stuttgart, 1981 and 1983); also H.P. Schwarz, *Vom Reich zur Bundesrepublik. Deutschland im Widerstreit aus der aussenpolitischen Konzeptionen in den Jahren der Besatzherrschaft 1945–49* (Neuwied, 1966); H.P. Schwarz (ed), *Adenauer und die Hohen*

Kommissare 1949–51 (Munich, 1990); H.P.Schwarz, 'Das aussenpolitische Konzept Adenauers', in R. Morsey and K. Repgen (eds), *Adenauer Studien* (Mainz, 1971), vol.1, pp. 71–108; and T. Schwarz, *From Occupation to Alliance*: *John J. McCloy and the Allied High Commission in the Federal Republic of Germany* (Ann Arbor, MI, 1985).

See also n. 35 below, which contains literature of particular relevance to Adenauer's French and European integration policies.

2 Adenauer's foreign policy objectives are summarized in H.P. Schwarz, 'Das aussenpolitische Konzept Adenauers', in R. Morsey and K. Repgen (eds), *Adenauer Studien* (Mainz, 1971), pp. 71–108. Also in his own *Erinnerungen* (see n. 1 above).

3 Baring, *Im Anfang*, 1982, p.64 & ff.; see also H.P. Schwarz (ed), *Adenauer und die Hohe Kommissare 1949–51* (Munich, 1990); J.J. McCloy, 'Adenauer und die Hohe Kommission', in Blumenwitz *et al.* (eds), *Adenauer und seine Zeit*, vol. 2. pp. 421–6; and T. Schwarz, *From Occupation to Alliance: John J. McCloy and the Allied High Commission in the Federal Republic of Germany* (Ann Arbor, MI, 1985).

4 *Verhandlungen des Deutschen Bundestages* [henceforth *VDB*], 20 September 1949.

5 Adenauer *Erinnerungen 1*, p. 259.

6 See, for example, W. Grewe, *Deutsche Aussenpolitik in der Nachkriegzeit* (Stuttgart, 1966), and other key books on foreign policy, n.1 above.

7 K. Birrenbach. 'Adenauer und die Vereinigten Staaten', in Blumenwitz *et al.* (eds), *Adenauer und seine Zeit,* vol. 2, pp. 477–509, and Lucius D. Clay, 'Adenauers Verhältnis zu den Amerikanern, und die deutsch-amerikanischen Beziehungen nach 1945', idem. pp.466-76; on Adenauer's close relationship with Dulles, see D. Oberndorfer, 'John Foster Dulles und Konrad Adenauer', idem. pp. 229–48.

8 D. Acheson, *Present at the Creation,* (London, 1969), p. 342.

9 On Adenauer's close relationship with McCloy, see T. Schwarz, *From Occupation to Alliance: John J. McCloy and the Allied High Commission in the Federal Republic of Germany* (Ann Arbor, MI 1985); John J. McCloy, 'Adenauer und die Hohe Kommissare', in Blumenwitz *et al.* (eds), *Adenauer und seine Zeit*, vol. 2 pp. 421–6; and Adenauer *Erinnerungen 1*, p. 263.

10 Baring, *Im Anfang*, 1982, pp. 155–75; Adenauer *Erinnerungen 1*, pp. 273–83.

11 On rearmament, see Baring, *Im Anfang*, 1982, pp. 175–208; on European integration, see the second part of this chapter, pp. 107–44.

12 For full details about Adenauer's dispute with Heinemann, see below, chapter 5, pp. 165–7.

13 On Adenauer's strong commitment to rearmament, see Adenauer *Erinnerungen 1*, pp. 398–420; for Schwarz's views, see Schwarz, 1995, pp. 554–69.

14 On 6 and 29 August 1950: see K. Schwabe, 'Adenauer und die Aufrüstung der Bundesrepublik Deutschland', in Blumenwitz *et al.* (eds), *Adenauer und seine Zeit*, vol 2. pp. 15–36.

15 On EDC, see below, pp. 98–100.

16 K. Adenauer, *Briefe 1949–51* (Berlin, 1984), p. 546.

17 D. Acheson, *Present at the Creation* (London, 1969), p. 436.

18 *Le Monde,* 16 November 1949.

19 *Le Monde*, 27 May 1952.

20 Adenauer *Erinnerungen 2*, pp. 270–300.

21 See also below, p. 107; and Adenauer *Erinnerungen 2*, pp. 307–54.

22 I shall refer to the May 1952 treaty as the General Treaty, and that of October 1954 as the German Treaty.

23 See below, pp. 101–3.

24 D. Acheson, *Present at the Creation* (London, 1969), p. 341.

25 *Europa Archiv,* 1952, p. 4404. On the Soviet Note offensive, see A. Hillgrüber, 'Adenauer und die Stalin-Noten von 1952' in Blumenwitz *et al.* (eds), *Adenauer und seine Zeit*, vol. 2, pp. 111–30; and for Adenauer's own views, Adenauer *Erinnerungen 2*, pp. 63–131.

26 Adenauer *Erinnerungen 2*, pp. 125–31.

27 *FAZ*, 11 April 1952; *Welt*, 12 April 1952; *Spiegel*, 17 April 1952.

28 Adenauer, *Erinnerungen 2*, p.130.

29 For importance of Federal Chancellor's Office in Adenauer's dominance of policy-making, see below, chapter 5, pp. 156–7.

30 For detailed coverage of the negotiations leading up to the General Treaty, see W. Grewe, *Deutsche Aussenpolitik in der Nachkriegzeit* (Stuttgart, 1966), chapter 4.

31 For information and discussion in this paragraph, see Baring, *Im Anfang*, 1982.

32 Interview with United Press, 22 May 1952.

33 Adenauer *Erinnerungen 1*, p. 550.

34 Adenauer *Erinnerungen 2*, pp. 341–54; and A. Eden, 'Von der EVG zur NATO', in Blum (ed.), *Adenauer und seine Zeit*, vol. 2. pp. 627–31.

35 Much of the literature referred to in note 1 above is also relevant to Part 2 of this chapter. In addition, the following books are of particular relevance to Franco-German reconciliation and Western European integration:

L. Herbst, *Option für den Westen. Vom Marshallplan bis zum deutsch-französischen Vertrag* (Munich, 1989); M. Koopmann, *Das schwierige Bündnis. Die deutsch-französischen Beziehungen und die Aussenpolitik der Bundesrepublik Deutschland 1958–65* (Baden-Baden, 2000); H. Kusterer, *Der Kanzler und der General* (Stuttgart, 1995); U. Lappenkuper, *Ein besonderes Verhältnis. Konrad Adenauer und Frankreich 1949–63* (Bad Honnof, 1997); L. Legoll, *Konrad Adenauer et l'idée européenne, 1948–50* (Paris, 1989); J. Monnet, *Memoirs* (transl. R. Mayne) (London, 1976); H. Müller-Roschach, *Die deutsche Europapolitik 1949–63* (Bonn, 1980); H. Müller and K. Hildebrand, *Die Bundesrepublik Deutschland und Frankreich. Dokumente 1949–63. Aussenpolitik und Diplomatie* (Munich,

1997) – a key source book with documents on rearmament, the Saar problem, the various treaties of the 1950s (ECSC, EDC, EEC, etc.) and the Franco-German Treaty, 1963; also foreign policy speeches by Adenauer, Schuman, de Gaulle *et al.*; R.H. Schmidt, *Saarpolitik 1945–57* (Munich, 1985); G. Schröder, *Decision for Europe* (London, 1964); H.P. Schwarz, *Erbfreundschaft. Adenauer und Frankreich* (Bonn, 1992); see also H.P. Schwarz books in note 1 above; W. Weidenfeld, *Konrad Adenauer und Europa. Die geistigen Grundlagen der westeuropäischen Integrationspolitik der ersten Bundeskanzlers* (Bonn, 1976); W. Weidenfeld, 'Die Europapolitik Konrad Adenauers', *Politische Studien*, 1979, vol. 1; G. Ziebura, *Die deutsch-französischen Beziehungen seit 1945* (Stuttgart, 1970).

36 See above, chapter 2, p. 33.

37 *Zeit*, 3 November 1949.

38 *Le Monde*, 6 November 1945.

39 *Journal Officiel*, 17 January 1946.

40 *Le Monde*, 23 February 1946.

41 *Le Monde*, 30 June 1946.

42 *Le Monde,* 29 March 1947.

43 On Marshall Aid and its consequences, see L. Herbst, *Option für den Westen. Vom Marshallplan bis zum deutsch-französischen Vertrag* (Munich, 1989); for a short discussion of Marshall Aid's effect on Germany, see A. Kramer, *The West German Economy, 1945–55* (Oxford, 1991), pp. 148–50.

44 *Journal Officiel*, 13 February 1948.

45 Cf. A. Kramer, *The West German Economy, 1945–55* (Oxford, 1991), p. 140.

46 *Le Monde*, 18 November 1948.

47 *Journal Officiel*, 25 July 1949

48 *Le Monde*, 14 August 1949.

49 *Le Monde*, 5 November 1949.

50 R. Schuman, *Pour l'Europe* (Paris, 1968), p. 130; for Adenauer's views on European integration, see *Erinnerungen 1*, pp. 295–340.

51 Adenauer, *Erinnerungen 1*, p. 300.

52 *Neue Zürcher Zeitung*, 8 March 1950.

53 For Adenauer's views on ECSC, see *Erinnerungen 1*, pp. 311–16; for Schuman's, *Pour L'Europe* (Paris, 1968); and for Monnet's, *Memoirs* (London, 1978).

54 Adenauer, *Erinnerungen 1*, p. 312.

55 R.Schuman, *Pour L'Europe* (Paris,1968), p. 166.

56 *Le Monde*, 11 May 1950.

57 Adenauer, *Erinnerungen 1*, p. 335.

58 Adenauer, *Erinnerungen 1*, p. 337.

59 On the Saarland problem, see R.H. Schmidt, *Saarpolitik 1945–57* (Munich, 1965).

60 Prittie, 1972, p. 177; Schwarz, 1997, p. 129.

61 Adenauer *Erinnerungen 1, p* 294

62 Adenauer *Erinnerungen 1*, p. 296.

63 *VDB*, 4 March 1950.

64 Cf. John J. McCloy, 'Adenauer und die Hohe Kommissare', in Blumenwitz *et al.* (eds), *Adenauer und seine Zeit*, vol. 2, p. 424.

65 *VDB*, 10 March 1950.

66 Adenauer *Erinnerungen 1*, p. 336.

67 *VDB*, 11 January 1952.

68 T. Prittie quoting his own article, *Manchester Guardian,*1 December 1952, in his biography of *Adenauer* (1972), p. 185.

69 For matters discussed in this paragraph, see T.Vögelsang, 'Politik zwischen Mendès-France und Adenauer', in Blumenwitz *et al* (eds), *Adenauer und seine Zeit*, vol. 2. pp. 37–52.

70 Adenauer *Erinnerungen 2*, p. 377.

71 On Adenauer's quarrel with the FDP, see below, chapter 5, pp. 175–7.

72 Adenauer *Erinnerungen 2*, p. 378.

73 Adenauer *Erinnerungen 2*, p. 377.

74 Quoted Schwarz, 1997, p. 187.

75 K. Carstens, 'Das Eingreifen Adenauers in die Europa-Verhandlungen', in Blumenwitz *et al.* (eds), *Adenauer und seine Zeit*, vol. 2, pp. 591–602.

76 D. Koerfer, *Kampf ums Kanzleramt. Erhard und Adenauer* (Stuttgart, 1987), p. 174.

77 *VDB*, 5 July 1957.

78 *Année Politique*, 1950: full text, pp. 718–19.

79 Adenauer *Erinnerungen 3*, p. 23.

80 *VDB*, 20 March 1957.

81 Interview with Erhard, *Le Monde,* 20 March 1957.

82 L. Erhard, *Prosperity through Competition* (London, 1958), p. 213.

83 Adenauer *Erinnerungen 3*, pp. 255–60.

84 See below, pp. 135–6.

85 *Handelsblatt*, 23 January 1957.

86 F.R. Willis, *France, Germany and the New Europe, 1945–63* (Oxford, 1965), p. 270.

87 *VDB*, 5 July 1957.

88 Adenauer *Erinnerungen 3*, p. 424 and ff.

89 Adenauer *Erinnerungen 3*, p. 435.

90 Adenauer *Erinnerungen 3*, p. 436.

91 K.J. Müller, *Adenauer and de Gaulle* (Oxford, Adenauer Memorial Lecture, 1992), p. 24.

92 See C. de Gaulle, *Le Fil de l'Epée* (1924) and *L'Armée de Métier* (1934).

93 Prittie, 1972, p. 265.

94 M. Koopmann, *Das schwierige Bündnis. Die deutsch-französischen Beziehungen und die Aussenpolitik der Bundesrepublik Deutschland 1958–65* (Baden-Baden, 2000), p. 296.

95 See D. Koerfer, *Kampf ums Kanzleramt. Erhard und Adenauer* (Stuttgart, 1987), p. 415.

96 L. Erhard, *Deutsche Wirtschaftspolitik* (Frankfurt-am-Main, 1962), p. 410.

97 D. Koerfer, *Kampf ums Kanzleramt. Erhard und Adenauer* (Stuttgart, 1987), p. 182.

98 Adenauer *Erinnerungen 3*, p. 432.

99 *VDB*, 17 January 1962.

100 *Journal Officiel*, 15 January 1959.

101 *Le Monde*, 7 May 1960.

102 *Die Zeit*, 17 May 1960.

103 *Le Monde*, September 1960.

104 *Le Monde*, 19 July 1961.

105 *Le Monde*, 7 February 1962.

106 *Le Monde*, 17 May 1962.

107 *Le Monde*, 7 September 1961.

108 *Le Monde*, 16 January 1963.

109 Adenauer *Erinnerungen 4*, p.163.

110 Adenauer *Erinnerungen 4*, p.164.

111 *FAZ,* 25 September 1962; and see G. Schröder, *Decision for Europe* (London, 1964), pp. 188–9.

112 Adenauer *Erinnerungen 4*, p. 165.

113 On Adenauer and the Franco-German Treaty, see T. Jansen, 'Die Entstehung des deutsch-französischen Vertrages von 22 januar 1963', in Blumenwitz *et al.* (eds), *Adenauer und seine Zeit,* vol. 2, pp. 249–74.

114 *Le Monde*, 24 January 1963.

115 *Le Monde*, 24 January 1963.

116 *Le Monde*, 29 January 1963.

117 E. Jouve, *Le Général de Gaulle et la Construction de l'Europe* (Paris, 1967), p. 103.

118 *Le Monde*, 29 January 1993 (looking back at the Franco-German Treaty after 30 years).

Chapter Five

Chancellor Democracy

Introduction

There is no doubt that Adenauer was *the* dominant figure in West German politics from 1949 to 1963. As we have seen, he controlled foreign policy, committing the Federal Republic decisively to the West. He gave his full support to modern capitalism through his endorsement of the social market economy. He helped to fashion the Federal Republic's particular brand of parliamentary democracy with its emphasis on a powerful Chancellorship, disciplined political parties and a distinctive blend of rivalry and cooperation in the Federal Parliament. Indeed, as has been emphasized, the years 1949–63 are often referred to as the 'Adenauer era'. Yet from early in his Chancellorship fears were expressed that Adenauer was *unduly dominant* in the governmental system. Might not Chancellor Adenauer – through his apparently insatiable desire to dominate and control – be undermining the very democracy he was so committed to building. No sooner had Adenauer won the general election in September 1953 than this very question began to be asked, and soon afterwards the epithet 'Chancellor democracy' (*Kanzlerdemokratie*) came into common usage.[1]

The debate about 'Chancellor democracy' is both complex and important. The epithet is of course strictly speaking an oxymoron, contrasting 'rule by one' with 'rule by many'. At first sight the debate may seem rather academic – like the equivalent debate about prime ministerial power in Britain. After all, in the second half of the twentieth century all liberal democracies experienced a major shift in power from the legislature to the executive. All became more 'presidential' (whatever the title of the head of the executive), as greater emphasis was placed on the power and personality of the head of government. And many liberal democracies, especially in Western Europe, also experienced significant changes in their party systems: in particular, there was a widespread move towards fewer, more disciplined parties, which tended to strengthen the executive further.

The Federal Republic not only experienced such changes, but also had a constitution which deliberately emphasized executive power, as the framers of the Basic Law (*Grundgesetz*) were determined to avoid the mistakes of the Weimar Republic. Thus Article 65 laid down that the Federal Chancellor was responsible for 'general policy guidelines', and Article 67 made it extremely difficult to overthrow a Chancellor during a legislative period, the name of the new Chancellor-candidate, together with an absolute majority of the members of the Bundestag, being required to achieve this end. (Only one 'constructive vote of no-confidence' was passed in the first fifty years of the Federal Republic, when Kohl replaced Schmidt in 1982.)

Yet, despite the general move towards increased executive power in liberal democracies, the debate about Chancellor democracy in Germany was, and is, important for historical, constitutional and political reasons. With recent memories of the abuse of executive power in the Third Reich, the concern was that the Germans were once again playing follow-my-leader to a powerful, charismatic leader who, despite his democratic claims, had an undoubted tendency to behave in an autocratic manner. Moreover, the *Grundgesetz* not surprisingly laid great emphasis on the concept of the *Rechtsstaat*, that is to say a governmental system which is subject to a higher form of law entrenched in the constitution and subject to the jurisdiction of a constitutional court (the *Bundesverfassungsgericht*). If Adenauer paid lip service to the concept of the *Rechtsstaat*, but in any way acted unconstitutionally, the charge against him would be a serious one. Even if he infringed the spirit of the constitution without actually breaking it, he could be accused of having harmed the fledgling democracy. Did Adenauer, then, infringe either the letter or the spirit of the constitution? Did he damage West German democracy by his style and actions as Chancellor? Was there too much Chancellor dominance and too little democratic participation in the Adenauer era?

We can attempt to answer these questions by examining Adenauer's personality and his relationship with his colleagues; by looking at the way he controlled the governmental machine and his party; and by analysing his style of electioneering and the way he formed his coalitions after elections. But we must also bear in mind the unusual political and social culture of the Adenauer years. We may well come to the conclusion that Adenauer did bully and criticize his colleagues excessively; that he was paranoid about criticism; and that he used underhand means to control his party, his cabinet and his parliamentary colleagues in order to retain power for himself. Nevertheless, there was a positive side to 'Chancellor democracy'. For Adenauer *could* work perfectly amicably with his colleagues and coalition partners – certainly this was generally true of the first half of his Chancellorship. Moreover, it can be argued that his unbending commitment to liberal democracy and to the West were positive political developments. Perhaps even more important, he converted many right-wing voters to supporting democracy for the first time, because they empathized with his strong, decisive leadership. Finally, as we shall see, his determination to pursue certain policies in defiance of the wishes of his colleagues was sometimes both understandable and statesmanlike.

Constraints on Chancellor democracy

Before discussing Adenauer's dominance of the executive, it is necessary to comment on the limitations to Chancellor power in the Federal Republic. Stephen Padgett has defined 'Chancellor democracy' as 'a deviant form of democracy in which the chief executive's powers were untrammelled by the usual constraints'.[2] Among the 'usual constraints' were (and are) the nature of German federalism; the power and influence of certain interest groups; the provisions of the constitution; and the distinctive electoral law and party system, which in turn tend to produce coalition governments, themselves of course a further constraint on executive power.

The dispersal of power throughout the Federal Republic did of course affect Adenauer's style of government, just as it has that of his successors. The *Land* governments had the advantage of having come into existence before the Federal Government. When Adenauer became Chancellor, several *Länder* had coalition governments which he did not like. However, Adenauer's attempt to 'impose' different coalitions on these *Länder* failed. In 1950 he asked Werner Hilpert, deputy premier of Hesse, and Günther Gereke, deputy premier of Lower Saxony, to give up their grand coalitions with the SPD and try to form centre-right coalitions like his in Bonn. Both men refused. And so, more famously, did Karl Arnold in North Rhine Westphalia. Despite much pressure from Adenauer, Arnold maintained his centre-left (CDU/SPD) coalition in Düsseldorf from 1947 until after the *Land* election in 1954. He then did form a coalition with the Liberals, but it broke up two years later when the Liberals switched sides and joined the Social Democrats, thus ending Arnold's nine-year premiership of North Rhine Westphalia. For five years Arnold had successfully defied the Chancellor in his own *Land*, for Adenauer's constituency, Bonn, and his home town, Rhöndorf, both lay in North Rhine Westphalia.

Periodically Adenauer complained that the Bundesrat, through which the *Land* governments could express their opposition to the Federal Government, was frustrating his wishes, notably over policing and culture, which were both devolved to the *Länder*. In 1950 Hans Ehard, the Christian Democratic premier of Bavaria (1946–54), led the resistance to Adenauer's attempt to circumvent the Bundesrat when the Chancellor wanted to set up a Federal Police Force. And a decade later it was the Christian Democratic premiers of Rhineland-Palatinate and Schleswig-Holstein, Peter Altmaier and Kai-Uwe von Hassel, who led the resistance to Adenauer's attempt to impose commercial television on the *Länder*, i.e. to intervene in a cultural matter. In 1960 the Chancellor had promised the media tycoons that his government would introduce a second (commercial) television channel. But he counted without the resistance of the *Land* governments, who rejected his proposal through their delegations in the Bundesrat. Moreover, the Federal Constitutional Court upheld the right of the *Land* governments to do what they had done. The commercial TV case of 1961 was, however, an exception. The norm in the Adenauer era was that there was a tacit agreement between the CDU regional leaders (whether *Land* premiers or chairmen) and the Chancellor: Adenauer did not interfere in matters devolved to the *Länder*, and they left him in charge of national policy-making.[3] Nevertheless, it is quite clear that the federal system did limit the Chancellor's power to some extent, although not in areas of national importance.

Like his successors, Adenauer was also constrained by the important part played by interest groups in the Federal Republic's decision-making process. Here the so-called 'social partners' were particularly influential, i.e. the trade unions, led by the *Deutscher Gewerkschaftsbund* (DGB), and the employers, led by the *Bundesverband der deutschen Industrie* (BDI). To a large extent Adenauer succeeded in 'neutralizing' this problem by working closely with the DGB, especially with its immediate post-war president, Hans Böckler, in resolving controversial problems such as the implementation of industrial codetermination (*Mitbestimmung*).[4] And he also took careful account of the views of leading industrialists and bankers – men such as Fritz Berg, president of the BDI, and bankers such as Robert Pferdemenges and Hermann Josef Abs, who remained members of his 'kitchen cabinet' throughout his years in government.[5]

Throughout this discussion of Chancellor democracy it is important to bear in mind the unusual political and social circumstances of the Adenauer years. For these undoubtedly favoured the Chancellor's political style. Most West Germans were only just beginning to get used to liberal democracy: they accepted its outward symbols such as elections, but were suspicious of its participative side. They had had their fill of 'participating' under the previous régime – whether in the Hitler Youth, the Nazi Party or the Armed Forces. Quite simply they wanted a peaceful life – security from fear, hunger and danger after the deprivation and destruction of the war. Moreover, there were twelve million only partially integrated refugees in West German society. If Adenauer could prevent aggression from the East and ensure social peace and adequate living standards at home, what did it matter if journalists and academics were concerned about the Chancellor's 'autocratic tendencies'? The post-war generation wanted the freedoms associated with liberal democracy, not its responsibilities. Participation in pressure groups and overt criticism of the government meant little to them: German liberal democracy in the full sense of that epithet only developed after the Adenauer era.[6] Whatever Adenauer may have said in his post-war speeches about his strong commitment to liberal democracy, he retained many of the attitudes of a bourgeois German of the Wilhelmine Empire. So did the majority of his fellow citizens. The deferential political culture and distinctive social attitudes, then, of the immediate post-war generation suited Adenauer ideally.[7] The fact that the Federal Republic's democratic roots remained dangerously shallow until after his Chancellorship was of little concern to Adenauer or his fellow citizens in the 1950s.

Returning to the general constraints on Chancellor power, the most important of these relate to the constitution and to the party system. By a variety of means Adenauer was able to 'bend' the former and dominate the latter, at least during the first half of his Chancellorship. His success in doing so of course owed much to the unusual political and social circumstances we have just discussed. But they also owed much to Adenauer's powerful personality and to the particular means by which he chose to control the governmental machine and his own party.

The Basic Law (*Grundgesetz*) had certainly boosted the powers of the executive.[8] However, with memories of the Weimar Republic, it had also tried to constrain them. Thus, although Article 65 stated that 'The Federal Chancellor shall determine, and be responsible for, the general policy guidelines (*Richtlinienkompetenz*)', it went to say that: 'Within the limits set by these guidelines, each Federal Minister shall conduct the affairs of his department autonomously and on his own responsibility [the *Ressortprinzip*]', and that 'The Federal Government shall decide on differences of opinion between Federal Ministers. The Federal Chancellor shall conduct the affairs of the Federal Government in accordance with rules of procedure adopted by it and approved by the Federal President.' Thus Article 65 not only gave the Chancellor wide general powers, but it also gave individual Ministers the right to run their departments autonomously. In addition, the Chancellor, like his Ministers, was supposedly constrained by the collegial principle, the *Kabinettprinzip*: once a decision had been made in Cabinet, it was binding on all members of the government. Every Federal Chancellor has had to balance these three principles (or competences). However, as the first Chancellor of the Federal Republic, Adenauer had greater leeway than his successors to interpret 'general policy guidelines' and thus to mould the Constitution in the way he wanted. He did so partly through his control of the governmental machine by his distinctive use of Federal Chancellor's Office and partly through his domination of his party.

Adenauer's control of the governmental machine through the Federal Chancellor's Office

The key institution, through which Adenauer dominated the whole governmental system, was the Federal Chancellor's Office (*Bundeskanzleramt*). Its role has been analysed by many scholars, and there is no doubt that it lay at the heart of the Adenauer power system.[9] There is no reference to the *Bundeskanzleramt* in the *Grundgesetz*. Yet before Adenauer formed his first Cabinet, he set up his Chancellor's Office. In Adenauer's time the Office was quite small, its staff never exceeding thirty-five. It was to expand greatly in the 1960s and 1970s, but no succeeding Chancellor dominated the governmental system as successfully as Adenauer did through it. By means of the *Bundeskanzleramt* Adenauer coordinated government policy, kept his Ministers in check, and exerted control over the Christian Democratic Party in the Bundestag. The State Secretary in charge of the Chancellor's Office in the Adenauer era was in a very real sense the Chancellor's right-hand man.

The first two State Secretaries were Franz-Josef Würmeling (1949–51) and Otto Lenz (1951–53). But the really important State Secretary in the Adenauer era was Hans Globke, the Chancellor's right-hand man from 1953 to 1963. Globke had one disadvantage. As a young lawyer he had written a commentary on the Nuremberg Race Laws in 1935. However, Globke had never been a member of the Nazi Party, and he was in fact an extremely able, knowledgeable and discreet colleague. Adenauer always trusted him implicitly and defended him against any attacks on his past record. Globke attended all Cabinet meetings and played a vital 'linkage role' between the executive and the legislature. His importance was shown in 1955, when Adenauer was ill for six weeks and Globke was asked by the Chancellor to take charge of the day-to-day running of the government.[10] One of Globke's most important duties was to keep Adenauer fully informed about what was going on in the various government Departments. He did this by maintaining a network of contacts in these Departments. In addition, he had almost daily discussions with Adenauer, often as they walked in the grounds of the Chancellor's official residence, the Palais Schaumburg. Thus, with the help of Globke and the Chancellor's Office, Adenauer was able to control his Cabinet and keep a watchful eye on all government Departments. Globke in turn was greatly helped throughout the 1950s by Adenauer's chief press officer and government spokesman, Felix von Eckardt, who had the good fortune to be head of the Federal Press and Information Office at a time when journalists were generally less critical than they were to become in the post-Adenauer years.

As regards the *Bundeskanzleramt,* then, it is difficult to disagree with a leading scholar in this field, who has written that in the period 1953–63 'Power and influence were decisively shaped' by the Chancellor's Office: 'In Konrad Adenauer's hands, the Chancellor's Office was the chief instrument of a dominant leadership style which at times bordered on being authoritarian.'[11]

Adenauer's control of the Christian Democratic Party

The other means by which Adenauer dominated policy-making was through his control of the Christian Democratic Party. Stephen Padgett has rightly emphasized that a Chancellor's power is closely related to the strength of his party and its loyalty to him.[12] Paradoxically, Adenauer controlled his party *in the country* by keeping it *weak*, or at least inactive except at election times. In contrast, he controlled his party *in the Bundestag* through two powerful and influential parliamentary party (*Fraktion*) chairmen, Heinrich von Brentano (1949–55 and 1961–64) and Heinrich Krone (1955–61).

In Brentano's first period as chairman of the *Fraktion*, the CDU/CSU was very loyal to the Chancellor with one or two minor exceptions, and Brentano, who was greatly respected by his party colleagues, had relatively little difficulty in controlling them. But, as we shall see, when Brentano was chairman between 1961 and 1964, things were very different, and he was to play an important part in the overthrow of Adenauer.[13]

The only other Christian Democratic *Fraktion* chairman in Adenauer's time was Heinrich Krone (1955–61). A very efficient administrator, Krone, like Hans Globke, kept in regular contact with Adenauer. Krone played a vital role in maintaining the loyalty and support of the parliamentary party, especially towards the end of Adenauer's Chancellorship, when the party was becoming increasingly restive. There seems no reason to doubt Schwarz's assessment of Krone's importance in these years: 'Between 1957 and 1961 Krone was the second most powerful man in the land … As Adenauer became more solitary, he trusted Krone increasingly, realizing his great value to him. Without Krone, Adenauer would not have been able to remain Chancellor for a further six years'(i.e. from 1957 to 1963).[14] This comment alone shows that Adenauer was not as dominant as his critics have suggested. The emperor certainly did not have feet of clay, but in his final years he could only survive with the help of a strong right-hand man.

Adenauer has often been accused of leading his party in an autocratic manner. However, he controlled his party in the country more by ignoring it than by dominating it. He visited the party headquarters in Nasse Street, Bonn, only once during his fourteen years as Chancellor. Moreover, he paid little attention to the resolutions passed at party congresses or the rules laid down in the party statutes.

As we have seen, the CDU's character was greatly influenced by the party's history, together with its electoral successes in the 1950s.[15] For as long as the party continued to move from one electoral victory to another there seemed to be no need for a strong organization. In the 1950s the CDU provided the unusual spectacle of a party which was highly disciplined, at least in terms of loyalty to its leader, yet weakly organized and with quite a small membership. The CDU seemed to be little more than an 'electors' party',[16] whose main purpose was to win elections for Chancellor Adenauer and then go into hibernation for another four years.

Interestingly, Adenauer originally favoured a highly organized, mass membership Christian Democratic Union.[17] The CDU was to be a nationwide social and political movement, not just a political party. But whereas in 1947 there were 650,000 CDU members, by 1954 there were only 215,000. The figure began to climb again in the 1960s to an average annual membership of about 300,000, but it was only in the post-Adenauer period that the CDU began to stress the importance of membership. Just as Adenauer lost interest in a mass membership party, so also he lost interest in a strongly organized party, having initially favoured that too. He soon found that as Party Chairman and Chancellor he could control the CDU without a strong national organization. And so long as he won elections, he and his followers were content.

When Adenauer was elected chairman of the CDU at the first National Congress in October 1950, with Kaiser and Holzapfel as his deputy chairmen, he tried to establish a powerful national secretariat. However, owing to the strongly federalist views of the *Land* associations, he did not get his way. Instead of a powerful party secretary-general the Congress established a five-man committee (*Fünfer-Ausschuss*) to run the party. The *Fünfer-Ausschuss* gave Christian Democrats of different backgrounds a chance to express their views, balancing representatives of the north and south, Catholics and Protestants, and progressives and conservatives. But it fell far short of the strong party secretariat which Adenauer had originally wanted. In 1950 the CDU federal offices were moved from Frankfurt to Bonn, and in 1952 Bruno Heck was appointed federal business manager (*Bundesgeschäftsführer*) to prepare the party for the 1953 general election. Heck retained this post till 1958, and was then replaced by Konrad Kraske (till 1971). However, the federal business manager was essentially a part-time *elections manager* rather than a full-time *administrative secretary*. Thus the CDU had neither a powerful secretary-general nor a strong party organization and, as it turned out, this suited Adenauer perfectly.

In theory the supreme organ in the CDU was the party congress (*Parteitag*). Its decisions were supposed to be binding on the parliamentary party (*Fraktion*) and on CDU-led governments. But Adenauer soon proved himself a pastmaster at using the party congress for his own ends. He simply made keynote speeches and then ignored any criticisms expressed by delegates: in any case, such criticisms were distinctly muted in the 1950s. Adenauer's foreign policy speeches and Erhard's economic speeches were usually greeted with rapturous applause by the delegates. Moreover, the CDU congress did not always even meet annually (as it was supposed to do) in the Adenauer years. The congress, then, was little more than a meeting of the party faithful, who dutifully endorsed the Chancellor's policies.

The other two main national organs of the CDU were the executive committee (*Vorstand*) and federal committee (*Bundesausschuss*). To a large degree Adenauer bypassed the former and used the latter as a liaison committee. The *Vorstand* consisted of the party chairman (Adenauer), the vice-chairmen, secretary, treasurer and chairman of the parliamentary group; it also included the *Land* chairmen and fifteen ex officio members elected for two years by the party congress. Adenauer had little difficulty in controlling this unwieldy committee of sixty members, which met every three months. The federal committee was even larger. It had 160 members – 60 elected by the party congress, 90 representing the *Länder*, and 10 others representing such groups as the party's research committee, young members (*Junge Union*), social committees (*Sozialausschüsse*), artisans and small businessmen (*Mittelstandvereinigung*), economic association (*Wirtschaftsvereinigung*) and refugees' association (*Union der Vertriebenen und Flüchtlingen*). The federal committee's main role in Adenauer's time was to transmit the Chancellor's views and policies to the CDU's nation-wide organization, i.e. its eleven *Land* associations, 390 regional associations (*Kreisverbände*) and 16,500 district associations (*Ortsverbände*). In theory, the federal committee was responsible for all the political and organizational tasks allocated to it by the national party. In practice, its influence was minimal in the Adenauer years owing to its large size and the irregularity of its meetings: it had a statutory obligation to meet at least twice per annum, but Adenauer rarely summoned it more than once a year, and in 1958 and 1959 it did not meet at all.

Adenauer claimed to be a great believer in democracy, but clearly, insofar as his own party was concerned, he was not. Yet he retained the loyalty of the CDU for over a decade. Put quite simply, his policies were theirs: there did not seem to be any need for 'great debates' in the 1950s, certainly not in the CDU. It was not until Adenauer's abortive Presidential candidature (1959) that the first serious criticisms of his style of leadership began to emerge.[18]

To summarize at this point, Adenauer retained strong, centralized control over government policy by stretching to the limit his general constitutional right as Chancellor to lead and direct national policy; by controlling his Cabinet and Departmental Ministries through the Chancellor's Office: here Hans Globke, his State Secretary, played a particularly important role and was probably more powerful than any Cabinet Minister; by his firm control over the parliamentary group through the two very able men who chaired it from 1949 to 1964, Heinrich von Brentano and Heinrich Krone; and by carrying out a pro-Western, anti-Communist foreign policy which united all Christian Democrats and the vast majority of the citizens of West Germany. Moreover, Adenauer had the good fortune to be Chancellor at a time of social and political deference. In addition, he presided over the 'economic miracle', and was able to win a series of elections which were dominated by economic and foreign policy issues.

Adenauer's personality and his relationship with his colleagues

Adenauer was undoubtedly a fairly domineering man. As we saw earlier, he was a very old-fashioned type of paterfamilias within his own family.[19] Moreover, as Mayor of Cologne, he had been used to getting his own way, and when he did not, he resorted to Machiavellian means to achieve his ends.[20] As Chancellor in the post-war period Adenauer displayed many of the characteristics he had shown in his Mayoral days, but he was now in a much more powerful position.

Adenauer was a surprisingly vain man considering his austere upbringing and lifestyle. He liked to be the centre of attention, running election campaigns as personal plebiscites. But it was not only at elections that he enjoyed adulation. Each year on his birthday, 5 January, there was a Louis XIV-style *levée* at the Chancellor's official residence, the Palais

Schaumburg. The day began with birthday greetings from his immediate family, his four sons and three daughters being given twenty minutes to pay their respects. Thereafter, each visitor or delegation received only five minutes. By the late 1950s and early 1960s all the important members of the 'establishment' of the Federal Republic paraded before *Der Alte*: the President of the Republic, the Presidents of the Bundestag and Bundesrat, the presidents of the trade unions and employers' associations, Catholic and Protestant bishops, the Ministers-President of the *Länder*, and many others. This extraordinary birthday parade lasted all day (with a break for lunch), and Adenauer not only enjoyed it but regarded it as politically important: it was a demonstration of his almost regal role in what was supposed to be a democratic republic.

Adenauer's fondness for self-publicity was also shown during the many state visits he made after the Federal Republic had achieved full sovereignty in 1955. He was always closely involved in the planning of these events. The apotheosis was reached with the state visits which he and de Gaulle exchanged in 1962, with the Chancellor visiting France in July and the President visiting Germany in September. These were of course important political occasions symbolizing Franco-German reconciliation and solidarity. But Adenauer and de Gaulle both quite clearly exploited the public adulation displayed at times like these, when both men behaved almost like Roman Emperors. There is of course nothing unusual about politicians making the most of media attention and public adulation. Indeed, this is the norm in modern liberal democracies. Adenauer and de Gaulle were certainly both skilful, early exploiters of this aspect of modern politics. Whether the German Chancellor focused excessively on his own personality is a matter of judgement, to which we shall return when discussing his electioneering style.

Meanwhile, although Adenauer generally behaved in a rather aloof manner, he nevertheless gradually won the confidence of his party and the electorate through the success of his economic and foreign policies. By the mid-1950s opinion polls showed that he was the most respected politician in Germany, even if his opponents thought him demagogic and his colleagues knew him to be remote, distrustful and often pessimistic. Even his most loyal supporters – Hans Globke, his State Secretary at the Chancellery from 1952 to 1963, Heinrich Krone, chairman of the parliamentary group from 1955 to 1961, and Anneliese Poppinga, his devoted secretary – admired, rather than loved, him.[21] Adenauer was often irritatingly arrogant, regarding those who disagreed with him as fools. Moreover, he rarely forgave those who questioned his judgement or his policies. He constantly criticized his colleagues, either behind their backs or openly. In Cabinet he saw himself very much as *primus inter pares*. He once remarked: 'What am I going to do with this Cabinet? The only man I can rely on is the Foreign Minister.'[22] At the time he was both Foreign Minister and Chancellor!

On innumerable occasions he was extremely impolite to and about Ludwig Erhard, his Minister of Economics and heir apparent.[23] Yet Erhard somehow retained his gentlemanly good manners throughout most of the time they were political colleagues. Heinrich von Brentano also remained very loyal to Adenauer, but Brentano's patience finally broke and, as we shall see, he led the parliamentary party in its overthrow of the Chancellor in April 1963.[24] Heinrich Krone, like Globke, remained close to Adenauer, but neither was ambitious for one of the great offices of state: hence, they did not constitute a threat to the Chancellor.

However, even Krone's patience was beginning to run out by the early 1960s, and it finally ended after the *Spiegel* Affair.[25] Krone's Diary shows that, in spite of his loyalty to the Chancellor, he often found Adenauer an extremely difficult man. In 1960 he wrote that Adenauer should stop writing so many critical letters to his colleagues: Erhard, Blank and Gerstenmeier, he claimed, were particularly upset by this practice.[26] Krone also tells a story which reveals much about his own character as well as Adenauer's. When he received one of Adenauer's highly critical letters, he decided to return it with the words: 'Dear Herr Bundeskanzler, I believe that it serves us best if I return your letter of this morning without any comment. As always, with friendly greetings, Heinrich Krone.' He then wrote in his Diary: 'The Chancellor is becoming more abrupt, biased and unfair. I have returned his letter to him. He is mistaken if he thinks I shall allow him to treat me in this way. In our next discussion I shall try to clear the air.'[27] On this occasion Krone succeeded, for a few days later Adenauer told him that he regarded their 'quarrel' (i.e. *his* criticism of Krone!) as over. The story illustrates Adenauer's increasing intolerance by the early 1960s as well as Krone's forbearance. For most of the years 1955–63, however, Adenauer worked amicably with Krone. He certainly had a very high opinion of him: in 1959 he suggested that Krone would make a suitable Presidential candidate and in 1963 that he should succeed him as Chancellor.[28]

Other more ambitious men lost patience with Adenauer in his later years: Eugen Gerstenmeier, President of the Bundestag (1954–69), and Gerhard Schröder, Minister of the Interior (1953–61) and Foreign Minister (1961–66), started as loyal supporters of the Chancellor, but ended by criticizing him for his unwillingness to listen to the advice of his colleagues. And, not surprisingly, the ambitious and outspoken Franz-Josef Strauss, Chairman of the CSU and Minister of Defence (1956–62), had a love–hate relationship with the Chancellor. We shall return to these personality clashes when discussing Adenauer's fall from power.[29]

In discussing 'Chancellor democracy', it is difficult to come to any precise conclusions about Adenauer's fractious relationships with his colleagues. Was he merely a tough manager of men, who inevitably clashed with ambitious politicians? Or was he something more sinister, a bully who abused his position of power? The answer would seem to be that he was both. Sometimes he was unnecessarily rude to his colleagues, and sometimes he interfered in the departmental business of his Ministers, thereby infringing the constitutional right of Ministers to run their own Departments. But at other times he got on well with his colleagues and left his Ministers to run their Departments. Adenauer certainly exhibited many of the characteristics of a chief executive who dislikes delegating. Since his time as Mayor of Cologne he had been fascinated by the details of policy, and as Chancellor he continued to examine Departmental and Cabinet papers with meticulous care. He was thus exceptionally well-informed, but his self-supposed mastery of every subject could lead to his being dogmatic and interfering, especially when it came to anything concerned, however indirectly, with foreign affairs. On the other hand, in areas such as economics, finance and agriculture, he generally did not interfere. He left agricultural policy almost entirely to Heinrich Lübke in the 1950s and, even although he had no personal liking for Fritz Schäffer, his Minister of Finance, and even less for Ludwig Erhard, his Minister of Economics, he generally left them with a free hand while periodically criticizing them.

The 'Gürzenich incident' of 1956 illustrates both Adenauer's interfering nature and his willingness to defer to the judgement of his Ministers, at least in economic and financial matters.[30] In May of that year Erhard and Schäffer decided to lower import duties. At their annual conference in the Gürzenich Hall in Cologne the employers association (BDI) complained that these tariff reductions would lead to a flood of imports which would damage German manufacturing industry. Adenauer, who had attended the conference, accepted the judgement of the employers, and at a Cabinet meeting soon afterwards he criticized Schäffer and Erhard in no uncertain terms for their decision to cut import duties. However, within a week, he deferred to his two Cabinet colleagues, who had stood up to him and refused to change their policy. The reality was that, when it came to the economy, Adenauer knew that he lacked the expertise of Erhard, Schäffer and the President of the Bundesbank (who had also suppported the Ministers of Economics and Finance).

Adenauer's profound interest in the characteristics and abilities of his colleagues undoubtedly had a positive side: it helped him to run a series of highly successful Coalition Governments, at least during the first half of his Chancellorship. He was particularly skilful at balancing politicians of different backgrounds, regions and religions in his Cabinets. And without his overall mastery of the government machine and his knowledge of those who ran it, Adenauer would not have been able to dominate as successfully as he did the heterogeneous Christian Democratic parliamentary group and his multi-party coalitions. However, he also got involved in a number of highly publicized quarrels with his party colleagues and coalition allies. Moreover, he rarely forgave anyone who crossed his path.

In his first four years as Chancellor (1949–53) Adenauer only had two major clashes with colleagues, but his disputes with Gustav Heinemann and Otto Lenz gave a foretaste of what was to come towards the end of his Chancellorship.

Gustav Heinemann was appointed Minister of the Interior by Adenauer in September 1949 and dismissed by him in October 1950 as a result of their dispute about rearmament. Heinemann's dismissal showed the ruthlessness with which Adenauer could act, even although his position as Chancellor was not nearly as strong in 1950 as it was to become after the 1953 general election. As well as being Minister of the Interior, Heinemann was the President of the All-German Synod of the Protestant Church, and he was a close friend of Martin Niemöller, a pastor who had resisted the Nazis courageously and become a pacifist after the war. As we have seen, in June 1950 Adenauer made his first proposal to the High Commissioners about a German defence contribution.[31] This was discussed in outline by the Cabinet on 25 August 1950. Heinemann was particularly involved in the question of defence, because his Ministry would have been responsible for Adenauer's proposed Federal Police Force. No decisions were made at the Cabinet meeting on 25 August, but on 29 August Adenauer unilaterally offered a defence contribution to the High Commissioners. On the following day he asked the Cabinet to make a decision about a defence contribution, although he had *already* told the High Commissioners that the Cabinet had agreed to one. Adenauer at first refused to admit that he had made the offer which he had, only reading extracts from the 'security memorandum' he had discussed with the High Commissioners.[32]

Heinemann, however, as Minister of the Interior, insisted on seeing the entire memorandum, and left the Cabinet room to read it. He returned in high dudgeon, because the memorandum showed that the 'Federal Government', i.e. Adenauer personally, had indeed offered to provide a German contingent (police or troops) to support the Western Allies in the event of a Communist attack. In spite of his high-handed action, Adenauer succeeded in winning the support of all of his Cabinet colleagues except Heinemann and initially Jakob Kaiser (although the latter soon rallied to the Chancellor). However, Heinemann did not. He contended that the setting up of *any* defence force might provoke a pre-emptive Soviet strike. In addition, he argued that a defence force, even in the form of a federal police force, would act as an obstacle to German reunification, which Heinemann and Kaiser, and of course the SPD, wanted before any commitment to the West. Adenauer, however, maintained that Stalin was a dictator just like Hitler, and that force – or the threat of force – was the only language such men understood. Adenauer also accused the pacifist Pastor Niemöller (and by implication his friend Heinemann) of 'naked treason',[33] and, after a number of furious arguments in Cabinet, the Chancellor finally dismissed Heinemann on 9 October 1950.

All the other members of the Cabinet supported Adenauer in this decision. But the incident illustrated two important points about Adenauer's style of government. Firstly, Heinemann was right: it *was* high-handed – indeed *unconstitutional* – for Adenauer to have offered defence forces to the High Commissioners *before* a decision had been taken in Cabinet, and in particular before he had consulted the Minister responsible for internal security. Secondly, although Adenauer could have dismissed Heinemann at the end of August 1950, he waited until mid-October, by which time he was sure that he had majority support not only in the Cabinet but also in the parliamentary party, where his actions had also been criticized. He then dismissed a Minister whom he had never wanted in the first place. It was, however, typical of Adenauer that he resented and criticized Heinemann for the rest of his political life. (After the failure of the pacifist party he set up in the early1950s, Heinemann joined the SPD in 1959 and eventually became a distinguished President of the Republic from 1969 to 1974).

Less than three years later Adenauer had a comparable, although less serious, dispute with Otto Lenz, State Secretary at the Chancellor's Office from 1951 to 1953. Shortly before the general election of 1953, Lenz rashly suggested to Adenauer that a government reshuffle would be desirable in the near future. In particular, he proposed that Krone should take over from Brentano as chairman of the parliamentary party, and that Brentano should become Foreign Minister. This was precisely what was to happen in 1955, but in 1953 Adenauer was determined to keep the Foreign Ministry for himself and was furious with Lenz for 'interfering'. He dismissed him forthwith and, in typical Adenauer style, never forgave him for his 'impudence'. The ostracism of Lenz illustrates rather neatly one very unpleasant aspect of Adenauer's character. He hated being criticized, even by a relatively unimportant man such as Lenz; certainly Lenz was unimportant compared with the senior politicians with whom Adenauer later clashed. Worse than that, he never forgave those with whom he had major clashes (and he alone decided what a 'major clash' was). The mishandling of a colleague like Lenz was, however, unusual during the first half of his Chancellorship. But, as we shall see, quarrels with party colleagues and coalition allies became much more common and bitter in the second half of his Chancellorship.[34]

Adenauer: electioneering and coalition formation, 1949–57

The way Adenauer ran general election campaigns and formed coalitions tells us a good deal about the nature of Chancellor democracy. The four general elections which Adenauer fought (1949, 1953, 1957 and 1961) have been analysed in Chapter 3, and here they will only be discussed insofar as they are relevant to the debate about Chancellor democracy.

Adenauer's first Cabinet in 1949 consisted of fourteen Ministers from four parties (counting the CDU/CSU as one), namely the CDU/CSU, FDP, DP and *Zentrum*. Two of his Cabinet appointees were prominent politicians who more or less selected themselves, namely Ludwig Erhard (CDU, Economics) and Fritz Schäffer (CSU, Finance). Although both generally supported Adenauer, neither was afraid to stand up to the Chancellor, as the 'Gürzenich incident' showed.[35]

The first Cabinet was basically united except over rearmament, which we have already discussed in connection with the dismissal of Heinemann. But, interestingly, Adenauer appointed four men whom his party forced upon him. One of these was in fact Heinemann: Adenauer had wanted to appoint the conservative Robert Lehr to the Ministry of the Interior, but he deferred to the wishes of his party's trade union wing, which wanted Heinemann. Secondly, he appointed Anton Storch Minister of Labour, again because the left wing of the CDU, supported him rather than Adenauer's preferred choice Theodor Blank, even alhough Blank was also a trade unionist. Thirdly, Jakob Kaiser became Minister of All-German Affairs, because the still influential Berlin CDU insisted on the appointment of Adenauer's old rival. And finally, Wilhelm Niklas was appointed Minister of Agriculture under pressure from the Bavarian CSU, although Adenauer had originally wanted to appoint an old friend and agricultural expert, Karl Müller. These Cabinet appointments show that, although Adenauer may have been determined to control foreign policy from the beginning, he was in no position to 'impose' a Cabinet upon the Christian Democrats and their coalition partners in 1949.

In contrast to the 1949 campaign, which was fought essentially on economic issues rather personalities (although of course Adenauer and the SPD leader Schumacher did clash in 1949), Adenauer fought his next three general elections (1953, 1957 and 1961) very much as personal plebiscites. However, in spite of his decisive victories in 1953 and 1957 (see Table 2, p. 62), he was not able to fashion his Cabinets as he wished; and he was even less able to do so after the 1961 election. So, whatever criticism may be levelled against Adenauer as an autocratic Chancellor, it can hardly be said that he dominated the process of coalition formation.

The election campaigns of the years 1953–61 did certainly show that Adenauer was a demagogic orator and a rather autocratic party leader. Indeed, there is no doubt that Adenauer, who saw so many issues in black and white, was in his element campaigning. He was quite happy to focus on his own merits and the failings of his opponents, and to hammer home a few simple truths (as he saw them). However, his critics were concerned that excessive focusing on the Chancellor was undermining democracy itself. This was a particular worry in the 1950s, when memories of Fascism were still vivid. Today we are so used to election campaigns focusing almost entirely on personalities that the criticisms of Adenauer's style seem unduly alarmist. But in his time, and especially in Germany, they were understandable.

At the 1953 general election, unlike that of 1949, *the* major focus was on Adenauer for the first time. Here was a 'Chancellor candidate' who was running on his record. Election posters put the main emphasis on the Chancellor. One large photograph of Adenauer had beneath it the slogan 'Our link to the free world'; and two others stated: 'A yes for Adenauer means our prosperity will continue' and 'Everyone is voting for Adenauer'.[36] Throughout the campaign Adenauer was a stickler for detail. If everything was not organized exactly as he wanted, he criticized his colleagues. He went round Germany in a special train, and at different times Hans Globke, Otto Lenz, Felix von Eckhardt and Bruno Heck were all upbraided by the Chancellor.

As usual, Adenauer cultivated the press assiduously. There was a reserved coach for journalists, and every evening he held informal meetings with these specially selected journalists over a glass of wine. Adenauer tended to be pessimistic when alone with his colleagues, but when speaking to journalists and voters he exuded self-confidence, focusing quite simply on his own ability as a leader, on national security and on economic prosperity. In contrast he emphasized that Kurt Schumacher, the SPD leader, lacked political judgement and experience and would be a threat to West Germany's security and prosperity. Herbert Blankenhorn, a close friend and adviser of Adenauer throughout the 1950s, accompanied him during the 1953 campaign and defended the Chancellor against the charge that he focused excessively on himself. Blankenhorn stressed that charisma was essential for a successful politician, and that it was perfectly justifiable to emphasize the outstanding ability of a political leader, provided that leader did not claim, as recent dictators had done, infallibility. In Blankenhorn's opinion, liberal democracy *positively* required *charismatic leadership*:

> We need a dynamic, powerful character who satisfies people's fantasies and their inner need for security. Without a shadow of doubt the Chancellor has something of these qualities ... It was astonishing how in small villages the refugees and ordinary people waved to him and shouted friendly greetings. ... When I accompanied Dr Adenauer in 1949, that did not happen. It is not just success, which has brought him to the forefront. It is his quiet patience, his clear powers of judgement, and his gift for understanding the psychology of people . And he projects himself without posturing. He is naturally self-assured and composed.[37]

After the Christian Democrats had won the election with 45 per cent of the poll, giving them an absolute majority of seats in the Bundestag, Blankenhorn again stressed Adenauer's key role in the campaign: 'We are all of the view that our success cannot be ascribed to the CDU so much as to the Chancellor personally. This election should be called "The Adenauer Election", because the mass of the people ... gave their vote to Adenauer personally.'[38] And the *Frankfurter Allgemeine Zeitung* came to the same conclusion: 'This is Dr Konrad Adenauer's victory.'[39]

Such comments were precisely what worried those who considered that 'Chancellor democracy' was getting out of hand. Shortly after the 1953 election Rudolf Augstein, the editor of *Der Spiegel*, speculated on whether an Adenauer-dominated state had come into being: 'Another victory like this', Augstein warned, ' and German democracy is doomed.'[40]

However, those who feared that the Federal Republic was about to become a 'CDU state' dominated by one man were proved wrong. For Adenauer decided to form a broad-based five-party coalition. Once again he invited the FDP (48), GB/BHE (27), DP (15) and Centre Party (3) to join the CDU/CSU (243 seats) in a coalition government. Together these parties had polled two-thirds of the vote. In theory Adenauer could have formed a coalition based only on his own supporters, because one Centre Party member had been elected on a joint CDU ticket; hence the Christian Democrats effectively had 244 seats out of 487. But after the 1953 election Adenauer behaved, in Schwarz's simile, like a 'fox' rather than a 'lion',[41] i.e. he formed a carefully balanced Cabinet rather than trying to go it alone.

Although the Liberal vote had fallen slightly (from 10 per cent to 9.5), he again gave the FDP four Cabinet posts. However, he unwisely sacked Thomas Dehler from the Ministry of Justice. Hitherto Dehler had been a strong supporter of Adenauer, but he never forgave the Chancellor for this decision. Dehler was elected chairman of the FDP parliamentary group shortly after the election, and he soon proved to be a thorn in Adenauer's side, as the FDP became increasingly critical of the Chancellor in the mid-1950s. However, Adenauer did appoint another Liberal, Fritz Neumayer, to the Ministry of Justice, and he retained Franz Blücher as Vice Chancellor. Somewhat surprisingly he kept Fritz Schäffer (CSU), with whom he had clashed on various occasions, at the Ministry of Finance. Ludwig Erhard, the CDU's biggest electoral asset after the Chancellor himself, was of course retained at Economics, and two Christian Democratic left-wingers, Jakob Kaiser (All-German Affairs) and Anton Storch (Labour), retained their Ministries. Another left-winger (in the sense that he believed in large state subsidies to farmers), Heinrich Lübke ('Red Lübke') replaced Wihelm Niklas at Agriculture, and proved to be a conspicuous success. Some talented younger politicians were also brought into the Cabinet, notably Franz-Josef Strauss (CSU) and Gerhard Schröder (CDU), who were appointed Ministers without Portfolio. Hans-Christoph Seebohm of the Protestant right-wing German Party (DP) retained his job at Transport. More controversially, Adenauer appointed two Refugees who had been Nazi party members to his Cabinet, the Northerner Waldemar Kraft and the Bavarian Theodor Oberländer. One of Adenauer's main reasons for bringing them into government was to 'absorb' them into the CDU/CSU in due course, for a number of the Refugee members of parliament were considered to be close to the SPD, including Oberländer who had previously served in the SPD-led government in Munich. The evidence provided by Adenauer's Cabinet selection in 1953 undoubtedly suggests that he was indeed a wily fox rather that a growling lion, a man who was determined to have a balanced, widely based Cabinet rather than one moulded after his own image.

By the time of the 1957 general election many changes had occurred in the Federal Republic. In particular it had become a sovereign state within the Western Alliance (May 1955) and its economy was booming. Moreover, the main opposition party, the SPD, had moderated both its foreign and economic policies. In addition, Adenauer's chief coalition ally from 1949 to 1956, the FDP, had left the government. Yet one thing had not changed. Adenauer, now aged eighty-one, remained the dominant political figure. One critic called him a 'demagogic patriarch',[42] and the whole campaign was once again run essentially as a plebiscite on the merits of the Chancellor. Yet, as in 1953, it is difficult to criticize Adenauer as someone who was in any sense 'undemocratic' either during the campaign or in the way he formed his government after the election. The main message in 1957 was simple: 'Trust the Chancellor'. Added to this was the famous slogan '*Keine Experimente*' ('no experiments') – in effect, 'do not rock the boat in economic or foreign policy when all is well in the hands of our trusted leader'.[43] Adenauer may have been over eighty, but he was unusually fit for his age, and he remained a witty, if limited, orator. He visited all the *Länder* of the Federal Republic, and in the end easily won his 'plebiscite against Herr Ollenhauer', as the *Frankfurter Allgemeine Zeitung* put it.[44]

By 1957 there was in fact very limited *real* opposition to Adenauer. For the SPD under Erich Ollenhauer had become a very different party from the SPD of Kurt Schumacher. Although Schumacher had died before the 1953 election, the SPD went into that campaign with his policies. These appeared to be diametrically opposed to Adenauer's in most areas, whereas the policy gap between Adenauer and Ollenhauer by 1957 was relatively narrow. Schumacher, for all his failings, had been a formidable opponent, whereas Ollenhauer was not. Schumacher's background made him very different from Adenauer. A West Prussian from beyond the Oder–Neisse Line, Schumacher had fought in the First World War, losing an arm as a young infantry officer. He had been a courageous opponent of Hitler and had spent ten years in concentration camps. As post-war leader of the SPD he had great moral authority, but he was also a sick and rather warped man. Worn out by imprisonment and wracked with pain, he had to have a leg amputated in 1949 and finally died of heart failure in 1952. Schumacher was in fact no less anti-Communist than Adenauer, but he had hoped that reunification could be achieved *before* Germany committed itself to the West. The SPD had therefore opposed the Federal Republic's entry into the Council of Europe, the European Coal and Steel Community and the European Defence Community. Schumacher had appeared to be much more nationalistic than Adenauer, partly because he was concerned that the Right would label the Left 'unpatriotic', as it had in the Weimar Republic. In reality Adenauer was just as 'patriotic' as Schumacher, fighting West Germany's corner against the High Commissioners and striving for the restoration of German sovereignty, which made Schumacher's jibe at Adenauer as 'the Chancellor of the Allies'[45] all the more inappropriate. Finally, Schumacher advocated a state-controlled economy, although after the initial success of Erhard's social market economy this objective became increasingly untenable.

The changed nature of the SPD under Ollenhauer in 1957 made Adenauer's task both more difficult and easier. It was difficult to attack a party whose foreign and domestic policies were relatively close to his own. Ollenhauer had accepted the Federal Republic's entry into the Western Alliance in 1955 and into the Common Market in 1957. And the SPD's criticisms of the social market economy were very muted by 1957; indeed two years later at Bad Godesberg the party finally dropped its commitment to the nationalization of the means of production. What these changes meant was that it was easy for Adenauer to argue in 1957 that it would be pointless to vote for the Social Democrats, as their policies were similar to the CDU's, but its leader, Ollenhauer, had no experience of national leadership. In his usual way Adenauer exaggerated the differences between his policies and the Opposition's during the campaign, claiming that the Social Democrats were crypto-Communists who could not be trusted with the Federal Republic's security or prosperity. But intelligent voters must have realized that there was a good deal of shadow-boxing going on. So it boiled down to a choice of *personalities* rather than policies. In the sense of the *personalization* of an election, 'Chancellor democracy' reached its apotheosis in 1957, with the campaign being fought like an American presidential election. Adenauer, as a successful Chancellor, inevitably had a headstart over Ollenhauer, who had neither the moral credit of his predecessor Schumacher nor the youthful charisma of his successor Brandt. Not surprisingly Adenauer had a triumphant electoral success in 1957, polling over 50 per cent of the vote and winning 270 seats out of 497 in the Bundestag (see Table 2, p. 62). But in 1957, as in 1953, there was nothing particularly 'undemocratic' about Adenauer's electioneering. He was simply a hard-hitting politician who exaggerated his own merits and his opponent's failings. The 1957 campaign, then, did not prove anything particular about 'Chancellor democracy'. There was less *policy* choice in 1957 than in 1949 or 1953. But there was a clearcut choice of *leaders* in what was otherwise a normal parliamentary election.

In spite of the magnitude of Adenauer's victory in 1957 the formation of the new government did not turn out to be an easy task. However, once again Adenauer did not 'dominate' the process of cabinet formation in the way that his critics claimed he could and would. There were now only four parties left in the Bundestag (counting the CDU/CSU as one). Moreover, two of the four, the SPD and FDP, were in opposition. Adenauer considered that he should include the German Party (DP) in his new Coalition, for this north German conservative party had participated loyally in his previous coalitions. He could of course have ignored the 17 members of the DP if he had really wanted to dominate his Cabinet, because he had a majority without them (270 out of 497 without, 287 with). But he had no wish to do so, as he hoped to 'absorb' the DP into the CDU now that the DP was in terminal decline (see Table 2, p. 62). Adenauer therefore decided to retain his two DP Cabinet Ministers, Joachim von Merkatz and Hans-Christoph Seebohm.

It was ironical that Adenauer, in spite of his comfortable majority, took over a month to form his government in 1957. But the very fact that he took so long shows that he was not as autocratic as his critics claimed. The main problem centred on two appointments. Adenauer was determined to remove Fritz Schäffer from the Finance Ministry and to keep Heinrich von Brentano at the Foreign Ministry. Schäffer had been a successful, but in Adenauer's opinion unduly thrifty, Finance Minister. Their most recent quarrel had occurred when Schäffer had queried the long-term cost of Adenauer's Pension Reform Act in January 1957.[46] In addition, both he and his Defence Minister, Franz-Josef Strauss, blamed the slow build-up of the Bundeswehr on Schäffer's financial niggardliness. However, Schäffer had been Finance Minister during eight years of economic growth, and his party, the CSU, had improved its position at the 1957 election. A place in the Cabinet therefore had to be found for Schäffer, and this could only be done by offering him the Ministry of Justice, which Adenauer had previously promised to Kurt-Georg Kiesinger. Adenauer simply dropped Kiesinger from his proposed Cabinet, and this outstanding debater and future Chancellor (1966–69) returned to Stuttgart to become Premier of Baden-Württemberg. Meanwhile Schäffer was appointed Minister of Justice.

Another prominent Christian Democrat missed out in 1957 was Eugen Gerstenmeier, who had been President of the Bundestag since 1954. Gerstenmeier wanted to become Foreign Minister, but Adenauer decided to keep the loyal Brentano as Foreign Minister, offering Gerstenmeier instead the relatively minor post of All-German Affairs. Gerstenmeier regarded this as an affront and opted to continue as President of the Bundestag, from which position he proved to be a dangerous critic of Adenauer over the next six years.

Adenauer's Cabinet of 1957–61 was in fact more centre-right than his previous ones had been, Theo Blank being the only representative of the left wing of the CDU. The Cabinet also had – perhaps unwisely – an unusually large number of men from North Rhine Westphalia in it, notably Franz Etzel (Finance), Gerhard Schröder (Interior), Heinrich Lübke (Agriculture) and of course the Chancellor himself. Swabians like Kiesinger and Gerstenmeier resented this Rhineland domination, although south Germany was well represented by the Bavarians Schäffer (Justice), Strauss (Defence) and Erhard (now Vice Chancellor as well as Minister of Economics). Still, Bavarians obviously did not compensate for the under-representation of politicians from central and northern Germany. Adenauer, then, had a Cabinet which was to a large extent a reflection of himself – Catholic, Rhenish and Conservative. He had acted more 'dominantly' than in 1953, but it can hardly be said that he had acted 'autocratically'. Whether he had chosen wisely is another matter. Some of his party colleagues felt excluded, while others were already preparing for his departure. The Chancellor was to find – as did Prime Minister Thatcher in Britain after the 1987 general election – that a large parliamentary majority and an outwardly homogeneous Cabinet were not necessarily a political advantage. Nevertheless, in 1957 (as at previous elections) the case against Adenauer as an over-dominant, 'autocratic' Chancellor remains unproven, both in relation to the election campaign and to the selection of his Cabinet thereafter.

Adenauer's final years as Chancellor, 1959–63: Introduction

By the time of Adenauer's last general election as Chancellor, 1961, the political situation was very different from 1957. Although Adenauer won the 1961 election, it was a Pyrrhic victory. The Liberals rejoined the Christian Democrats in government, but their main objective from now on was to get rid of the eighty-five-year-old Chancellor. Indeed, Adenauer's overall political strength had been significantly undermined by his break with the FDP in 1956. Confidence in *der Alte* declined further at the time of the 1959 Presidential Election; continued with the 1961 General Election setback; and went into a downward spiral after the *Spiegel* Affair (late 1962). Most important of all, by late 1962–early 1963 Adenauer had lost the confidence of the Christian Democratic parliamentary party. Some leading figures, notably Heinrich Krone and Hans Globke, remained fundamentally loyal to Adenauer, but important politicians like Ludwig Erhard, Eugen Gerstenmeier, Gerhard Schröder, Franz-Josef Strauss and even Heinrich von Brentano, now considered that it was time for Adenauer to stand down. To illustrate the decline and fall of Adenauer, we can focus firstly on his break with his erstwhile coalition ally, the Liberal Party; secondly on the 1959 Presidential Election; and thirdly on his loss of control of his party after the 1961 general election.

Adenauer's break with the Liberals (FDP)

The break with the FDP went back to 1956 and, although a formal truce came about after the 1961 election, the strong Christian Democratic–

Liberal alliance of the first half of Adenauer's Chancellorship had ended in the mid-1950s, leaving Adenauer considerably weakened in spite of his triumphal re-election in 1957.[47]

The CDU's split with the FDP certainly cannot all be blamed on Adenauer. Nevertheless his high-handed treatment of his main coalition ally after 1953 undoubtedly contributed significantly to the divorce which occurred in February 1956. Adenauer's first mistake had been to dismiss Thomas Dehler from the Ministry of Justice in 1953 without offering him another Cabinet post. Dehler was a leading FDP politician and the party's foreign policy expert. In 1955 he criticized the Chancellor over the Saar Statute, claiming that, if implemented, it would entail the loss of German territory. If Adenauer were prepared to sacrifice the Saarland, would he also be prepared to sacrifice Germany's Eastern territories? Dehler's perfectly legitimate question touched a raw nerve: Adenauer was furious with the FDP parliamentary leader for daring to criticize his foreign policy. In December 1955 he met the FDP parliamentary group and demanded that there should be no more criticism of his foreign policy. In addition, he reprimanded Dehler personally for not keeping his party under control. He then threatened to drop the Liberals from his Coalition if they did not support him unconditionally in future. This was Adenauer at his most arrogant and 'Chancellor democracy' at its worst.

Early in 1956 Adenauer took his vendetta against the FDP a stage further by threatening to change the electoral law by removing its proportional element. This would have been very damaging to the FDP (and other small parties). As it turned out, the threat proved counter-productive, only rallying the FDP around Dehler and alienating it further from the CDU/CSU. It was in this sour political atmosphere that the so-called 'Young Turks' of the FDP made their crucial decision to switch sides from the CDU to the SPD in North Rhine Westphalia.[48] Shortly afterwards the FDP left the Coalition in Bonn, although Franz Blücher (hitherto Vice Chancellor) and fifteen right-wing Liberals broke with the rest of the parliamentary group and continued to support Adenauer. They formed the Free People's Party (*Freie Volkspartei*, FVP), which in turn merged with the German Party (DP) in January 1957, but the combined DP/FVP was only moderately successful at the 1957 general election, winning 17 seats compared with the 15 the DP had won in 1953.

Meanwhile, the mainstream Liberals, whether in government or in opposition, became a constant thorn in Adenauer's side in the late 1950s and early 1960s. They criticized the Chancellor over the Treaty of Rome – it was too protectionist; over his endorsement of France's rejection of Britain from the Common Market – it showed that he favoured an inward-looking 'Little Europe'; over the Franco-German Treaty – it showed that he was wholly subservient to de Gaulle; and over his *Ostpolitik* – they considered that Adenauer's unbending anti-Communism was preventing any movement towards better relations with the East. However, in spite of all these political differences, there is no doubt that Adenauer's highly critical attitude towards the FDP was short-sighted. It was one thing for Adenauer to disagree periodically with the FDP, quite another to pursue a vendetta against an essentially conservative party which should have been his natural ally.

The years 1955–56 were undoubtedly a crucial time in CDU/FDP relations. It is true that after the conservative Erich Mende became FDP chairman in 1960, a partial reconciliation with Adenauer – or at least with the Christian Democrats – occurred. But most Liberals never forgave Adenauer for threatening to destroy their party by changing the electoral law, and they remained firm critics of his Gaullist *Westpolitik* and rigid *Ostpolitik*. In the long term Adenauer's haughty treatment of the FDP proved to be extremely unwise, for after the 1961 election the Liberals were determined to get rid of the Chancellor, even although they joined his final government.

The Presidential Election of 1959

The 1959 Presidential Election tells us a great deal about Chancellor democracy in Adenauer's declining years. It showed that Adenauer had lost his old political judgement; that he was becoming increasingly cantankerous and devious; that he was prepared to ignore the advice of his close colleagues; and that he was determined to hold on to the Chancellorship, however damaging this might be for his successor and his party. Indeed, the Presidential election of 1959 showed how damaging 'Chancellor democracy' could be.[49]

The Liberal Theodor Heuss had served two five-year terms as President with considerable distinction by 1959. In accordance with the Basic Law a successor was now required. As the FDP was no longer in government, a Liberal candidate was out of the question. The SPD initially put forward the distinguished lawyer and elder statesman, Carlo Schmid, as its candidate. Eugen Gerstenmeier was suggested as a possible CDU candidate, but Adenauer never liked the President of the Bundestag and thought that he might encourage a grand coalition (a Christian Democratic–Social Democratic government). This was still anathema to Adenauer. At the end of February 1959 Adenauer's favoured candidate was Ludwig Erhard. Although not particularly interested in the Presidency, Erhard was prepared to stand if the parliamentary party wanted him to do so. Erhard knew that he could also count on the support of most of the Liberals. Adenauer, in his Machiavellian way, had decided that Erhard would be an ideal President, because he would then be excluded from the Chancellorship.

On 24 February 1959 Adenauer asked Erhard if he would be prepared to stand for the Presidency. Erhard asked for time to consider the matter. However, the next day Adenauer told the press that Erhard was going to be the Christian Democratic candidate. He counted without the Christian Democratic parliamentary group, which at once made it clear that it was against Erhard standing for the Presidency, as it wanted him to be the next Chancellor. Moreover, public opinion favoured Erhard continuing as Minister of Economics until he was ready to take over the Chancellorship. Erhard therefore wrote to Adenauer explaining that in the circumstances he did not wish to stand, whereupon Adenauer made a furious attack upon Erhard for vacillating and on Eugen Gerstenmeier, the President of the Bundestag, for supporting Erhard in his refusal to be a candidate.

The matter lay dormant for over a month. Then on 7 April 1959 Adenauer suddenly and unexpectedly announced that *he* would stand for the Presidency. On the face of it this seemed a sensible decision. After all, his old friends Herbert Blankenhorn and Robert Pferdemenges both considered that it would be ideal for an elder statesman like Adenauer to become Head of State at the end of a long life of public service. Moreover, the Christian Democratic parliamentary group supported the proposal. And Gerstenmeier, the President of the Bundestag, suggested that it would be ideal if Adenauer were to become President, Erhard Chancellor, and Krone Vice Chancellor (Krone's administrative capacity making up for Erhard's supposed lack of this). In addition, Adenauer's loyal colleagues, Krone and Globke, encouraged him to stand. So on 8 April Adenauer, the newly announced Presidential candidate, set off for a holiday in Cadenabbia, Lake Como, holding a copy of the Basic Law, and opining that a future President could exercise greater political power than Heuss had done.

At the end of April, however, Adenauer returned from Cadenabbia, having decided to withdraw his candidature. Why? He realized that he would have no influence over foreign policy as President, and this was a sine qua non for him. In addition, he was totally opposed to Erhard becoming Chancellor, and the more the parliamentary group stressed its enthusiasm for this (as it had done throughout April), the more Adenauer was determined to prevent it happening. He did not think that Erhard had the necessary political skills for the job, and above all he believed that Erhard would encourage the transformation of the Common Market into a free trade area and undermine the Federal Republic's special relationship with France. Already Adenauer was very much under the spell of de Gaulle; Erhard on the other hand was an Atlanticist and a free trader.

Adenauer lacked the courage to withdraw his Presidential candidature until Erhard was in the United States at the beginning of June, at which point he made his decision public. Even the loyal Krone's patience was tested to the limit, for Adenauer had criticized him as well as Erhard and Gerstenmeier for having encouraged his candidature, which he now realized had been a mistake. In fact Adenauer *alone* had made the decision to stand, albeit with the support of the above men. The whole parliamentary group also felt humiliated by the Chancellor's volte-face: indeed Krone offered to resign as its chairman. Meanwhile Gerstenmeier justifiably criticized Adenauer for treating a revered public office in such a cavalier manner.

In the end Heinrich Lübke, the efficient but uncharismatic Minister of Agriculture, was elected President in July 1959. In the short term the popularity of Adenauer and of the Christian Democrats dropped sharply, but by the end of the year their poll ratings were moving up again. Nevertheless, the Presidential fiasco indicated that it was time for Adenauer to go. Both friends and critics judged that Chancellor dominance had gone too far. Adenauer had treated his colleagues and close advisers with disdain. He seemed to have lost his political judgement. And he had given the unfortunate impression that he could treat his party with contempt and get away with it. Worse still, the Presidential fiasco showed how difficult it was going to be to get rid of Adenauer when this finally became necessary.

ADENAUER

The 1961 electoral setback and its consequences

By the time of the 1961 general election and the formation of another Adenauer-led Coalition, *der Alte* really should have been prepared to hand over to Erhard. Yet he insisted on holding on to power, and continued to treat his colleagues badly and to pursue policies which his parliamentary party could not support, in particular his blind pursuit of his special relationship with General de Gaulle.[50]

At the general election of September 1961 the Christian Democrats polled 45.4 per cent (compared with 50.2 per cent in 1957), the Social Democrats 36.2 per cent (compared with 31.8 per cent), and the Liberals 12.8 per cent (compared with 7.7 per cent) (see Electoral Table 2, p. 62).

As usual, Adenauer strove to personalize the campaign. However, this did not work as well as previously, since the eighty-five year old Chancellor obviously did not have the charisma of the youthful Willy Brandt (then aged forty-eight). Moreover, in the middle of the campaign the Berlin Wall was unexpectedly built by the East Germans (13 August 1961). The Mayor of West Berlin, Brandt, appeared calm and states-manlike, while the Chancellor seemed to be indecisive. Understandably Adenauer did not want to provoke the crisis further, but he should have gone to Berlin at once to have emphasized his solidarity with the West Berliners. Instead, he gave the impression that he was more interested in electioneering than he was in the fate of Berlin. Both Franz-Josef Strauss and Gerhard Schröder later wrote that this was the moment when they finally lost confidence in Adenauer. As Schröder put it: 'Adenauer had lost his once instinctive, ultra-swift power of judgement ... He ought to have gone at once to Berlin.'[51] He did eventually go, but not until ten days after the Wall went up, by which time the damage had been done. Adenauer's attacks on 'Brandt, alias Frahm' (frequently repeated during the election campaign) were cheap and unworthy (alluding to Brandt's illegitimate birth and his exile during the Third Reich), but in the midst of the Berlin crisis they simply looked like the ill-judged rantings of an old man.

As we have seen, the charismatic Brandt was a much more difficult Chancellor-candidate to attack than his predecessors.[52] In addition, the SPD's economic and social policies after the Bad Godesberg Congress of 1959 were not very different from the CDU's. And although Brandt was as firmly anti-Communist as Adenauer, he was prepared to consider a more flexible Eastern policy. So also was Erich Mende, the FDP's influential leader, who campaigned for the renewal of a centre-right Coalition, but *without* Adenauer as Chancellor. The voters seemed to endorse this objective, as the FDP's vote went up from 2.3 million in 1957 to 4.1 million in 1961. At the same time, Adenauer began to look increasingly like an old-fashioned Cold Warrior.

The 1961 election, then, seemed to show that the voters wanted a renewed Christian Democratic–Liberal Coalition, but without Adenauer as Chancellor. The six weeks of coalition bargaining which followed the 1961 election did no credit to Adenauer, only providing his critics with further ammunition with which to criticize the Chancellor-dominated political system. Almost everyone, with the exception of Adenauer himself, regarded his fourth Chancellorship as inappropriate and transitional. But Adenauer had lost neither his appetite for power nor his Machiavellian cunning. The first thing he did was to persuade the Liberals to support him, although they had spent the whole election campaign claiming that they wanted to get rid of him. Secondly, he succeeded in isolating Strauss, the powerful CSU leader, who immediately after the election had stated that he favoured a Christian Democratic–Liberal Coalition led by Erhard.[53]

On 18 September Adenauer pre-empted any challenge from his own parliamentary party by informing it that he would retire in two years' time, leaving his successor with adequate time to prepare for the 1965 general election. He also assured Erhard that he would make way for him within two years. He conveyed the same information to Gerstenmeier and Brentano. But significantly he refused to make a public statement about these matters. By making his 'promises' to Erhard and the other CDU leaders, Adenauer eliminated the possibility of a serious challenge from within his own party. Then, on 19 September, Adenauer let Mende know that if the FDP persisted in demanding an Erhard-led government, he would open negotiations with the SPD with a view to a grand coalition. As Adenauer had spent all his political life opposing such a coalition, and had just waged a virulent election campaign against the SPD, his threat showed how cynical he had become and how desperate he was to hold on to power. But it was no idle threat, for on 25 September he invited three senior Social Democrats, Ollenhauer, Wehner and Erler, for talks. In fact they discussed the *political situation in general*, and no specific offer of a grand coalition was made. However, when Adenauer met Mende immediately afterwards, he implied that such an offer had been made, and that if a grand coalition came into being, it would amend the (essentially) proportional electoral law to a majority one with drastic consequences for the FDP.[54]

On 21 September the CDU/CSU parliamentary group, including Strauss, decided that it was satisfied with Adenauer's two-year 'promise', and voted to continue its support for him as Chancellor. This decision – together with Mende's wish to get back into government and at all costs to avoid a grand coalition – encouraged the FDP leader's volte-face. The negotiations between Adenauer and Mende, however, took several weeks to complete. The Chancellor and the chairman of the FDP were agreed that the Federal Republic should maintain its strong commitment to NATO; thus, service in the *Bundeswehr* should be increased from twelve to eighteen months. Mende also endorsed the main thrust of Adenauer's hard-line policy towards the Communists. However, the Liberals were determined that Adenauer should show some signs of flexibility in his Eastern policy. And to ensure that this happened, they insisted that Gerhard Schröder should replace Brentano (who was regarded as Adenauer's puppet) as Foreign Minister. This was an important decision. For Schröder combined flexibility with a high degree of intelligence. Indeed, the nuances in Schröder's foreign policy in the early 1960s were too subtle for Adenauer to grasp in his declining years, and the two men soon fell out. Schröder, for instance, believed in a tough stance vis-à-vis the Soviet Union, but he wanted to modify the 'policy of strength' and progress towards what became known as the 'policy of movement', i.e. to move towards better relations with the East. Schröder was also in favour of Franco-German reconciliation, but, as we have seen, he was against the Chancellor's subservience (as he saw it) to de Gaulle. In addition, Schröder was a strong supporter of a widened European Community, favouring British entry into that organization. He was therefore an 'Atlanticist' rather than a 'Gaullist'. He thus found himself on a collision course with Adenauer, whose European views had become increasingly 'Gaullist,' even if his long-term commitment to the US-led Western Alliance had not changed. By the time Adenauer left office (October 1963) the rift between the two was complete. Moreover, true to form, Adenauer continued his vendetta against Schröder for the next three years – Schröder remaining Foreign Minister until 1966, when he was replaced by Brandt on the formation of the Grand Coalition under Kiesinger.

By the autumn of 1962 Adenauer had fallen out not only with Erhard and Schröder but also with Josef Hermann Dufhues, the executive chairman of the CDU who had rashly speculated about the post-Adenauer era at a press conference. He was immediately reprimanded by the Chancellor, who from now on was determined to prevent Dufhues from succeeding him as chairman of the CDU. Even more serious, Adenauer fell out with two other senior Christian Democratic politicians in late 1962, namely Franz-Josef Strauss, chairman of the CSU and Minister of Defence (1956–62), and Heinrich von Brentano, chairman of the parliamentary party. Thus by late 1962–early 1963 it was true to say that 'Adenauer, the great man of CDU party integration, had become the chief of a minority within his own party'.[55]

The *Spiegel* Affair and the CDU's final loss of confidence in Adenauer

The break with Strauss occurred over the *Spiegel* Affair.[56] Adenauer had always had a love–hate relationship with Strauss. Although temperamentally the relatively youthful Strauss (aged forty-seven in 1962) and the eighty-six-year-old Chancellor were very different, they had a number of common characteristics. Both, for example, were clever, unscrupulous and devious. Their similarities led to Adenauer admiring, but never trusting, Strauss. Recognizing Strauss's ability, Adenauer had appointed him Minister without Portfolio in 1953, although his portfolio soon became Nuclear Policy. Strauss made no secret of his desire to become Minister of Defence, and in October 1956 Adenauer replaced the relatively ineffective Blank with Strauss.

Strauss was in fact a very effective Minister of Defence. In particular he helped to create a successful *Bundeswehr* (Federal Defence Force). Blank had been dilatory in getting the new army organized. But Strauss, with the full support of Adenauer, opted for a smaller *Bundeswehr* (360,000 instead of 500,000 men), which both men wanted to be equipped in due course with tactical nuclear weapons. Adenauer's first open quarrel with his Minister of Defence occurred immediately after the 1961 general election when Strauss stated that he agreed with Mende that Adenauer should stand down in favour of Erhard.[57] As we have seen, that suggestion came to nothing, but Adenauer never forgave Strauss for conniving with the leader of the FDP. In the spring of 1962 Strauss was elected chairman of the CSU, whereupon Adenauer proposed that he should return to Munich and become Prime Minister of Bavaria: Strauss was not amused. Finally, in the autumn of that year, Adenauer told Krone that he was contemplating dismissing Strauss (and Erhard and Schröder!) in a major Cabinet reshuffle.[58] Again nothing happened.

When the *Spiegel* Affair broke in October 1962, Adenauer and Strauss at first stood by each other. However, at the end of the Affair the Chancellor sacked Strauss as a sop to the FDP. Although Adenauer and Strauss denied it at the time, they acted in collusion over the raid on the *Spiegel* offices in Hamburg on 26 October. On 18 October Strauss had told Adenauer that he intended acting against the *Spiegel*, which had queried the effectiveness of the *Bundeswehr* and criticized his own enthusiasm for tactical nuclear weapons. Strauss also believed that the *Spiegel* was in possession of secret official documents. On 22 October Adenauer and Strauss conspired to 'circumvent' Wolfgang Stammberger, the FDP Minister of Justice, who thus knew nothing about the decision to raid the *Spiegel* offices. However, when armed police entered the offices on 26 October, they failed to find any secret documents. Nevertheless, on 27 October Rudolf Augstein, the editor of the *Spiegel*, was arrested and, very controversially, Conrad Ahlers, the journalist who had written the article, when he was on holiday in Spain.

It soon became apparent that Strauss had lied to the Bundestag over various matters to do with the raid. However, at this stage Adenauer supported Strauss, claiming on 7 November that the Federal Republic was in 'an abyss of treason'.[59] Not surprisingly, there was a public outcry against Strauss for his high-handed actions and against Adenauer for supporting him. In the *Spiegel*'s view 'Chancellor democracy' had come close to 'Chancellor dictatorship'.[60]

On 19 November the FDP Ministers, furious at Strauss's treatment of Stammberger, resigned en bloc from the Government. However, they counted without the wiliness of the Chancellor, who was helped by the fact that President Lübke was on a state visit to India and was not due back until 5 December. So no action about a new Chancellor could be taken before then. This gave Adenauer a vital breathing space to extricate himself from a very awkward situation. Using all his old political skills and deviousness, he played off the SPD against the FDP, offering the former a chance to enter a grand coalition under him, while telling the latter that, if they did not return to his coalition, he would go ahead with a grand coalition and destroy them by amending the electoral law.

Confronted with this threat, Mende agreed to rejoin Adenauer's Coalition. But the FDP made its return conditional upon the dismissal of Strauss. Adenauer accepted this, and on 6 December a furious Strauss was replaced at the Ministry of Defence by Kai-Uwe von Hassel. On the same day the FDP rejoined the Coalition.

In spite of his apparent 'success', Adenauer was clearly shaken by this governmental crisis, because on 6 December – uncharacteristically – he asked his two most trusted colleagues, Krone and Globke, what he should do next. They both advised him to resign by mid-1963 at the latest, and somewhat surprisingly Adenauer agreed to do this.[61] It was thus not the FDP but his own Christian Democratic colleagues who exacted Adenauer's agreement to resign. The *Spiegel* Affair was, then, the *direct* cause of the fall of Strauss and the *indirect* cause of that of Adenauer. However, the *underlying* cause of Adenauer's fall was neither the Affair nor the demands of the FDP, but the fact that he had lost the confidence of his own party. That was what Krone and Globke told him in no uncertain terms on 6 December 1962.

The *coup de grâce* was administered in April 1963, although Adenauer did not finally hand over the Chancellorship to Erhard until October 1963. That Heinrich von Brentano presided over the *coup de grâce* was indeed ironical for, although never a yes-man, Brentano had been a loyal supporter of Adenauer throughout most of his Chancellorship. During his first period as chairman of the parliamentary party (1949–55), Brentano had occasionally questioned the Chancellor's judgement, for example over his unilateral offer of financial compensation to Israel in 1951.[62] But an incident in 1953 taught him that it was dangerous to question the Chancellor's judgement. After that year's general election Brentano unwisely told a journalist that he expected Adenauer to offer him the Foreign Ministry. Adenauer reprimanded him for his presumption, and made Brentano issue the following humiliating statement to the press: 'The decision of the German people on 6 September has unambiguously endorsed the continuation of foreign policy under the Chancellor ... The surrender of the leadership of the Foreign Ministry by the Federal Chancellor, Dr Adenauer, is thus out of the question.'[63]

As Foreign Minister between 1955 and 1961, Brentano had had little option but to support Adenauer fully. However, this was not difficult, as both men were firmly committed to Franco-German reconciliation, Western European integration and close cooperation with the United

States. Nevertheless, Adenauer did make it clear that he expected Brentano to follow his lead in all foreign policy matters, telling him on his appointment: 'I will keep in my hands the leadership of European affairs and all matters to do with the United States and the Soviet Union.' Adenauer went on to say that he expected to be 'kept informed of every-thing', and 'You must tell me in good time of any steps you intend to take. Correspondingly I will keep you appropriately informed ... The Head of Government, as in other countries, will speak for the Government in the area of foreign policy, unless there are compelling reasons for him not to do so.'[64] Adenauer was nothing if not blunt in his dealings with Brentano. But the relationship worked well until 1961.

Then, as we have seen, Adenauer had to dismiss Brentano and replace him with Schröder in order to persuade the FDP to re-join a Coalition under him.[65] Adenauer had no wish to dismiss Brentano, but he was pre-pared to sacrifice Brentano in order to retain the Chancellorship for him-self. Brentano, who had always been so loyal to Adenauer, found it difficult to forgive the Chancellor for this decision. However, owing to his popularity in the parliamentary party (which he had chaired from 1949 to 1955), he was immediately re-elected chairman of the CDU/CSU *Fraktion*, a position which he retained until forced to retire through ill-health in 1964.

The overthrow of Adenauer by the Christian Democratic parliamen-tary group was certainly not a simple matter of revenge on the part of Brentano. Rather his overthrow came about because the Chancellor had finally lost the confidence of the vast majority of the *Fraktion*. Brentano was simply implementing the will of the parliamentary party, but he did so with decision and conviction. Brentano knew that Adenauer had 'promised' Krone and Globke in December 1962 that he would leave office before the middle of 1963. Moreover, Adenauer's personal opinion poll ratings had dropped steadily in the first few months of 1963 (from 47 per cent in January to 35 per cent in April). In addition, the CDU had polled badly in the Rhineland-Palatinate *Land* election in March 1963, with the SPD and FDP both gaining significantly. The politicians in Adenauer's own party now knew that the Chancellor had become an electoral liability, and all the leading Christian Democrats agreed with Brentano that Adenauer must be removed. On 23 April 1963 the executive of the parlia-mentary party made it clear that this was what it wanted. However, even at this late stage, Adenauer stalled, claiming that Brentano, Krone or

Schröder were all better suited to the Chancellorship than Erhard. But all three refused to stand against Erhard. Adenauer then stated that, if Erhard received the support of the parliamentary party, he would accept their decision, adding grudgingly: 'I do not regard this man, with whom I have worked for fourteen years, and whose achievements are outstanding, as suitable for the position he now wants.'[66] Brentano, with the support of Strauss, the chairman of the CSU, then called for a vote in favour of Erhard replacing Adenauer as Chancellor. In a secret ballot on 24 April 1963 the Christian Democratic group supported Brentano's resolution by 159 votes to 47 with 19 abstentions. Thus, 'The first Chancellor was finally thrown out of office by the party he had made great.'[67]

It was a rather melodramatic end to a bitter old man's career. Even after formally handing over the Chancellorship to Erhard in October 1963, Adenauer continued to resent the decision of the Christian Democratic group, claiming that his dismissal was the worst of the three he had experienced (the other two having been at the hands of the Nazis and the British, i.e. his sackings as Mayor of Cologne in 1933 and 1945). Adenauer continued to rant against Chancellor Erhard, Foreign Minister Schröder, and his own party for betraying him. But after October 1963 he no longer had any real influence over the government of his country. His harping criticisms of Erhard may have undermined the Chancellor's standing somewhat, but they had no direct bearing on Erhard's fall from the Chancellorship in the autumn of 1966. That occurred as a result of the economic recession of 1966 and owed little to Adenauer's sniping at the Chancellor and his Foreign Minister. Nevertheless, to his discredit, Adenauer made a point of making a special visit to the Bundestag on 30 November 1966, the day on which Erhard's Government fell, to gloat over the failure of his despised successor.[68]

The positive side of Chancellor democracy

In spite of the criticisms which can be made of Adenauer as an over-dominant head of the executive, it can be argued that 'Chancellor democracy' brought significant benefits to the Federal Republic. For a start, Adenauer's decision in favour of a so-called small coalition – a 'bourgeois', non-socialist coalition – marked the political style of West Germany in an important way. For it emphasized from the beginning the concept of government *and* opposition, something which had never really developed in the Weimar Republic. Moreover, if Adenauer had not dominated his coalition governments in the way he did, and fought elections on personalities and black-and-white issues, this important concept might not have developed as strongly as it did. The transformation from the dictatorship of the Third Reich to the liberal democratic system of the Bonn Republic was therefore paradoxically helped by the Chancellor playing an unusually dominant role. The electorate, especially the conservative electorate who had never accepted Weimar democracy and had fallen for the simple appeal of strong leadership in the Third Reich, would probably not have accepted the Bonn Republic if it had turned out to be a 'weak' regime. Adenauer's dominant style and decisive leadership, then, encouraged many Germans, especially conservatives, to accept liberal democracy for the first time.

Adenauer's dominant style of government produced another obvious benefit. In a number of areas Adenauer pushed through policies which, although criticized at the time, were undoubtedly beneficial in the long term. In domestic policy, three such examples were the 1951 Industrial Codetermination Law, the 1952 Equalization of (War) Burdens Law and the 1957 Pensions Law. In foreign affairs, an important example of an Adenauer-led policy, which was by no means universally popular, but which undoubtedly had beneficial long-term effects, was the German–Israeli Compensation Treaty of 1952.

Workers' participation in the Federal Republic takes two forms, that which is embodied in the works council (*Betriebsrat*) legislation of 1952 and 1972, and that which is embodied in the codetermination (*Mitbestimmung*) legislation of 1951 and 1976.[69] Broadly speaking the Christian Democrats were united in their support for the former but were much more critical of the latter. There is no need to discuss the relatively uncontroversial works council legislation here. The 1952 law set up consultative works councils in all firms with five or more employees. Although these councils did not (and do not) play a part in running the firm, they ensure that employees are kept informed about working conditions and management decisions.

Much more controversial was the *Mitbestimmung* legislation of 1951. Adenauer used his full powers as Chancellor to push through this legislation against the wishes of the majority of his Cabinet. On the face of it Adenauer's 'left-wing' role over this matter seems surprising, because he was a free marketeer and had been adamantly against the proposals put forward by the SPD, DGB and left-wing Christian Democrats for the nationalization of industry in the immediate post-war period. At first he regarded codetermination as a similarly utopian proposal concocted by the Social Democrats and the German Trade Union Confederation (*Deutscher Gewerkschaftsbund*, DGB).

Throughout 1950 Adenauer had avoided tackling this divisive problem, but when the DGB called for a strike in the coal and steel industries in February 1951 in favour of codetermination, he could no longer ignore it. Adenauer was genuinely apprehensive about industrial unrest, as he had vivid memories of this in the Ruhr in the 1920s. But, quite apart from possible industrial unrest, Adenauer was determined to win the support of the DGB for the Schuman Plan (the European Coal and Steel Community). The SPD had come out against the Plan; but Adenauer was anxious to win the support of the main trade union confederation, as the Coal and Steel Community was one of the cornerstones of his Western-orientated foreign policy. As regards codetermination, Adenauer was well aware that if too much influence were given to the trade unions in the running of German industry, he might split his own party and even bring down the government. In the event, he acted with statesmanlike vision in dealing with this delicate problem in 1951. Although he upset the business wing of the CDU/CSU and encountered the outspoken opposition of the Liberals, he managed to work out a compromise, which satisfied the trade unions, and at the same time won their support for the ECSC. His personal friendship with Hans Böckler, president of the DGB, played a key part in achieving this compromise. Adenauer was also greatly helped by the negotiating skills of Gerhard Schröder, then the young member of parliament for Düsseldorf, whose contribution to the 1951 compromise Adenauer did not forget when forming his government in 1953.

The industrial codetermination bill applying to the coal and steel industries (*Montanmitbestimmung*) became law in April 1951 thanks to the strong support it received from Adenauer, the Social Democrats and left-wing Christian Democrats. However, Adenauer's coalition partners, the FDP and German Party, voted against it, while the majority of conservative Christian Democrats, led by Finance Minister Schäffer and Economics Minister Erhard, abstained. The final vote was 196 for the Codetermination Bill, 151 against, with 45 abstentions.[70] The legislation provided that all coal and steel companies with payrolls of over a thousand should be 'comanaged', that is to say run by a supervisory board

(*Aufsichtsrat*) of eleven, half of whose members were appointed by share-holders, while the other half were appointed by the employees. An eleventh 'neutral person' was coopted with the approval of the share-holders and workers representatives. The *Aufsichtsrat* was responsible for general policy making, while the everyday running of the company was left to an executive board (*Vorstand*) of three. The *Vorstand* consisted of the managing director, production director and labour director. In practice the *Vorstand* was the key managing body, but in the final analysis it was responsible to the *Aufsichtsrat*. Overall, this was a significant move towards worker participation, although not, as Schäffer and Erhard feared, the first step towards workers' control. Moreover, it applied only to the coal and steel industries. Nevertheless, the codetermination law of 1951 constitutes a very interesting example of Adenauer using all his Chancellor's powers to act as a conciliator. The law was only passed after bitter arguments in his own party and in the Coalition between January and April 1951. Although it is true that Adenauer reverted to his tra-ditional conservatism in 1952, when he rejected the DGB's demand that the coal and steel legislation should be extended to other industries, in 1951 Adenauer had used his Chancellor's powers decisively and surpris-ingly as a reformer and a peacemaker.

Adenauer acted comparably in 1952 over the Equalization of (war) Burdens legislation (*Lastenausgleichgesetz*). The background to this law was that approximately ten million Germans had been driven out of their lands beyond the Oder–Neisse line, as well as from the Sudetenland, in 1945–46. In addition, between two and three million other Germans had moved westwards from the Soviet Zone. The refugee problem was thus a major one in the early 1950s – approximately 12.5 million expellees and refugees had arrived in the West, most of them initially without jobs or possessions. The issue came to a head in 1952, when the Refugee Party (*Block der Heimatvertriebenen und Entrechteten*, BHE), organized a number of major demonstrations to bring attention to their plight.[71]

Against the wishes of Fritz Schäffer, the CSU Finance Minister, and the conservative wing of his own Christian Democratic Party, Adenauer sided with those who advocated a generous package for the refugees (the pack-age also applied to Westerners who had lost their property as a result of the war). Adenauer of course had a strong political motive for wanting to retain the support of the refugees, as his long-term objective was to win them over to his own party. So his generosity was not exactly altruistic.

Nevertheless, the Equalization of Burdens Law of August 1952 showed that Adenauer was prepared to act decisively and generously in the face of considerable opposition from within his own party, if he believed that a particular course of action was required for social peace and economic justice. The Equalization of Burdens Law did not meet the demands of the refugees in full. But a special fifty per cent levy was made on all surviving pre-war assets. This meant that those who had come out of the war with property and/or capital relatively intact had to pay compensation to their less fortunate co-citizens. Over the years this levy amounted to the huge sum of DM50,000 million. It cost the fortunate survivors of the war a significant amount in extra tax, but in the end the pain for taxpayers was greatly reduced owing to the economic boom of the 1950s. Above all the Equalization of Burdens Law showed that once again Adenauer was quite prepared to use his considerable powers as Chancellor in the interests of social peace and solidarity.

A final example of Adenauer exerting his personal power to achieve a domestic reform opposed by the economists and financiers in his Coalition was the Pensions Act of January 1957. Again, Adenauer showed a mixture of political realism and social altruism in advocating an expensive pensions reform with such obstinate determination. For Adenauer, like Bismarck, was genuinely interested in social legislation, even if foreign policy was the main concern of both statesmen. After the Federal Republic had achieved full sovereignty in 1955 and Adenauer had officially handed over foreign policy to Brentano, he set up a social affairs commission under his own chairmanship, telling the CDU executive that he intended concentrating more on social affairs. In practice he concentrated on pensions. The argument about pensions reform was complex and went on for over a year. But, after bitter debates in Cabinet, the CDU executive and the Bundestag, Adenauer's will prevailed. The result was the Pensions Act of January 1957. The Federal Republic introduced a nationwide system of index-linked pensions, with the working generation paying for the pensions of those who had retired. Each month a percentage of each employee's gross income was paid into a national pension fund, from which the retired generation received their pensions. These were fixed at a level which reflected the current cost of living, and were not related, as previously, to the contributions the pensioners had made during their working lives. This was an excellent deal for pensioners. Nevertheless, it was surprising that Adenauer advocated this scheme so strongly, because Fritz Schäffer, the Finance Minister, and Ludwig Erhard, the Economics Minister, were against it. They pointed out – quite rightly – that, although such a scheme might work well in times of economic growth, it would incur enormous costs on the Federal budget in times of recession or zero growth. Adenauer, as we have seen, was instinctively conservative in economic and financial matters. Yet his relatively humble background gave him an understanding of the security concerns of ordinary citizens. In the great pensions debate of 1956–57 Adenauer was at first in a minority in his own party when he advocated the expensive new scheme. But in his usual dogged way, once he had set his mind on something, he stuck to it, eventually winning over the Cabinet (just) and the CDU parliamentary party (by a small majority). In practice the new Pensions Law of January 1957 proved very popular, if in the long run very costly. It undoubtedly helped the Christian Democrats to win the 1957 general election, which was clearly one of Adenauer's objectives. Thus, there is no reason to question Schwarz's contention that 'without the determined resolution of the Chancellor' the 1957 Pensions Act would never have reached the statute book: 'It is justifiable therefore to speak of it as Adenauer's Pension Reform Act.'[72]

Adenauer and Israel

If an important aspect of 'Chancellor democracy' was unilateral action by the Chancellor without consulting his Cabinet or parliamentary party, then the German–Israeli Compensation Treaty of September 1952 provides a perfect example of Adenauer acting in this way. Yet, with the hindsight of history, his high-handed behaviour over this matter was fully justified, or at least fully comprehensible. Of course, Adenauer consulted his Cabinet and colleagues about the background to and final details of the Treaty. But on two occasions his personal role in the policy-making process was crucial, and on both occasions he made vital decisions unilaterally. The first was in December 1951, when he met Nahum Goldmann, President of the World Jewish Congress, in London and made an important decision about the level of compensation. The second was in May 1952 when he acted in a similar way to unblock the negotiations which had stalled as a result of financial disagreements. The full story of German–Israeli relations in the Adenauer years and the Compensation

Treaty of September 1952 need not concern us here, except insofar as they illustrate 'Chancellor democracy' working in a positive way.[73]

One of the ironies of Hitler's Jewish policy was that German Jews had in general been better assimilated than those in any other part of Europe before the Nazis came to power. But in spite of the high degree of assimilation of German Jews, the Jewish community was more or less eliminated during the Third Reich. In 1945 only 30,000 of the 600,000 German Jews of 1933 were still alive, and Adenauer, unlike some Germans, felt deep shame about the Holocaust, which had cost the lives of up to 6 million European Jews.

In the immediate post-war period it was almost impossible to conceive how the Jews could ever be reconciled to the Germans. Moreover, many Jews had no wish to be reconciled. Any notion of financial compensation – 'money' for 'blood' – was anathema to them. Yet Israel, whither most of the survivors of the Holocaust had gone, had one thing in common with Germany. Its economy was in desperate straits for several years after the founding of the State of Israel (1948). Indeed by 1951 its problems were much worse than those of West Germany, and Ben Gurion, Israel's first Prime Minister, realized that, however repugnant it might be, German money could help Israel to survive. Meanwhile, Adenauer was determined to try to compensate the Jews for past wrongs, although he realized that material compensation, however great, could never make up for the crimes committed by the Nazis.

As early as November 1949 Adenauer had stated that 'The State of Israel has come to represent Jewry as a whole. The Federal Government, as an earnest of its intention to make amends for the wrongs which Germany has inflicted upon the Jews, will put development aid at Israel's disposal.'[74] The problem came to a head in 1951, for although by that year West Germany had already begun to compensate *individual* Jewish claims, neither it nor East Germany could under international law be compelled to pay compensation to the State of Israel, which had not even existed when the Nazis committed their crimes against the Jews. Moreover, there had been no pressure from the Allies to compensate Israel, because there was a general view that any form of reparations would prevent the revival of the German economy. If monetary compensation had been agreed, the Germans simply could not have paid anything owing to their own severe economic problems up to 1951. As the Americans realized, it would be *their* taxpayers who would have to pay the compensation, with Marshall

Aid in practice being siphoned off from Germany to Israel. Nevertheless, the problem was urgent by 1951, as West Germany was in the process of negotiating full sovereignty. If this were achieved, it would be difficult for the Allies to pressurize the Germans into paying compensation to Israel.

On 16 January 1951 the Israeli Government sent a formal Note to the Four Allies protesting about the lack of compensation except that paid to individual Jews. This was followed on 16 March by a Note demanding that Germany pay the (then) enormous sum of 1,500 million US dollars (1,000 million from West Germany and 500 million from East Germany) to offset the costs of settling the half million Jews who had arrived in Israel as a direct or indirect result of Nazi persecution. The Russians did not reply (they were intent on taking all they could in reparations for themselves) and the Western Allies, reluctant to pressurize a weak West Germany, proposed direct negotiations with the Germans, although such negotiations were anathema to most Jews. Adenauer, however, insisted on responding positively to the Israeli Note of 16 March 1951. At first this response could only be made in secret, because the subject was too sensitive for the Germans and the Israelis to discuss openly, but Adenauer's close adviser, Herbert Blankenhorn, held preliminary discussions in London with Noah Barou of the Jewish World Congress in the summer of 1951. After further indirect discussions with Nahum Goldmann, President of the same Congress, and Ben Gurion, Prime Minister of Israel, Adenauer announced to the Bundestag on 27 September 1951 that the Federal Government was ready to open negotiations about compensation with the Israeli Government and representatives of world Jewish organizations. He added that, although the German people could not be held collectively responsible for the crimes committed by the Nazis, the German Government had a moral obligation to provide compensation not only to the Jews but to other victims of the Nazis, including the twelve million German refugees expelled from the East.[75]

The response to Adenauer's speech was at first low-key. Most Israelis were very doubtful about the morality of accepting anything from the blood-stained hands of the Germans, while most Germans were too engrossed in rebuilding their country to pay any attention to Adenauer's important offer. But the impoverished Israeli Government was very interested in Adenauer's offer, and after further discreet contacts Adenauer met Nahum Goldmann, by now President of the Jewish Claims Conference (set up in October 1951 to coordinate the claims of the twenty organizations with claims against Germany) as well as of the World Jewish Conference, in London.

By all accounts the secret meeting between Adenauer and Goldmann in Claridge's Hotel on 6 December 1951 was not only an emotional one – the two men knew exactly what they were talking about – but a politically significant one.[76] Adenauer and Goldmann immediately established a high degree of empathy and trust. Adenauer asked Goldmann to present his case first. In a short statement Goldmann admitted that Israel could not compel Germany under international law to pay compensation. However, he believed that if Germany were to make a large sum of money available, this would be a very important moral gesture which would act as a catalyst in the healing process. The gesture would have to be financially significant and without strings, or it should not be made at all. Adenauer tells us that he was deeply moved by Goldmann's appeal, and at once asked him to draft the letter he (Goldmann) would like to receive from him (Adenauer). Without consulting his Cabinet, Adenauer agreed to the wording of the letter drafted by Goldmann. The key sentence was: 'The Federal Government is prepared to accept the claims made by the State of Israel in its Note of 16 March 1951.'[77] Thus Adenauer personally made the decision to negotiate with the Israeli Government on the basis of its March 1951 demand for 1,500 million US dollars in compensation. In Israel there were violent demonstrations against the offer, and Goldmann's life was threatened. But the Knesset voted in favour of negotiations by 60–31. Meanwhile, in Germany Adenauer was fiercely criticized for making such a large financial commitment without consulting his colleagues. In particular Vice-Chancellor Blücher and most of the FDP, as well as Fritz Schäffer, the Finance Minister, contended that Germany could not afford to pay such a huge sum of money without seriously undermining its own economic recovery. Meanwhile, Heinrich von Brentano, on behalf of the parliamentary group, criticized the Chancellor for making this commitment without consulting his Cabinet, although the group was not necessarily against the offer as such.[78]

When negotiations about the details of the compensation package opened in The Hague in March 1952, the German delegation was led by Franz Böhm, a Frankfurt Law Professor, and the Israeli delegation by Felix Shinnar. One of the biggest problems was that in London another German delegation, led by the banker Hermann Josef Abs, was trying to minimize Germany's payments at an international conference on Germany's pre-

and post-war debts. Abs found it difficult to claim that Germany could not afford to pay more than a proportion of the 'reparations' demanded at the London Debts Conference attended by thirty claimant nations, while Böhm was apparently on the verge of agreeing to pay a huge sum to Israel at The Hague. Abs, not unreasonably, wanted either to postpone the Israeli negotiations till after agreement had been reached in London, so that Germany would know what it could reasonably afford to pay, or to include Israel in the London negotiations.

At an important meeting on 5 April 1952 attended by Adenauer, Erhard, Abs, Böhm and Hallstein, Adenauer insisted that the compensation to be paid to Israel was different in kind from all the others; therefore the negotiations should be kept separate. In addition, he contended that if an agreement were reached with the Israelis, the Americans would put pressure on the participants at the London conference to moderate their demands. The Americans, he said, would do this, because the Israeli Government appeared to be on the verge of collapse owing to its desperate financial situation. At this meeting Erhard, in contrast to the line taken by Abs and Schäffer, argued that West Germany *could* pay Israel approximately what was being demanded, *provided* the bulk of the payment was in goods spread over several years. He maintained that, although the Federal Republic was very short of foreign currency, the economy was definitely improving (in 1951 the balance of payments had been in the black for the first time since the war); moreover, production would be stimulated further if the Israelis were provided with appropriate capital goods. Although the German taxpayer would of course have to pay for these, there would be economic spin-off in the long term: German industry would benefit, while the Israelis would get what they desperately needed. Nevertheless, the Federal Government was in a difficult position. There is no question that Adenauer himself did want to make a generous gesture towards Israel. But it was awkward for him to do so in the middle of the London Debts Conference, and also at a time when the negotiations over the European Defence Community and German sovereignty (the General Treaty) were reaching their climax.[79] Adenauer was concerned that the Federal Republic might not achieve the signing of these Treaties (they were in fact signed on 26–27 May 1952), if satisfactory agreements could not be reached in London and The Hague about German debts and Israeli compensation.

On 20 April 1952 Adenauer and Goldmann met in private at Rhöndorf to try to resolve the deadlock at The Hague. Goldmann asked if the

Germans were going to renege on Adenauer's promises of December 1951. Adenauer told Goldmann that the Germans were not going to renege, but it was necessary to work out what they could realistically pay. Meanwhile, in London, Abs worsened the situation by telling Felix Shinnar, the chief Israeli delegate at The Hague, that Germany could not possibly afford the sums 'agreed' by Adenauer and Goldmann in December 1951. Instead he offered approximately half of the 'agreed' figure. Shinnar rejected this offer, and Goldmann wrote at once to Adenauer: 'The contrast between Abs's proposal and all that you, Herr Bundeskanzler, have told me in private conversations is so extraordinary that I cannot believe it represents your views.'[80] In his *Memoirs* Adenauer claims that he had no prior knowledge of Abs's offer.[81] So he decided to intervene personally at this point without consulting his Cabinet. He immediately sent Böhm to meet Goldmann in Paris (23 May 1952) with a specific offer of 760 million US dollars in goods spread over 8–12 years plus 150 million US dollars to be given to the Israeli Government for distribution among the Jewish relief organizations. The total offered was approximately three-fifths of what Adenauer had 'promised' in London in December 1951. Nevertheless, it was a huge offer in terms of the monetary values of the early 1950s. Goldmann therefore agreed to accept it on behalf of the Israeli Government. Finally, on 10 September 1952 Adenauer and Goldmann signed the German–Israeli Compensation Treaty in Luxembourg (it could not be signed in Germany owing to threats from Jewish extremists). It was ratified soon afterwards in the Israeli Knesset and on 4 March 1953 in the German Bundestag. Adenauer spoke decisively in favour of the Treaty as a significant, if inadequate, step towards reconciliation. He received the unanimous support of the SPD, but the Communists and two small right-wing parties voted against it, while 86 members of his Coalition, including Fritz Schäffer, the Finance Minister, and the whole of the Bavarian CSU, abstained. The final vote was carried by 288–35 with 86 abstentions. After the vote all members of the Bundestag stood and observed a minute's silence.

Overall, the German–Israeli Compensation Treaty of 1952 was a major achievement. It constituted an example of the beneficial side of 'Chancellor democracy', because two unilateral decisions by Adenauer (in December 1951 and in May 1952) played a vital part in achieving the agreement. In the next twelve years the Federal Republic made a significant economic contribution to the young State of Israel. The West

Germans provided the Israelis with almost their entire fleet (60 passenger ships, 41 merchantmen and 4 oil tankers), a floating dock, a copper smelting works, a steel works, and thousands of vehicles and machine tools. Perhaps as important as this huge financial package was the moral gesture, which opened the way to a remarkable degree of German–Israeli reconciliation. No sum of money could ever expunge the past. But Adenauer personally had acted with great moral and political courage. Arguably he promised too much and granted more than was wise in the economic circumstances of the time. But in this case fortune favoured the bold, for from 1953 West German prosperity began to increase dramatically. There is no doubt that Adenauer's conduct over compensation to the Jews was motivated to some degree by realpolitik, especially by the Chancellor's desire to win the support and approval of the United States, including its large Jewish community. But it is difficult to disagree with Nahum Goldmann, who considered that Adenauer put morals before politics in dealing with compensation for the Jews.[82] It was one of those areas of policy-making in which he exercised his Chancellor's powers to the full – indeed at times beyond the full – to the long-term benefit of both sides.

Conclusion

As pointed out at the beginning of this chapter, the debate about 'Chancellor democracy' is complex but important. Adenauer can justifiably be criticized for his autocratic style, and he did occasionally act unconstitutionally. But he was not a 'democratic dictator', to use the epithet of one of his more critical biographers.[83] Adenauer was certainly domineering, over-critical and devious. But he was also sincerely committed to liberal democracy. If he had not been so determined to make German democracy work at the second attempt, he would have remained at Rhöndorf growing roses in 1945 when he was already in his seventieth year. It is true that he acted unconstitutionally over defence in 1950, over Israeli compensation in 1951 and during the *Spiegel* Affair in 1962. It is also true that he waged endless vendettas against anyone who criticized him, whether they were political opponents (Schumacher and Brandt), colleagues (Erhard, Schröder and Gerstenmaier), or political allies (the Liberals from 1955 to 1963). Moreover, Adenauer undoubtedly often acted in a 'presidential' manner, regarding elections as personal plebiscites and courting public adulation at other times, but acting in a 'presidential' manner hardly made him into a quasi-dictator.

We should always remember that, however much he tried, Adenauer could not 'control' the new Republic. He was constrained both by the constitution and by the federal system. And, as we have seen, Adenauer could not and did not dominate his Cabinets. There were five parties in his coalitions of 1949 and 1953, four in that of 1957, and three in that of 1961, in each case counting the CDU and CSU as separate parties, which strictly speaking they were, even although they formed one parliamentary group. But even if the CDU/CSU is regarded as one Christian Democratic Party, all Adenauer's governments were *coalitions*. Throughout his Chancellorship he had to take account not only of the frequently critical views of the CSU but also of those of his other coalition partners, notably the FDP, who for example insisted on the appointment of Schröder to Foreign Affairs in 1961 and the dismissal of Strauss from Defence in 1962. In addition, Adenauer was very dependent on Krone and Globke during the last six years of his Chancellorship. And most important of all, the fact that he was overthrown by his own parliamentary party (just like Mrs Thatcher in Britain in 1990) showed that parliamentary democracy was fully functional in the Federal Republic by the end of the 'Adenauer era'. It may have taken an unconscionable time to get rid of *der Alte*, but he went quietly enough in the end after the *Fraktion* voted against him.

In the last analysis, then, we can certainly say that Adenauer – in spite of his *personal* autocratic tendencies – was genuinely committed to liberal democracy, and that for 95 per cent of the time he acted within the parameters of the *Grundgesetz* and the *Rechtsstaat*. 'Chancellor democracy' existed in the sense that the Federal Republic had a very powerful chief executive in the Adenauer years (1949–63), or, to be more precise, it had such a person until 1961. It did not exist in the sense of its having an *autocratic* Chancellor.[84]

Notes and references

1 There is a considerable literature on Chancellor Democracy. See especially A. Baring, *Im Anfang war Adenauer. Die Entstehung der Kanzlerdemokratie* (Munich, 1982) [henceforth Baring, *Im Anfang*, 1982]; K.D. Bracher, 'Die Kanzlerdemokratie', in R. Löwenthal and H.P. Schwarz, *Die Zweite Republik. 25 Jahre Bundesrepublik Deutschlands. Eine Bilanz* (Stuttgart, 1974), pp. 172–202; J. Domes, *Mehrheitsfraktion und Bundesregierung. Aspekte*

des Verhältnisses der Fraktion der CDU/CSU zum Kabinett Adenauer (Cologne, 1964); K. Dreher, *Das Weg zum Kanzler. Adenauers Griff nach der Macht* (Düsseldorf, 1972); T. Ellwein and J.J. Hesse, *Der Regierungssystem der Bundesrepublik Deutschland* (Opladen, 1987); K. Gotto (ed.), *Der Staatssekretär Adenauers. Persönlichkeit und politisches Wirken Hans Globkes* (Stuttgart, 1980); P. Haungs, 'Kanzlerdemokratie in der Bundesrepublik Deutschland von Adenauer bis Kohl', *Zeitschrift für Politik*, 1986, vol. 33; A.J. Heidenheimer, 'Der starke Regierungschef und das Parteiensystem. Der Kanzlereffekt in der Bundesrepublik', *Politische Vierteljahresschrift*, 1961, vol. 2; W. Hennis, *Richtlinienkompetenz und Regierungstechnik* (Tübingen 1964); W. Jäger, 'Von der Kanzlerdemokratie zur Koordinationsdemokratie', *Zeitschrift fur Politik*, 1988, vol. 35; E.U. Junker, *Die Richtlinienkompetenz des Bundeskanzlers* (Tübingen 1965); J. Küpper, *Die Kanzlerdemokratie. Voraussetzungen, Strukturen und Änderungen des Regierungsstiles in der Ära Adenauer* (Frankfurt, 1985); R. Mayntz, 'Executive leadership in Germany: dispersion of power or Kanzlerdemokratie?', in R. Rose and E.N. Suleiman (eds), *Presidents and Prime Ministers* (Washington, DC, 1980); K. Niclauss, *Kanzlerdemokratie. Bonner Regierungspraxis von Konrad Adenauer bis Helmut Kohl* (Stuttgart, 1988); S. Padgett (ed.), *The Development of the German Chancellorship: Adenauer to Kohl* (London, 1994) [henceforth, S. Padgett (ed.), *The German Chancellorship*, 1994] G.P. Pridham, *Christian Democracy in Western Germany* (London, 1977).

2 S. Padgett (ed.), *The German Chancellorship,* 1994, p. 18.

3 G.P. Pridham, *Christian Democracy in Western Germany* (London, 1977), pp. 246–7.

4 See below, pp. 188–90.

5 H. Abromeit, in S. Padgett (ed), *The German Chancellorship* , 1994, pp. 160–1.

6 See, for example, W.E. Paterson, 'From the Bonn Republic to the Berlin Republic', *German Politics*, April 2000, pp. 23–39.

7 See especially R. Dahrendorf, *Society and Democracy in Germany* (London, 1967).

8 See, for example, E.U. Junker, *Die Richtlinienkompetenz des Bundeskanzlers* (Tubingen, 1965).

9 For key role of *Bundeskanzleramt*, see especially A. Baring, 1982; J. Küpper, 1985; and K. Otto, 1980, all in note 1 above.

10 G. Pridham, *Christian Democracy in Western Germany* (London, 1977), p. 106, n. 14

11 F. Müller-Rommel, in S. Padgett (ed.), *The German Chancellorship*, 1994, p. 113.

12 S. Padgett (ed.), *The German Chancellorship*, 1994, chapter 2, pp. 44–77.

13 See below, p. 186–7.

14 See, for example, Schwarz, 1997, pp.19–22, pp. 155–7, & pp. 410–15.

15 See above, pp. 60–82.

16 On party typology, see M. Duverger, *Political Parties* (London, 1954).

17 A. Heidenheimer, *Adenauer and the CDU* (The Hague, 1960), pp. 50–2.

18 See below, pp. 177–9.

19 See above, pp. 22–3.

20 See above, p. 34.

21 Cf. A. Poppinga, 1970.

22 Otto Lenz Diary, quoted Schwarz, 1995, p. 60.

23 For discussion of Adenauer–Erhard feuds, see above, pp. 178–9, and below, pp. 185–7; see also D. Koerfer, *Kampf ums Kanzleramt. Erhard und Adenauer* (Stuttgart, 1987) and V. Hentschel, *Ludwig Erhard. Ein Politikerleben* (Munich, 1996).

24 See below, p. 185.

25 See below, pp. 183–4.

26 Krone Diary, 15 July 1960, quoted Schwarz, 1997, p. 289. On the previous day he had written: 'It is crazy the way the Chancellor treats his Ministers.'

27 Quoted Schwarz, 1997, p. 289.

28 See below, p. 186.

29 See below, pp. 183–6.

30 For full details about the Gürzenich incident, see Koch, 1985, pp. 458–60.

31 See above, p. 96.

32 For full details of Heinemann's dismissal, see Koch, 1985, pp. 259–64.

33 Adenauer in Cabinet, quoted in Schwarz, 1995, p. 552.

34 See below, pp. 175–86.

35 See above, n. 30.

36 For a thorough analysis of the 1953 Election, see H. Köhler, *Adenauer* (Frankfurt-am-Main, 1994), pp. 775–85.

37 Blankenhorn Diary, 28 August 1953, quoted Schwarz, 1997, p. 76.

38 Ibid, p. 81.

39 *FAZ*, 8 September 1953.

40 *Spiegel*, 16 September 1953.

41 On this analogy, see Schwarz, 1997, p. 94 & ff.

42 R. Augstein, *Spiegel,* 14 September 1957.

43 There is an excellent analysis of the 1957 election in English: U. Kitzinger, *German Electoral Politics: a study of the 1957 campaign* (Oxford, 1960).

44 *FAZ*, 17 September 1957.

45 *VDB*, 24 November 1949.

46 On Pension Reform Act, see below, p. 191.

47 On Adenauer's relations with FDP, see above, p. 171.

48 See above, pp. 60–1

49 The election is discussed in detail in W. Wagner, *Die Bundestagspräsidentenwahl 1959* (Mainz, 1972).

50 See above, pp. 134–43.

51 A. Schröder, *Mein Bruder, Gerhard Schröder*, p. 221; F.J. Strauss, *Erinnerungen* (Berlin, 1988), p. 397.

52 See above, p. 82.

53 F.J. Strauss, *Erinnerungen* (Berlin, 1988), p. 401.

54 Schwarz, 1997, pp. 552–7.

55 Schwarz, 1997, p. 595.

56 For detailed discussion of the Spiegel Affair, see A. Grosser and J. Seifert, *Die Spiegel Affäre* (Freiburg, 1966); and in English, D. Schoenbrun, *The Spiegel Affair* (New York, 1968).

57 F.J. Strauss, *Erinnerungen* (Berlin, 1988), p. 401.

58 Koch, 1985, p. 454.

59 *VDB*, 7 November 1962.

60 *Spiegel*, 24 November 1962.

61 Schwarz, 1997, p. 659.

62 See below, p. 195.

63 *FAZ*, 7 September 1953.

64 Adenauer to Brentano, in A. Baring (ed.), *Sehr verehrter Herr Bundeskanzler! Heinrich Brentano im Briefwechsel mit Konrad Adenauer 1949–64* (Hamburg, 1974), p. 151.

65 See above, p. 182.

66 Adenauer to CDU/CSU *Fraktion*, 23 April 1963, quoted Schwarz, 1997, p. 686.

67 Schwarz, 1997, p. 687.

68 William Paterson, now Professor William Paterson, Director of the Institute of German Studies, University of Birmingham, witnessed this incident on 30 November 1966.

69 See H.E. Jahn (ed.) *CDU und Mitbestimmung* (Stuttgart, 1969) and G. Müller-List (ed.) *Montanmitbestimmung* (Düsseldorf, 1969).

70 *VDB*, 10 April 1951.

71 See F. Neumann, *Der Block der Heimatvertriebenen und Entrechteten 1950–60* (Meisenheim, 1968).

72 Schwarz, 1997, p. 224.

73 For documentation about relations between the Federal Republic and Israel, see R. Vogel (ed.), *Deutschlands Weg nach Israel* (Stuttgart, 1967). On Adenauer's determination to push through the settlement with Israel, see especially H. Köhler, *Adenauer* (Frankfurt-am-Main, 1994), pp. 698–722; also F. Böhm, 'Das deutsch-israelische Abkommen 1952', in Blumenwitz *et al.* (eds), *Adenauer und seine Zeit*, 1976, p. 434 & ff.; N. Goldmann, 'Adenauer und das jüdische Volk', in ibid. pp. 427–36; L. Gardner-Feldman, *The Special Relationship between West Germany and Israel* (Boston, MA, 1984); G. Gillessen, *Konrad Adenauer and Israel* (Adenauer Memorial Lecture, Oxford, 1986); and N. Goldmann, *Memories* (London, 1960).

74 *FAZ*, 11 November 1949.

75 *VDB*, 27 September 1951.

76 N. Goldmann, *Memories* (London, 1960), p. 260, and Adenauer *Erinnerungen 2*, p. 131.

77 Adenauer *Erinnerungen 2*, p. 138.

78 Schwarz, 1997, p. 659.

79 See above, pp. 99–101.

80 Goldmann letter of 19 May 1951 in Adenauer *Erinnerungen 2*, p. 146.

81 Adenauer *Erinnerungen 2*, p. 146.

82 N. Goldmann, *Memories* (London, 1960), p. 318.

83 C. Wighton, *Adenauer – Democratic Dictator: a critical biography* (London, 1963).

84 See in particular W. Jäger, 'Von der Kanzlerdemokratie zur Koordinationsdemokratie', *Zeitschrift für Politik*, 1988, vol. 35.

Conclusion

Now is the time to try to answer the two questions posed in the Introduction. How far was Adenauer merely the product of his times? And how far did he influence the era which bears his name?

Firstly, of course, we have to bear in mind Wordsworth's truism: the child is indeed the father of the man. Adenauer inherited from his parents certain characteristics which he never lost: his Catholicism, his conservatism, his regulated lifestyle. From his father specifically, he inherited his love of his country, his devotion to duty, his self-discipline, his courage, but also his domineering nature, short temper and pettiness. And from his mother, his determination and thriftiness, but also his sense of insecurity. Throughout his long life he tended to be dour, pessimistic and distrustful. If he had had more faith in his colleagues, he would have been more willing to delegate. But, even when on holiday, he insisted on daily contact with Bonn, never trusting his Ministers fully. Like his parents, he was a very private person. Apart from politics, his only interests were solitary ones – gardening, walking (usually on his own), listening to music, reading. He was of course a devoted, albeit old-fashioned, husband and father. He only had a few close friends – Dannie Heineman, Robert Pferdemenges, Hans Globke and Heinrich Krone. Otherwise, he was not a sociable person – except with his immediate family.

Yet Adenauer had many admirable qualities. He was ambitious, conscientious, relentless in his pursuit of what he believed to be right. He also exhibited some of the defects of his qualities: certainly in his later years he became extremely obstinate, refusing to listen to the advice of friends and colleagues with regard to both home and foreign policy. Given Adenauer's renowned deviousness, it may seem paradoxical to say that he was a man of *high moral principles*. But he was such a man. For most politicians power comes well ahead of principles. And of course Adenauer realized that without power a politician can never achieve anything. Nor can it be denied that he held on to power for far too long. However, Nahum Goldmann was right when he stressed that Adenauer had been so shocked by all that had happened in the Third Reich (and not just in relation to the Jews) that henceforth he had a strong *moral* commitment to create a better world.[1] He was determined to ensure that the basic human rights enshrined in the German Constitution would not be abused in future. Meanwhile, his foreign policy – in particular his desire for reconciliation with France – was part of his moral crusade for a new, democratic Europe. He also believed strongly that he and his fellow European 'crusaders' needed a shield to protect themselves from the Communist 'infidels' in the East. That shield was NATO, and even in his most 'Gaullist' phase Adenauer never wavered from his total commitment to the United States-led Western Alliance.

It is easy to be cynical about Adenauer. Did he himself not betray those very moral principles to which he was in theory so committed by infringing the Constitution – indeed by his whole style of governing? The answer is that it is perfectly possible to be a sinner, and yet to remain wholly committed to one's faith. This was precisely Adenauer's situation. After the Hitler régime a major change *did* occur in Adenauer's *political values*, if not in his *personality*. He remained the man he was – a middle-class Catholic Rhinelander, born in Wilhelmine Germany. Yet after the war he was no less than a *revolutionary* – and I use the word advisedly. Adenauer was a revolutionary in his utter determination that his country should make a new beginning. He was one of those Germans who really did believe that 1945 was 'year zero'. Shakespeare (through Henry V) tells us that 'old men forget'. Adenauer did not forget. His whole post-war political career was motivated by his determination to ensure that the past should not repeat itself. Paradoxically, with his mind on the *past*, he became extremely *forward-looking*. He was convinced that democrats could no longer afford to temporize in defending liberal democracy, as had so many from his class and background in the Weimar Republic. His fellow citizens could no longer afford to appease dictators, be they of the Right or the Left. Catholics and Protestants could no longer afford to argue about denominational schools, when Christian civilization was itself under threat from totalitarianism.

It can of course be argued that Adenauer was no more than a man who was wholly in touch with the spirit of his times, the distinctive Zeitgeist of post-war West Germany. And that if he had not become Chancellor, someone with comparable principles and objectives would have taken his place. This is like saying that Churchill was 'inevitable' in 1940, which he certainly was not.[2]

It is difficult to deny that foreign policy 'made' the two German States, rather than vice-versa. Even if Schumacher had become Chancellor of the Federal Republic in 1949, it seems inconceivable that he would not have joined the West. He would soon have concluded that reunification *before* commitment to the West was not a viable option, given the geopolitical situation during the Cold War. However, Adenauer – even if in a sense he made an 'inevitable' choice – marked West German foreign policy with his distinctive personality and values: notably his unbending anti-Communism and his desire for Franco-German reconciliation, both of which went back to the 1920s. These long-held attitudes led naturally to his particular enthusiasm for rearmament and his strong determination to join the Atlantic Alliance as soon as possible. Adenauer, then, gave a *particular emphasis* to West Geman foreign policy in the 1950s, even if he did not determine it. And that emphasis was overwhelmingly supported by public opinion. However, by the early 1960s Adenauer began to lose touch with the new Zeitgeist which favoured détente.

No doubt, too, the Federal Republic would have opted for a free market economy once it became part of the capitalist world. But it might have done so in a rather different way without Adenauer. If Schumacher had become Chancellor in 1949, or if a grand coalition had been formed in that year, it is perfectly possible that the German economy might have been run on French lines, with considerably more state intervention. However, Adenauer and Erhard gave a particular slant to German capitalism with their strong commitment to the *Sozialmarktwirtschaft,* which, in spite of its name, always put more emphasis on free enterprise than on social solidarity.

Again, it can be argued that the times were ripe for the establishment of the type of political party which Adenauer and his fellow-politicians created – namely an inter-class, inter-confessional, bourgeois-orientated *Volkspartei* like the Christian Democratic Union. Indeed, if a party like the CDU had *not* come into being, it is hard to see how Germany's second attempt at parliamentary democracy could have succeeded. It was essential to draw the middle classes and the peasantry into the party system if Bonn's political future were to be different from Weimar's. The CDU became *the* vehicle through which German conservatives of all classes, regions and religions embraced liberal democracy for the first time. However, there is no doubt that Adenaeur did mark and mould the CDU *personally*. It could quite easily have developed into a more left-wing party, for it is perfectly possible that, but for Adenauer, the battle with the 'Social Christians' in 1948–49 could have gone the other way. Again, it is perfectly possible that the Christian Democrats could have opted for a grand coalition with the Social Democrats in 1949. Powerful figures in the CDU such as Karl Arnold and Jakob Kaiser wanted precisely that, believing that a 'government of national unity' would be best able to resolve the country's economic and social problems and defend its interests in the face of the Allied High Commissioners. Adenauer, however, was determined to keep the Social Democrats out of government. And his decision had a significant long-term political effect on the Federal Republic. For it encouraged the development of the important concept of government *and* opposition – a concept which had never developed in the Weimar Republic, at least not in the sense of a *loyal* opposition. There was of course a downside to Adenauer's dominance of the Federal Republic's political system and control of the Christian Democratic Party. For there is little doubt that 'Chancellor Democracy' held back the development of participative politics and responsible party government in the 1950s. Thus, the Bonn Republic had to be founded twice – firstly in 1949 in a formal constitutional sense, and secondly in 1969 with the arrival in power of the Brandt Government and the beginnings of a more participative democracy.[3]

In achieving liberal democracy at home and reconciliation abroad, Adenauer certainly enjoyed a considerable measure of good fortune. He was lucky to be dismissed by the British from the Mayorship of Cologne in late 1945, thus freeing him for national politics at exactly the right time. He was lucky that his country was divided in the way it was, for, with a fifty–fifty confessional balance in the West, a party like the CDU became possible for the first time in German history. He was lucky that his main political opponent was Kurt Schumacher, whose backward-looking views contrasted with his own forward-looking vision. Moreover, Schumacher then played right into Adenauer's hands by choosing the 'wrong' foreign and economic policies. Adenauer was thus able to govern from 1949 to 1959 almost in a political vacuum: the opposition was non-existent or at best ineffective. This suited Adenauer's dominant style of leadership perfectly. He was lucky too in having privileged access to the Allied High Commissioners in the early years of his Chancellorship, and he then guarded his special relationship with them until full sovereignty was achieved in 1955. Meanwhile, the Bundestag was relatively docile in those

ADENAUER

years, leaving the Chancellor to control the governmental machine
through the Federal Chancellor's Office. The Adenauer era was, as it were,
a bridge between the autocratic Third Reich and the participative post-
1969 Bonn Republic. During this transitional phase the citizens of the
Federal Republic wanted security and prosperity, not participation or
responsibility. They were quite content to leave the running of the country
to their powerful Chancellor. They had become used to strong leadership,
and Adenauer continued to give it to them, even though the political
system now called itself – and indeed *was* – a liberal democracy based on
the rule of law. Moreover, Adenauer's 'strong' régime helped millions of
Germans to adapt to a form of government which hitherto they had never
accepted. Adenauer was exactly suited to this unique period in German
history. No future Chancellor would govern in a 'time warp' like the
period 1945–60. Nor would any future Chancellor be able to 'bend' the
Constitution or dominate policy-making in the way which Adenauer was
able to do as first Chancellor.

If a statesman is defined as a politician with vision – together with the
determination to realize that vision, then Adenauer was indeed a statesman. For, in spite of his autocratic tendencies and good fortune, *real vision*
was precisely what this conservative old man showed in abundance in the
two decades after 'year zero'. Adenauer demonstrated that he really had
learnt from the past. His vision in 1945 was truly remarkable. Indeed, it
was vital for the future of his country. If he had not been wholly committed to implementing that vision, Adenauer would have opted for a quiet
life as a pensioner in Rhöndorf. Instead, he devoted fourteen years to
ensuring that his beloved Fatherland became a fully fledged Western liberal democracy.

Notes and references

1   N. Goldmann, *Memories* (London, 1970), p. 318.
2   See, for example, H.R. Trevor-Roper's brilliant valedictory lecture as Regius Professor of
    Modern History at the University of Oxford, 'History and the imagination', in H. Lloyd-Jones
    et al., *History and the Imagination* (London, 1981), pp. 356–69.
3   See, for example, H. Doring and G. Smith (eds), *Party Government and Political Culture in
    Western Germany* (London, 1982), and W.E. Paterson, 'From the Bonn Republic to the
    Berlin Republic', *German Politics*, April 2000, pp. 23–39.

Bibliography

Abs, H.J., *Entscheidungen 1949–53. Die Entstehung des Londoner Schuldabkommens* (Mainz, 1991).

Adenauer, K., *Erinnerungen* (Stuttgart, 1965–68), 4 vols (1945–53; 1953–55; 1955–59; 1959–63). The last volume consists only of fragments, but has a very useful Index covering both persons and events. The first volume was translated into English by Beate von Oppen as Adenauer, K., *Memoirs, 1945–53* (London, 1966).

Adenauer, K., *Briefe*, 7 vols (1945–47; 1947–49; 1949–51; 1951–53; 1953–55; 1955–57; 1957–59), edited by H.P. Mensing, R. Morsey and H.P. Schwarz (Berlin, 1983–88).

Adenauer, K., *Briefe über Deutschland 1945–55*, edited by H.P. Mensing (Berlin, 1999).

Adenauer, K., *Teegespräche*, 9 vols (4 cover years 1950–63), edited by R. Morsey and H.P. Schwarz (Berlin, 1984–92). A collection of interviews/discussions with German and foreign journalists, often in the presence of eminent politicians and/or members of Adenauer's Chancellor's Office.

Adenauer, K., (Preface by), *Regierung Adenauer 1949–63* (Bonn, 1963).

Adenauer, K., *Reden 1917–67*, edited by H.P. Schwarz (Stuttgart, 1975).

Adenauer, K., Stiftung (ed.), *Konrad Adenauer und die CDU der britischen Besatzungszone 1946–49. Dokumente zur Gründungsgeschichte der CDU Deutschlands* (Bonn, 1975).

Acheson, Dean, *Present at the Creation: My Years in the State Department* (London, 1969).

Allemann, F., *Bonn ist nicht Weimar* (Cologne, 1956).

Augstein, R. (ed.), transl. W. Wallich, *Konrad Adenauer* (London, 1964).

Baring, A., *Aussenpolitik in Adenauers Kanzlerdemokratie* (Munich, 1969).

Baring, A., *Im Anfang war Adenauer. Die Entstehung der Kanzlerdemokratie* (Munich, 1982), second, virtually unchanged, ed. of Baring (1969).

Baring, A., (ed.), *Sehr verehrter Herr Bundeskanzler! Heinrich Brentano im Briefwechsel mit Konrad Adenauer 1949–64* (Hamburg, 1974).

Becker F. (ed.), Konrad Adenauer, *'Die Demokratie ist für uns eine Weltanschauung'. Reden und Gespräche 1946–67* (Cologne, 1998).

Becker, F. (ed.), *Kleine Geschichte der CDU* (Stuttgart, 1995).

Becker, W., *CDU und CSU 1945–50. Vorläufer, Gründung und regionale Entwicklung bis zum Entstehen des CDU-Partei* (Mainz, 1987). Very useful collection of key speeches by Adenauer.

Berghahn V. and Karsten, D., *Industrial Relations in West Germany* (Oxford, 1987).

Besson, W., *Die Aussenpolitik der Bundesrepublik* (Munich, 1970).

Blankenhorn, H., *Verständnis und Verständigung. Blätter eines politischen Tagebuchs 1949–79* (Cologne, 1998).

Blumenwitz, D., K. Gotto, H. Maier, K. Repgen and H.P. Schwarz (eds), *Konrad Adenauer und seine Zeit. Politik und Persönlichkeit des ersten Bundeskanzlers*, 2 vols (Stuttgart, 1976).

Bracher, K.D., *Das deutsche Dilemma. Leidenswege der politischen Emanzipation* (Munich, 1971). English translation: *The German Dilemma* (London, 1973).

Bracher, K.D., 'Die Kanzlerdemokratie', in R. Löwenthal and H.P. Schwarz (eds), *Die Zweite Republik. 25 Jahre Bundesrepublik Deutschland. Eine Bilanz* (Stuttgart, 1974) pp.179–202.

Brentano, H. von, *Germany and Europe: Reflections on German Foreign Policy* (London, 1964)

Buchstab, D. (ed.), *Die Protokolle des CDU-Bundesvorstandes, 1950–65*, 4 vols (Düsseldorf, 1986–1998).

Bührer, W. (ed.), *Die Adenauer Ära, 1949–63* (Munich, 1993).

Cary, N.D., *The Path to Christian Democracy: German Catholics and the Party System from Windthorst to Adenauer* (Cambridge, MA., 1996).

Conze, W., *Jakob Kaiser. Politiker zwischen Ost und West, 1945–49* (Stuttgart, 1969).

Conze, E. and G. Metzler (eds.), *Fünfzig Jahre Bundesrepublik Deutschland* (Stuttgart, 1999).

Craig, G.A., *Germany 1866–1945* (Oxford, 1978).

Dahrendorf, R., *Gesellschaft und Demokratie in Deutschland* (Munich, 1965). English translation: *Society and Democracy in Germany* (London, 1967).

Doering-Manteuffel, A., *Die Bundesrepublik Deutschland in der Ära Adenauer. Aussenpolitik und innere Entwicklung 1949–63* (Darmstadt, 2nd edn, 1988).

Doering-Manteuffel, A., *Adenauerzeit. Stand, Perspektiven und methodische Aufgaben der Zeitgeschichtsforschung 1945–67* (Bonn, 1993).

Domes, J., *Mehrheitsfraktion und Bundesregierung. Aspekte des Verhältnisses des Fraktion der CDU/CSU zum Kabinett Adenauer* (Cologne, 1964).

Dönhoff, M., *Deutschland, deine Kanzler. Die Geschichte der Bundesrepublik 1949–99* (Munich, 1999).

Doring, H. and G. Smith, *Party Government and Political Culture in West Germany* (London, 1982).

Dreher, K., *Der Weg zum Kanzler. Adenauers Griff nach der Macht* (Düsseldorf, 1972).

Eckardt, F. von, *Ein unordentliches Leben. Lebenserinnerungen* (Düsseldorf, 1967).

Eden, A., *Full Circle* (London, 1960).

Edinger, L.J., *Kurt Schumacher* (Stanford, CA, 1965).

Ellwein T. and J.J. Jesse, *Der Regierungssystem des Bundesrepublik Deutschland* (Opladen, 1987).

Erhard, L., *Gedanken aus fünf Jahrzehnten* (Düsseldorf, 1988).

Erhard, L., *Deutsche Wirtschaftspolitik. Der Weg der Sozialen Marktwirtschaft* (Frankfurt-am-Main, 1962).

Erhard, L., *Prosperity through Competition* (London 1958).

Eschenburg, T., *Jahre der Besatzung 1945–49* (Stuttgart, 1983).

Erdmann, K.D., *Adenauer in der Rheinlandpolitik nach dem ersten Weltkrieg* (Stuttgart, 1966).

Feldkamp, D., *Der Parlamentarische Rat 1948–49. Die Entstehung des Grundgesetzes* (Göttingen, 1998).

Flechtheim, O.K., *Die Parteien der Bundesrepublik Deutschland* (Hamburg, 1973).

Flechtheim, O.K. (ed.), *Dokumente zur parteipolitischen Entwicklung in Deutschland seit 1945*, 9 vols (Berlin, 1962 & ff.).

Foschepoth, J. (ed.), *Adenauer und die deutsche Frage* (Göttingen, 2nd edn, 1990).

Frank-Planitz, U., *Konrad Adenauer. Eine Biographie in Bild und Wort* (Stuttgart, 1990).

Gillessen, G., *Konrad Adenauer and Israel* (Adenauer memorial lecture, Oxford, 1986).

Goldmann, N., *Memories* (London, 1960).

Gotto, K. (ed.), *Der Staatssekretär Adenauers. Persönlichkeit und politisches Wirken Hans Globkes* (Stuttgart, 1980).

Gotto, K., H. Maier, R. Morsey and H.P. Schwarz, *Konrad Adenauer. Seine Deutschland und Aussenpolitik 1945–64* (Munich, 1975).

Gortemacher, M., *Geschichte der Bundesrepublik Deutschland. Von der Gründung bis zur Gegenwart* (Munich, 1999).

Hacke, C., *Weltmacht wider Willen. Die Aussenpolitik der Bundesrepublik* (Stuttgart, 1988).

Hanrieder, W., *West German Foreign Policy 1949–63* (Stanford, CA, 1987).

Hallstein, W., *United Europe: Challenge and Opportunity* (London, 1962).

Haungs, H., 'Kanzlerdemokratie in der Bundesrepublik Deutschland von Adenauer bis Kohl', *Zeitschrift für Politik*, 1986, vol. 33, pp. 47–88.

Heidenheimer, A.J., *Adenauer and the CDU: the rise of the leader and the integration of the party* (The Hague, 1960).

Heidemeyer, H., *Die CDU/CSU Fraktion im Deutschen Bundestag 1949–53* (Düsseldorf, 1998).

Hennis, W., *Richtlinienkompetenz und Regierungstechnik* (Tübingen, 1964).

Hentschel, V., *Ludwig Erhard. Ein Politikerleben* (Munich, 1996).

Herbst, L., *Option für den Westen. Vom Marshallplan bis zum deutsch-französischen Vertrag* (Munich, 1989).

Hirsch, F., 'Stresemann and Adenauer: two great leaders of German democracy in times of crisis', in A.O. Sarkissian, *Studies in Diplomatic History in Honour of G.P. Gooch* (London, 1961).

Hiscocks, R., *Germany Revived: an appraisal of the Adenauer era* (London, 1966).

Hübsch, R., *Als die Mauer wuchs. Zur Deutschlandpolitik der Christdemokraten 1945–70* (Potsdam 1998).

Irving, R.E.M., *The Christian Democratic Parties of Western Europe* (London, 1979).

Jäger, W. 'Von der Kanzlerdemokratie zur Koordinationsdemokratie', *Zeitschrift für Politik*, 1988, vol.35.

Junker, E.U., *Die Richtlinienkompetenz des Bundeskanzlers* (Tübingen, 1965).

Kaack, H., *Geschichte und Struktur des deutschen Parteiensystem* (Opladen, 1971).

Kaiser, K. and R. Morgan (eds), *Britain and West Germany: changing societies and the future of foreign policy* (Oxford, 1971).

Kedward, H.R., *Fascism in Western Europe* (Glasgow, 1969).

Kirchner F., and J. Sperling (eds), *The Federal Republic and NATO* (London, 1992).

Kirkpatrick, I., *The Inner Circle* (London, 1959).

Knipping K., and K.J. Müller (eds), *Aus der Ohnmacht zur Bündnismacht. Das Machtproblem in der Bundesrepublik Deutschland in der Ära Adenauer 1945–60* (Paderborn, 1995).

Koch, P., *Konrad Adenauer. Eine politische Biographie* (Hamburg, 1985).

Koerfer, D., *Kampf ums Kanzleramt. Erhard und Adenauer* (Stuttgart, 1987).

Köhler, H., *Adenauer. Eine politische Biographie* (Frankfurt-am-Main, 1994).

Koopmann, M., *Das schwierige Bündnis. Die deutsch-französischen Beziehungen und die Aussenpolitik der Bundesrepublik Deutschland 1958–65* (Baden-Baden, 2000).

Kupper, J., Die *Kanzlerdemokratie. Voraussetzungen, Strukturen und Änderungen des Regierungsstiles in der Ära Adenauer* (Frankfurt-am-Main, 1985).

Kusterer, H., *Der Kanzler und der General* (Stuttgart, 1995).

Lappenkuper, U., *Ein besonderes Verhältnis. Konrad Adenauer und Frankreich 1949–63* (Bad Honnef, 1997).

Legoll, L., *Konrad Adenauer et l'idée européenne, 1948–50* (Paris, 1989).

Loewenberg, G., *Parliament in the German Political System* (Ithaca, NY, 1967).

Maier K. and B. Thoss (eds), *Westintegration, Sicherheit und deutsche Frage. Quellen zur Aussenpolitik in der Ära Adenauer 1949–63* (Darmstadt, 1994).

Mensing, H.P., (ed.), *Konrad Adenauer und Theodor Heuss. Unter vier Augen. Gespräche aus den Grunderjahren 1949–59* (Berlin, 1997).

Merkl, P.H., 'Equilibrium, structure of interests and leadership: Adenauer's survival as Chancellor', *American Political Science Review*, 1962 (56.3).

Mintzel, A., *Die CSU. Anatomie einer konservativen Partei, 1945–72* (Opladen, 1975).

Moeller, R. (ed.), *West Germany under Construction: politics, society and culture in the Adenauer era* (Ann Arbor, MI, 1997).

Monnet, J., *Memoirs* (transl. R.Mayne) (London, 1976).

Morgan, R., *The United States and West Germany, 1945–73* (Oxford, 1974).

Morsey, R., *Die Bundesrepublik Deutschland – Entstehung und Entwicklung bis 1969* (Munich, 2000).

Morsey R., *Konrad Adenauer und die Gründung der Bundesrepublik Deutschland* (Stuttgart, 1979).

Morsey, R., *Die Rolle Konrad Adenauers im Parlamentarischen Rat 1948–49* (Bad Honnef, 1998).

Morsey, R., *Die Deutschlandpolitik Adenauers. Alte Thesen und neue Fakten* (Opladen, 1991).

Morsey, R. and K. Repgen (eds), *Adenauer Studien*, 5 vols (Mainz, 1971–86).

Müchler, G., *CDU/CSU. Das schwierige Bündnis* (Munich, 1976).

Müller-Roschach, H., *Die deutsche Europapolitik 1949–63* (Bonn, 1980).

Neumann, F., *Der Block der Heimatvertriebenen und Entrechteten 1950–1960* (Meisenheim, 1968).

Nicholls, A.J., *The Bonn Republic: West German Democracy 1945–1990* (London, 1997).

Nicholls, A.J., *Freedom and Responsibility: the Social Market Economy, 1918–1960* (Oxford, 1994).

Nicholls, A.J., 'Konrad Adenauer', in *History Makers* Lord Longford and Sir John Wheeler-Bennett (eds), (London, 1973).

Nicholls A.J. and E.Matthias (eds), *German Democracy and the Triumph of Hitler* (London, 1971).

Niclauss, K., *Kanzlerdemokratie. Bonner Regieurungspraxis von Konrad Adenauer bis Helmut Kohl* (Stuttgart, 1988).

Niclauss, K., *Der Weg zum Grundgesetz. Demokratiegründung in Westdeutschland 1945–49* (Stuttgart, 1998).

Osterheld, H., *Konrad Adenauer. Ein Charakterbild* (Stuttgart, 1987).

Padgett, S., (ed.), *The Development of the German Chancellorship: Adenauer to Kohl* (London, 1994).

Paterson, W.E., and Southern, D., *Governing Germany* (Oxford, 1991).

Paterson, W.E., 'The changing context of German foreign policy', in Smith, G., *et al* (eds.), *Developments in German Politics* (London, 1992).

Paterson, W.E., 'From the Bonn Republic to the Berlin Republic', *German Politics*, April 2000, pp. 23–39.

Pohl, H., (ed.) *Adenauers Verhältnis zur Wirtschaft und Gesellschaft* (Bonn, 1992).

Pommerin, R., (ed.), *The American Impact on Postwar Germany* (Providence, RI, 1995).

Poppinga, A., *Meine Erinnerungen an Konrad Adenauer* (Stuttgart, 1970).

Poppinga, A., *Konrad Adenauer. Geschichtsverständnis, Weltanschauung und politische Praxis* (Stuttgart, 1975).

Poppinga, A. (intro. R. Morsey), *Konrad Adenauer. Eine Chronik in Daten, Zitaten und Bildern* (Bad Honnef, 1987).

Poppinga, A., '*Das wichtigste ist der Mut'. Konrad Adenauer – die letzten fünf Kanzlerjahre* (Bergisch Gladbach, 1994).

Poppinga, A. (ed.), '*Seid wach für die kommenden Jahre'. Grundsatze, Erfahrungen, Einsichten von Konrad Adenauer* (Bergisch Gladbach, 1997).

Pridham, G.P., *Christian Democracy in Western Germany* (London, 1977).

Prittie, T., *Konrad Adenauer 1876–1967: a study in fortitude* (London, 1972).

Prittie, T., H. Osterheld and F. Seydoux (transl P. Crampton), *Konrad Adenauer* (Stuttgart, 1983).

Pütz, H., *Die CDU. Entwicklung, Aufbau und Politik der Christlichen Demokratischen Union Deutschlands* (Düsseldorf, 1976).

Ruhl, K.J., *Die Ära Adenauer, 1949–63* (Munich, 1985).

Schmidt, R.H., *Saarpolitik 1945–57* (Munich, 1985).

Schröder, G., *Decision for Europe* (London, 1964).

Schumacher, F., *Stufen des Lebens. Erinnerungen eines Baumeisters* (Berlin, 1935).

Schuman, R., *Pour L'Europe* (Paris, 1968).

Schwarz, H.P., *Die Ära Adenauer 1949–57* (Stuttgart, 1981).

Schwarz, H.P., *Die Ära Adenauer 1957–63* (Stuttgart, 1983).

Schwarz, H.P. (ed.), *Adenauer und die Hohen Kommissare 1949–51* (Munich 1990).

Schwarz, H.P. (ed.), *Konrad Adenauers Regierungsstil* (Bonn, 1991).

Schwarz, H.P., *Erbfreundschaft. Adenauer und Frankreich* (Bonn, 1992).

Schwarz, H.P., *Adenauer. Der Aufstieg, 1876–1952* (Stuttgart, 1986). English translation: *Konrad Adenauer: From the German Empire to the Federal Republic* (Providence, RI, 1995).

Schwarz, H.P., *Adenauer. Der Staatsmann, 1952–67* (Stuttgart, 1991). English translation: *Adenauer: the Statesman* (Providence, RI, 1997).

Schwarz, H.P., 'Konrad Adenauer', *Die grossen Deutsche unserer Epoche* (Berlin, 1995), pp. 156–72 in L. Gall (ed.).

Schwarz, T., *From Occupation to Alliance: John J. McCloy and the Allied High Commission in the Federal Republic of Germany* (Ann Arbor, MI, 1985).

Selbach, J. (ed.), *Konrad Adenauer. Bundestagsreden* (Bonn, 1967).

Sontheimer, K., *Die Ära Adenauer. Grundlegung der Bundesrepublik* (Munich, 1991).

Stehkamper, H. (ed.), *Konrad Adenauer. Oberbürgermeister von Köln* (Cologne, 1976).

Stöss, R., *Parteien Handbuch. Die Parteien in der Bundesrepublik Deutschland*, 2 vols (Opladen, 1983).

Sternburg, W. von, *Adenauer. Eine deutsche Legende* (Frankfurt-am Main, 2nd edn., 2001).

Strauss, F.J., *Die Erinnerungen* (Berlin, 1988).

Streeck, W., *Industrial Relations in West Germany* (New York 1984)

Stresemann, W., *Mein Vater, Gustav Stresemann* (Munich, 1979).

Strobel, R., *Adenauer und der Weg Deutschlands* (Frankfurt-am-Main, 1965).

Thum, H., *Mitbestimmung in der Montanindustrie* (Frankfurt-am-Main, 1985).

Uexkull, G. von, *Adenauer* (Hamburg, 1976).

Vögel, R. (ed.), *Deutschlands Weg nach Israel. Eine Dokumentation* (Stuttgart, 1967).

Wagner, W., *Die Bundespräsidentenwahl 1959* (Mainz, 1972).

Weidenfeld, W., *Konrad Adenauer und Europa* (Bonn, 1976).

Weidenfeld, W., 'Die Europapolitik Konrad Adenauers', *Politische Studien*, 1979, vol. 1.

Weilemann, P.R., H.J. Kusters and G. Buchstab (eds), *Macht und Zeitkritik. Festschrift für Hans-Peter Schwarz zum 65 Geburtstag* (Paderborn, 1999).

Weymar, P., *Konrad Adenauer. Die autorisierte Biographie* (Munich, 1972). English translation: *Adenauer: the authorised biography* (London, 1957).

Wighton, C., *Adenauer – Democratic Dictator: a critical biography* (London, 1963).

Wilkens, A., *Jean Monnet, Konrad Adenauer und die Europapolitik 1950–57* (Bonn, 1999).

Williams, C., *Adenauer: the Father of the New Germany* (London, 2000).

Willis, F.R., *France, Germany and the New Europe, 1945–63* (Oxford, 1965).

Ziebura, G., *Die deutsch-französischen Beziehungen seit 1945* (Stuttgart, 1970).

INDEX

INDEX